THE DEMON WITHIN

A Study of John Cowper Powys's Novels

THE DEMON WITHIN
A Study of
John Cowper Powys's Novels

John A. Brebner

MACDONALD · LONDON

First published in Great Britain in 1973 by
Macdonald and Jane's
49 Poland Street
London W1

Printed in Great Britain by
Redwood Press Limited
Trowbridge, Wiltshire

ISBN 0 356 04531 5

The composers of fiction aim at an aesthetic veri-similitude which seldom corresponds to the much more eccentric and chaotic dispositions of Nature. Only rarely are such writers so torn and rent by the Demon within them that they can add their own touch to the wave-crests of *real actuality* as these foam up, bringing wreckage and sea-tangle and living and dead ocean monsters and bloody spume and bottom silt into the rainbow spray!

A Glastonbury Romance

Acknowledgement is made to the University of Wales Press and to Belinda Humfrey, the editor, for permission to reprint some of the material, in altered form, from the author's contribution to *Essays on John Cowper Powys, 1972*

The Extracts from the works of John Cowper Powys are reproduced by kind permission of Francis Powys, Executor of the Estate of the late John Cowper Powys, and Messrs. Laurence Pollinger Limited.

Contents

Preface	ix
CHAPTER I	1
CHAPTER II	38
CHAPTER III	91
CHAPTER IV	141
CHAPTER V	194
CHAPTER VI	226
Bibliography	235
Index	239

Preface

My main objective in this study has been to demonstrate the importance of J.C. Powys's novels in terms of their literary achievement and their contemporary relevance. What little Powys-criticism there is has never dealt adequately with his fiction, considering it from a biographical point of view or as a part of his total literary output. A few theses have been written on Powys but these have failed to make a significant statement; published work has concentrated on the *oeuvre* and the man rather than on the novels. Because these approaches have dominated, I have looked upon secondary material and biographical detail as essential background study but, otherwise, as quite extraneous to my purpose. My method throughout has been inductive: it has emphasized conclusions, not introductions. That is why I have preferred to open my discussion immediately with an analysis of Powys's first novel instead of with a formal introduction which would obviously have been at odds with my method.

By building up my argument from chapter to chapter, I have attempted to show the development and importance of Powys's novels chronologically, pointing to the way in which their visionary intent has evolved while incorporating structural and stylistic commentary into the overall discussion. My conclusion offers a tentative evaluation of Powys's art and ideas as they express the compass of his imagination. I hope, in this exploratory study, to have laid the groundwork for future research into specific areas which, given my present purpose, I could only suggest in passing.

None of this work would have been possible without the continued generosity of the Canada Council from whom I received a Doctoral Fellowship which enabled me to spend two years of research in Britain. While there I benefited from the assistance of the Library of the University College of South Wales and Monmouthshire where Mr. Richard Bell extended invaluable service by obtaining scarce materials for my consideration; I was also privileged through Dr. M.A. Hoskin's kindness to use the extensive collection of Powysiana at The Library, Churchill College, Cambridge. My personal debts are many: especially to Mr. G.D. Klingopulos, Senior Lecturer at University College, Cardiff, who helped me decide on the exact scope of my book; to Professor Gwyn Jones whose reminiscences furthered my understanding of Powys's exceptional imaginative abilities; to Mrs. Adelaide Ross who answered questions about her late husband's book, *John Cowper Powys: Letters to Nicholas Ross* (Bertram Rota, 1971), and whose thoughtfulness has continued to the present; to Mr. J.C. Mahanti whose comments on the final draft of this book were most useful; also to various members of the English Department of the University of New Brunswick.

All that I owe to Professor G. Wilson Knight for encouragement and advice cannot be summed up in a few words; suffice it to say that he has been extremely helpful.

My last words of gratitude, my strongest, are to Pat: editor, critic and friend.

Note on the editions of Powys's novels used and the reference form employed: I have referred to the most accessible editions of Powys's novels; these bear, in most cases, the imprint of Macdonald & Co. (Publishers) Ltd.,

London; otherwise, I have used the first American editions which appeared before British ones, with the exception of *Morwyn or the Vengeance of God* which was published only in Britain by Cassell & Co. Ltd. I mention these bibliographical details briefly in my first reference to the novel under discussion. Throughout I have referred to J.C. Powys's novels by chapter and page. In so doing, I hope to have lessened the confusion which might result from the different pagination of American and British editions.

Barker's Point,   J.A.B.
1973

I

Wood and Stone is constructed around a conjunction. The word "and" provides a clue to the ambiguous attitude which determines the failure as well as the success of John Cowper Powys's first novel. Title, preface, and opening chapter spell out the main theme of the book: the relationship between the will to Power and the will to Sacrifice. These two "mythologies", as they are called, are objectified in the materials of stone and wood. The story's general setting draws our attention to two particular instances: Leo's Hill, a "brute mass of inert sandstone", is a focus of spiritual and economic power; opposing it is thickly wooded Nevilton Mount where the Holy Rood of Waltham, a Christian standard of sacrifice, was reputedly discovered.

At the foot of the Mount lies the small village of Nevilton, whose inhabitants gain their livelihood by working the nearby sandstone quarries. They are thus united by residence and by occupation to the conflicting ideologies. At this point, however, we must be wary of facile classifications; for *Wood and Stone* is more than a simple confrontation between Pagan (evil) and Christian (good) forces. It is not, in fact, so much a "novel of ideas" as one of character analysis. It examines people living in a tightly enclosed society, striving to establish new or to retain old relationships with one another. Mortimer Romer, owner of the stone quarries, is a central figure in this struggle. His position of wealth and power enables him to exert considerable influence in both the public and private spheres of village life. He is a successful politician, easily defeating a crusading evangelist in a local election; he initiates industrial developments for strictly economic reasons; he also exhibits the dilettantish interest in art and literature proper to a citizen of his comfortably upholstered social standing. Yet we discover that the characteristics which achieve public success are not always adaptable to the demands of private life. When Romer's authoritarian drives are transferred to the personal plane they quickly assume the forms of dominance and manipulation. He exults in this sense of power over his family and acquaintances, arranging their lives according to his own whims or purposes. His decision to secure Ralph Dangelis, an American artist, as a prospective husband for his daughter Gladys is a basic plot-catalyst as is his persecution of Lacrima Traffio and Maurice Quincunx, both of whom are almost entirely dependent on him for their sustenance. Slightly outside the range of Romer's direct influence but nevertheless touched by its remoter vibrations are the members of the village gentry – Vennie Seldom and her mother; Hugh Clavering, the Vicar; and Francis Taxater, a Roman Catholic theologian and gentleman of leisure.

Of the other characters involved, the Andersen brothers, James and Luke, are of central importance. These two self-educated stone-cutters rise above Romer's designs by totally disregarding them. In consequence, they serve as a balancing-force throughout the novel – James's rather abstract concerns and Luke's rich sensuality opposing the industrialist's economic power-structure. Their other implied function – to act, in a general way, as mediators between the upper levels of the community and the lower – is poorly realized, however, for the majority of local villagers play only small parts in the unfolding story. Despite strongly individualized traits, the brothers remain somewhat unsatisfactory. They flout local conventions with *bourgeois* ease, exhibit exceptional literacy, and seem strangely removed from economic hardship. Quite simply, they do not fit the roles which the author has designed for them.

The motivation of the characters is determined, in most cases, by an intense process of introspection which stems from feelings of attraction to or repulsion from some other person. Men and women live in a tortuous tangle of love, lust, and hate: Lacrima, for example, loves Maurice, who appears indifferent to her; hates John Goring, who desires her; and is loved by James, who is loved by someone else. There are numerous other twists in this knot of frustrated passion. The generated tension is usually worked out in a series of internal adjustments rather than through a course of external action: a character's thoughts frequently reveal much more of his personality than anything he says or does. In depicting this evolving mental texture, Powys violates the aesthetics of "telling and showing". He ranges freely through the minds of his characters, pointing with sympathetic tenderness to some oddity or perhaps with blundering heaviness towards an object of scorn. Going even further, he is always ready to add a paragraph or two in his own voice, to speculate on an interesting aspect of the story. Although these interpolations are rarely dull, they tend to distract from the steady build up of the characterisation and too often blunt the natural force of events. The death of James Andersen provides us with a striking instance of intrusive comment by the author:

> Meanwhile . . . an event of tragic significance had occurred. It will be remembered that the last Lacrima had seen of James Andersen was the wild final gesticulation he made, . . . before he vanished from sight on the further side of Claudy's Leap. This vanishing, just

at that point, meant no more to Lacrima than that he had probably
taken a lower path, but had Gladys or Mr. Goring witnessed it, . . . a
much more startling conclusion would have been inevitable. Nor
would such a conclusion have been incorrect.

The unfortunate man, forgetting, in his excitement, the existence
of the other quarry . . . had stepped heedlessly backwards . . . and
fallen, without a cry, straight into the gulf.

The height of his fall would, in any case, have probably killed
him, but as it was 'he dashed his head,' in the language of the Bible,
'against a stone'; and in less than a second after his last cry, his soul,
to use the expression of a more pagan scripture, 'was driven,
murmuring, into the Shades.'

(XXI, 570)[1]

We may use this quotation to make two other distinct
points: first, it illustrates Powys's prose-style at its worst
(equally appalling passages are to be found throughout the
book); second, its final paragraph reminds us of the basic
religious ambiguity underlying the entire novel. Which is
more important — wood or stone, Christianity or Industry,
power or sacrifice? How are we to consider the relationship between the lecherous Reverend Clavering and the
beliefs he professes? Why is George Wone, the Christian
candidate, defeated at the polls by the godless Romer?
What are we to think as we read about the ghost voices of
Nevilton Churchyard debating the relative significance of
lust and love?

Some answers to these questions should be forthcoming
in the book-length dialogue between Luke Andersen and
Francis Taxater. The former is as eloquent in his denun-
ciation of religious orthodoxy as the latter is reasonable in
his support of it. Whereas Francis is cautious and bookish
in his explanation of Church doctrine (we are told rather
than shown this), Luke is adamant in his affirmation of
life-values. He extols the integrity of the self and rejects
the petty inhibitions of society. It is lightly implied that he
enjoys more than the company of village girls; nor is he

very concerned when he discovers that he has caused
Gladys's pregnancy. His subsequent proposal and marriage
to another girl result from a bachelor's desire for a more
convenient life, not from any sense of obligation. Spiritual
matters — including superstition and astrology — are of
only speculative interest to him. He unequivocally denies
any form of after-life. Although Luke's earthy attitude
contrasts sharply with Taxater's reasoned acceptance of
Catholicism, neither is condemned. It seems fitting that
the novel's final chapter should concern itself with a
description of these two men, sitting together in a public-
house, discussing the world, religion, sex, and politics. All
judgement has been suspended. Powys's lack of dogmatism
is one of the most attractive features of *Wood and Stone;*
however, we are left wondering whether his scepticism
results from objective detachment or from an artistic
attempt at fence-sitting.

Looking elsewhere in the novel, we begin to suspect that
its religious ambiguity is symptomatic of an even greater
and more disturbing problem; namely, of an overall
ambiguity which is accidental rather than intentional. Powys
may have been seeking a way out of this confusion in his
handling of Maurice Quincunx, the "Pariah". During most
of the novel, this character's intransigent stoicism repels
Lacrima's gentle advances and Romer's economic pressures. He cultivates his garden with vegetable-like passivity
— perhaps the cabbage leaves he wears to protect his neck
from the sun confirm the association. An opportunity to
change his way of life occurs when he is roused to rescue
the orphan-child Dolores from a shoddy travelling circus.
He acts quickly and effectively, but his courage is short-
lived. Only external coercion and guarantees of economic
freedom induce him to complete plans which involve
leaving England with Dolores and Lacrima. Even then he is
not without selfishness and, just prior to departure, wishes

that Lacrima were dead (she is his prospective bride!) so
that he might be alone with the child. Are there implied
sexual aberrations here?[2] and if so, what part do they play
in the total thematic structure?

Sex is certainly a dominant theme in the book; nor is it
confined to human activity. There is a general natural
fecundity. People are "surrounded by a riotous revel of
leafy exuberance"; they feel "the seething sap of these
incomparable days"; they catch "the indescribably sweet
scent of honey-suckle" which is "almost overpowering in
its penetrating voluptuous approach." Water and sun
conspire in this world of potency: Gladys is a "practised
swimmer" and enjoys a "matutinal plunge"; she basks in
"voluptuous contentment" on "sun-warmed" stones. The
most impressive handling of sun and water imagery is in
Chapter XXII. Visiting Weymouth, Luke wanders through
the streets enjoying the "smell of sea-weed, the sound of
the waves on the beach", "the sun-bathed atmosphere",
and the "salt-burdened sun-filled air." His eventual decision to swim in the sea is the natural culmination of his
desire to integrate himself as fully as possible with his
surroundings.

> Luke hurriedly undressed, and standing for a moment, a slim golden
> figure, in the horizontal sunlight, swung himself lightly down over the
> rock's edge and struck out boldly for the open sea.
>
> With vigorous strokes he wrestled with the inflowing tide. Wave
> after wave splashed against his face. Pieces of floating sea-weed and
> wisps of surf clung to his arms and hair. But he held resolutely on,
> breathing deep breaths of liberty and exultation, and drinking in, as if
> from a vast wide-brimmed cup, the thrilling spaciousness of air and
> sky.
>
> Girls, love-making, marriage, — the whole complication of the
> cloying erotic world, — fell away from him, like the too-soft petals of
> some great stifling velvet-bosomed flower; and naked of desire, as he
> was naked of human clothes, he gave himself up to the free, pure
> elements . . . . (XXII, 589)

Set against this sun-sparked vitality are the moon-lit graveyards and their interesting inhabitants. There is a hint of the macabre as the Andersen brothers make love to different women among the tombstones. (XIX,492-6, 513-15) This slightly odd or off-centre interpretation of what is so often called "the normal" is responsible for much of the merit of *Wood and Stone*: otherwise this would read like so many other stories of frustrated or satisfied passion. Once the possibility of the supernatural, of the unknown or unknowable, is admitted in the context of everyday activity, the levels of thematic complexity are multiplied. Consider, for example, James Andersen's belief in the power of stone. He is convinced that a special rapport has developed between himself and the material with which he has worked for so many years, that its soul has passed into his own soul, and that, like lovers, they respond to each other. (XVII,440)[3] When examined in this light, his subsequent death in the quarries appears a fitting fulfilment and justification of his life.

James and Luke represent extremes on the scale of human experience: the former is darkly introspective, struggling for sanity under a double burden of sexual frustration and moral idealism; the latter carelessly extro-verted, satisfied with the pleasure of living and desiring nothing more. Between these lies a middle way – the amoral, asexual, autonomous world of art. Ralph Dangelis embodies this aspect. He comes to Nevilton Manor as Romer's guest. His introduction as "the only son of one of Toledo's most 'prominent' citizens, a gentleman actively and effectively engaged in furthering the progress of civilization by the manufacturing of automobiles" is one of Powys's thankfully rare attempts to use verbal irony as social comment. (VII,II2) Besides being "a prospective, if not an actual millionaire", Dangelis is an artist of some renown and soon becomes more involved with capturing

Gladys's beauty on canvas than with his role as her suitor.
Eventually he sees her selfish nature and rejects her, but
not before he has understood the essential beauty of her
form. "She was the very epitome and incarnation of all
those sunward striving forces and impulses, which, rising
from the creative heart of the universe, struggle upwards
through the resisting darkness. She was a Sun-child, a
creature of air and earth and fire . . . ." (XI,239) Dangelis's
detachment from people and from their intrigues
apparently intended to serve as a kind of objective
commentary on them. This is not realized in the novel
because of the absence of the artist from so much of the
action. His trips to London and Weymouth are rather
inexplicable while his presence is sporadic and often
unremarked by persons with whom he should have some
connection.

The relation of character to place and time brings us to
yet another damning ambiguity in *Wood and Stone*. Time
is depicted as both chronological and psychological, but
there seems to be slight connection between the two types.
Events which are carefully documented with descriptions
of seasonal change have little specific reference to their
natural contexts and occur almost entirely within the
larger, psychological framework of the novel. A similar
difficulty appears in the treatment of place. Concrete
settings, whether towns, villages, or lakes, are rarely
particularized according to spatial dimensions; instead they
take their shapes from the informing attitudes of one or
more of the characters – or from Powys's own comments.
Perhaps some attempt was made to endow the village of
Nevilton with global significance by creating a vague sense
of depth or perspective through the rather haphazard
reiteration of place names such as London, Rome, Spain,
Peru, China, and the like.[4] Regardless of his aim, however,
Powys fails to convey an adequate sense of either place or
time. His inability to separate the measurable from the

mental results in confusion.

Wood and Stone is an interesting book, but, is it a good novel? A number of characters and events are memorable; certain nature-descriptions are forceful; the theme is significant. No doubt much must be said in favour of a narrative technique which deals with the "mythologies" of "Power" and "Sacrifice" in a way that sympathizes with both but avoids outright condemnation of either. Nevertheless, the question must be put: where does this novel lead? What is the point of all this character analysis, of these descriptions, of this theme? It leads nowhere: there is no point. This book is a collection of fragments of lyrical prose, of philosophical speculation, of entertaining characterization; but nothing unifies these bits of writing. Granted there is a thin story-line involving the somewhat forced achievement of freedom for the two pariahs Lacrima and Quincunx. However, apart from stories of thwarted love, the novel lacks vision or direction. As I have indicated above, spatial and temporal dimensions are inadequately co-related; characters often gesture without purpose; the prose rambles in digressions and repeats itself in arguments. *Wood and Stone* has no centre: it is constructed according to a principle of thematic duality and informed by an attitude of scepticism. The author appears to have had little idea of where he was going: the reader fares no better.

To point out that an author's first novel usually contains the most promising qualities as well as the most serious defects of his later work has become a standard cliché of the literary hack: nonetheless it is often a just observation. *Rodmoor* (1916), Powys's second novel, is shorter than its predecessor and, although the characters are as odd, they are less numerous, more sharply conceived. So too in story terms, *Rodmoor* is a much more dramatically executed work, being relatively free of the rambling digressions so characteristic of *Wood and Stone*. There is a sense of the particular in place and of the individual in person.

This concreteness of detail is obvious from the first chapter which describes a scene between two newly acquainted lovers. They are sitting on a bench in Kensington Park. The woman, Nance Herrick, is attempting to assimilate a few of the very strange things her lover has told her about himself. Adrian Sorio, as he is called, has been discussing both the past — his recent mental breakdown suffered in New York, his neurotic inability to work since arriving in London — and the future — a chance invitation to visit an old friend, Baltazar Stork, who lives in the small village of Rodmoor on the North Sea. The name of this village has fascinated him and given him premonitions of what he is to expect there. Later, after the pair have left the park, Adrian tells Nance about a sort of vision he has seen, of an human shape which appeared one evening on the wall of his room and then vanished when the word "Rodmoor" was spoken by someone in the room adjoining his.

It is not surprising that Nance should feel so uneasy in her response to Adrian's disclosures. She is a practical girl who supports herself, her half-sister Linda, and an old friend of her dead mother's, Rachel Doorm, by working at a dressmaker's; it is also the spring and she is in love for the first time. However, there is another, deeper reason for her apprehension. Before she knew of Adrian's planned visit to Rodmoor, she herself had been offered the opportunity of going there with Linda as the companion of Rachel Doorm whose father had recently died, leaving his daughter a house on the outskirts of the village. Although initially pleased with their coincidental prospects, Nance now experiences a vague sense of foreboding.

Adrian, on the other hand, is not concerned with the trivialities of day-to-day existence. He is totally absorbed by his own thoughts and accepts his friend's invitation to Rodmoor as a welcome release from the necessity of supporting himself. When he learns that Nance has had a like offer, he assumes her acceptance as already accomplished. The idea of Rodmoor has fast become an obsession: it governs his speculations and hopes with a fatalistic nearness which seems to him closer than memory or anticipation. His thought processes are centripetal: everything spirals inwards to the single, formalizing concept of Rodmoor which has "related itself, dimly, obscurely, and with the incoherence of a half-learnt language, to the wildest and most pregnant symbols of his life." (I,9)[5]

What stands out by the end of this first chapter is the dominating strength of Adrian's mind and, although the locality of action shifts from London to Rodmoor as the second chapter begins, it is Adrian's mind that has been fixed as the centre of the novel, not a geographical context. Various characters and situations are described in the course of this narrative but all are related in some way or the other to one constant — the mind of Adrian Sorio. Hence Rodmoor exists less as a physical presence than as a mental atmosphere — I shall have more to say about this towards the end of my discussion of the novel — and in this atmosphere two things contend for superiority in Adrian's thoughts: love for his son Baptiste who is in New York, and plans for a book which will be " 'a revelation of how the essence of life is found in the instinct of destruction' ". (VIII,111). In these two extremes, the one a positive manifestation of the continuance of life, the other a negative argument contrary to life, is to be discovered the same theme of dualism examined in *Wood and Stone*. Here again, the individual is being forced to choose, or if not able to choose, to be sundered, between the conflicting forces.

Duality is emphasized everywhere in this novel: by the pairing of characters as brother and sister, clergyman and doctor, sister and half-sister, protector and friend; nor is this sense of duality confined to persons; places are also paired: houses, land and sea, sun and moon. Such a deliberate pattern is not achieved without a certain loss of variety, and the frequent adjustments in situation needed to maintain conversations à *deux* often turn what should be structural emphasis into a monotonous device.[6] However, other advantages than those in dialogue are gained through the use of polarities. Of these, one of the most successful is the thematic fusion of antipodal relationships into the consciousness of the central character. We may begin our examination of this technique by considering the personality of Adrian's host in Rodmoor.

Baltazar Stork is a son of Walter Pater[7] and brother to Dorian Gray in many ways. As a bachelor whose pleasures are apparently cerebral, he has surrounded himself with prints, china, and statuary. His most cherished possession is "a portrait of a young man in a Venetian cloak, with a broad, smooth forehead, heavy-lidded penetrating eyes and pouting disdainful mouth." (V,58-59) A definite complicity is suggested between Stork and the portrait: on one occasion it seems to assist him in mocking Nance Herrick by tantalizing her sister Linda; on another it appears to stimulate his desire for suicide. (XI,145-51; XXIII,372-3; XXV,420) It addition to intellectual enjoyment, the portrait also gives him a certain sensuous delight: Baltazar finds his "Venetian boy" "delicious". We are not surprised to learn that he is "constitutionally immune from susceptibility to feminine charm". (XI,145) Other characteristics of dress and behaviour point back to the fashions of the 1890s.

More important than his appearance, however, is the

philosophy of life evolved by Stork the aesthete. As first suggested by Pater but later dissipated by Wilde, the formal structure imposed through art on both mind and body serves as an intricately designed surface under which seethe the grotesque unknowables of chaos.[8] Baltazar is fully conscious of the precariousness of his carefully ordered life which he frequently visualizes as "an immense, empty plain — a plain of steely-blue ice under a grey sky — and in the centre of this plain a bottomless crevasse, also of steely-blue ice, and on the edge of this crevasse, gradually relinquishing their hold from exhaustion, two human hands." (XX, 293; also XXIII, 366-7, 370) The final expression of his life-weariness inevitably involves itself in a ritual of self-destruction.

The details of Stork's characterization are commonplace; what is significant, however, is the distance and completeness with which his attitudes are delineated. Despite our sympathy with his predicament, we cannot fail to note either the cruel determination with which he torments those he dislikes or the perverse selfishness by which he is led to cause Adrian's permanent mental breakdown in order to thwart Nance's plans for marriage. An outcast by birth — he is a bastard — Baltazar remains an oddity throughout his life. His artistic and aesthetic interests are debilitating both to his own person and to those about him. Even in death, he maintains his solipsistic arrogance by leaving a will "of so strange a character, taking indeed the shape of something like a defiant and shameless 'confession', that . . . the appointed executors . . . hurriedly hid it out of sight." The portrait of Flambard is bequeathed "at the end of an astonishing panegyric, 'to our unknown Hippolytus, Mr. Baptiste Sorio, of New York City.' " (XXVI,432)

Who is "our unknown Hippolytus"? Is it coincidental that his initials are likewise those of his benefactor? Is he

too a bastard, an artist, and a beautiful boy? Were it not
mentioned that Baptiste sends a cable to Nance from New
York, Adrian's son might be nothing but a mental
construct; in any case, his entire character in the novel
exists in the thoughts of his father and in the speculations
of others. Only once is his mother described — "a
Frenchwoman of the coast of Brittany" — in reference to
the similarity of her appearance to that of her son.
Although he is apparently legitimate — his father wonders
at one point about Baptiste's reaction to his marrying
"again" — he seems a sort of spiritual bastard, cut off as he
is from any actual sense of a personal past. As regards his
present occupation, the reader is informed that he has, "a
good place in New York"; just what this "position"
entails remains vague. Rather, it is as an embodiment of
the projected desires and ideals of those who know of him
that the character of Baptiste Sorio is most fully emphasized. Hence, Adrian thinks of him as the "angel" who
stands at the centre of his philosophic dreams; for Baltazar
he is "an extraordinarily beautiful youth"; while to Nance
he is a saviour of "unearthly beauty and endowed with a
mysterious supernatural power". (XXI,326; XV,210;
XXVI,433) His place in the novel is symbolic: he is the
promise of youth and beauty; he is the hope of life and the
fulfilment of ambition. As such he must never enter the
novel as an active participant. His failure to reach
Rodmoor in order to effect any changes is again necessary.
For the ideal can never be realized: that is evident by
definition. Only once do Baptiste's symbolic and actual
roles unite: a few seconds before his death Adrian
experiences a short respite from his madness: "For one
brief miraculous moment his brain became clear and an
ecstatic feeling of triumph and unconquerable joy swept
through him." He shouts the word "Baptiste" twice.
(XXVII,458)

We have come full circle. Baltazar Stork encouraged
Adrian's insanity so as to prevent his friend from finding
happiness elsewhere; but in so doing he destroyed the
purpose and meaning of his own life. In Baptiste, Stork
sees an *alter-ego* , an innocent-self of the past — Hippolytus — who still has a permanent place in Adrian's thought.
The bestowal of the portrait is an attempt to identify
himself with and perpetuate himself in Baptiste. However,
it is not the actual Baptiste with whom Adrian is
preoccupied: it is with the " 'angel of that large, cool,
quiet place' " which " 'is beyond the limit, beyond the
extremest verge, beyond the point where every living thing
ceases to exist and *becomes nothing!*' " (XXI,326) In this
imagined region the negative influence of Baltazar fuses
with the positive force of Baptiste to give Adrian his
moment of "unconquerable joy".

The counterbalancing effects of Baltazar and Baptiste
upon the personality of Adrian Sorio is one of the best
illustrations in *Rodmoor* of Powys's technique of synthesis; but what of the components of other patterns of
relationship in this novel? If taken individually, each
person can be regarded as self-sufficient; in his relation to
others, as being contrasted with them. Thus the interplay
of action and reaction is permutable, often working itself
through various — and at times rather obvious and formal
— combinations. It is at this point that method and
meaning become one. For it is not towards the solution of
any of these opposites that this novel is moving; instead it
attempts to depict meaning in the very tensions it
describes.

An example of this process-as-meaning may be found in
the presentation of Brand Renshaw and his sister Philippa
who, with an ageing mother, live in their ancestral home
called Oakguard. (This living arrangement, incidentally,
parallels that of Nance, Linda, and Rachel who inhabit

nearby Dyke House.) Brother and sister are bound by an intimacy which exceeds ordinary family ties. Indeed, they are initially united by what appears to be an incestuous fascination. At least, it is difficult to interpret otherwise sentences such as the following: "Tightly and almost savagely he held her, pressing her lithe body against his own and caressing it with little,deep-voiced mutterings as if he were soothing a desperate child. She submitted passively to his endearments and then, with a sound that was something between a moan and a laugh, she whispered brokenly into his ear . . . ." (IV,54) [9] Incest in fiction is not new, but here another twist is given to the relationship. Philippa is described as a "fragile thing . . . whose tender form and tight-braided, dusky hair might have belonged to a masquerading boy"; elsewhere she is described as "boyish" and "androgynous". (III,44;IV,49) [10] In such a light, Brand's attraction to his sister becomes paradoxically homosexual. Perhaps this is an unspoken reason for Brand's conviction that he and his half-brother Baltazar are "bound together for life". Whichever way one chooses to regard this brother-sister relationship, it retains its symbiotic unity and, consequently, is self sufficient.

Nevertheless, each partner shows strong heterosexual interests. Brand's affair with Linda Herrick develops in a fairly straightforward manner; he meets her, seduces her, and leaves her pregnant. It is very tempting to make Brand Renshaw the villain of the piece. Linda is an innocent, sheltered girl of seventeen: she plays the local church organ as pastime and occupation. These are the apparent circumstances. But an examination of the lovers' conduct reveals a different level of activity. When they first meet, Nance, who is present, is quick to note "that there had leapt into being, magnetically, mysteriously, irresistibly, one of those sudden attractions between a man and a girl that so often imply . . . the emergence of tragedy upon the horizon". (VII,93) Yet something greater than a simply physical infatuation is being described here. The very elements are soon evoked in a ritual of fear and captivity whereby Brand binds Linda to himself: at the edge of the sea he flings sea-foam in her face while a cloud, blood-red in the sunset, takes the shape of a hand with forefinger extended. (VII, 96) Whether this sign is to be interpreted as a benediction or admonition remains ambiguous in itself, but, when a similar token appears moments before Brand impregnates Linda, there can be no doubt as to its symbolic nature.An elemental unity which was fittingly begun with the event of darkness grows to maturity and rises fecund out of the sea to envelop the lovers in a universal life-experience. They cease to be individuals playing out their own designs; rather they participate in the primordial mystery of creation. This is how Powys describes them "when through an eastward gap between the trees the sun rose above the mist. It sent towards them a long blood-coloured finger that stained the cedar trunks and caused the strangely shaped head of the stooping man to look as if it had been dipped in blood. It made the girl's mouth scarlet-red and threw an indescribable flush over her face, a flush delicate and diaphanous as that which tinges the petals of wild hedge roses." (XXVII,230-1) Another synthesis has been achieved. Although Brand abandons Linda after this, he has fulfilled his role: the life-force has been affirmed once again as the central aspect of all human relationships.

Here we have arrived at a crucial point in the plot of *Rodmoor*. The romance between Brand and Linda has run its course; Brand has been thrown back into his former association with Philippa. At this point action in the novel rests. There is an interlude of re-establishment, of almost idyllic *rapprochement*, wherein the characters appear to be moving towards a final and happy resolution of their differences. Three separate chapters (XVIII-XX) are used to engender this deceptive sense of security: the first deals principally with the two sisters, the second with Brand and Philippa, and the last with Nance and Adrian. It is especially with this last chapter entitled "Ravelston Grange" that we must be concerned. In it Nance and Adrian achieve an unprecedented degree of reciprocity. They journey to Mundham on a Saturday afternoon where, seated in a small tea-shop under the contemplative gaze of a "large blue-china cow", the lovers confide in each other. When they eventually leave the shop, they do so "in a mood of delicate and delicious harmony". Their happiness is short-lived. Soon Adrian reacts according to "that law which is perhaps the deepest in the universe, the law of *ebb and flow*." (XX, 301)

The effects of this "law" on human emotions and situations are so aptly chronicled by Powys that even the most bizarre happenings become assured of credibility. What often governs the outcome of events is the chance intervention of some seemingly insignificant incident. Hence, human conduct is not so much determined by the heavy-handed intervention of fate as by the way things are; in other words, the merest caprice of thought can change or even reverse the anticipated result in any set of circumstances. By acknowledging this unpredictable variable in all of his characters' affairs, by making the very unruliness of chance subservient to his greater design, Powys has managed to incorporate one of the most evasive aspects of observable reality into the plot of *Rodmoor*. This formation of causal patterns according to apparently random associations gives to the overall structure of the novel a finality which develops from an inexorable inner necessity.

And so it is. Between the time Nance and Adrian leave the tea-shop and their train departs, the entire serenity of the preceding action is reversed. When they visit a local church, Adrian, unlike his companion, is annoyed by the singing of a hymn in English: he finds it melodramatic, preferring the "passionate aloofness" of Latin. This minor difference between the couple increases after their decision to walk along the river in search of Ravelston Grange, the former home of a celebrated East Anglian painter. Despite Nance's foreboding and the lateness of the hour, Adrian insists on pursuing their investigations further. They finally arrive, not at the Grange, which turns out to be on the other side of the river, but at the County Asylum.

We remember the first chapter of the novel, Nance's fear of Adrian's obsessions, and above all, Adrian's fascination with the importance of the word "Rodmoor" in relation to his own mental-balance. Once again the movement of events has turned in upon itself, and in this convoluted schema everything returns to its centre: the mind of Adrian Sorio.

These three chapters of *détente* can now be seen as much more than a lull or breathing space for both reader and author; indeed they recapitulate and emphasize earlier motifs and themes, they gather the diverse strands of the secondary material — the entire cast of characters is regrouped and re-assessed at one point or the other during this interval — and shape it towards the now inevitable *dénouement*. Nance Herrick, our standard of normality and common-sense throughout the book, is unable to cope with Adrian's eccentricities. Although she attempts to maintain a semblance of confidence in her plans for a secure marriage, she has been defeated. All this is evident in spite of her rather frenzied determination that it be otherwise. Hereafter, the pace of the novel drives forward with an unmitigated compulsion which reduces Nance's feeble actions to inconsequential gestures.

The excursion to Mundham took place in late August.

The action which follows occurs during a period from
early September until the first week in November. During
these two months, a strange concatenation of events
results in Adrian's complete and fatal insanity. Some of
the related incidents have already been discussed –
Baltazar Stork's suicide and the consequent summoning of
Baptiste Sorio – but both of these are more caused by
than causes of Adrian's madness. There are however a
series of happenings which bear directly on Adrian's
extreme behaviour and eventual confinement in the
Asylum: his discovery of Rachel Doorm's corpse; his
formal proposal of marriage to Nance; his reaction to
Linda's disclosure of pregnancy; his violent assault on
Brand and near strangulation of Nance. All of these things
are linked by one underlying connecting factor: Adrian
Sorio's attitude to Philippa Renshaw or, perhaps more
precisely, his attitude to her avowal of absolute love for
him.

   Earlier, when describing Philippa's involvement with her
brother, I mentioned the underlying masculinity which
gave their relationship a homosexual, almost fraternal,
character; at the same time I stressed the essentially
self-sufficient nature of their personalities acting as a single
unit against the intrusion of strangers: Renshaw *versus* the
world, so to speak. What has happened to that bond
between brother and sister? In "The Listeners", the second
of the "three chapters of *détente*", we observe Brand and
Philippa engaging in a kind of mental duel, each testing out
the other's most secret and cherished aspirations: Philippa
taunts Brand about Linda and marriage while he, in turn,
accuses her of hating their mother enough to kill her.
These dark speculations are stopped by the arrival of two
visitors but later Philippa is described as "laughing as
merrily as a little girl" and Brand comments that his sister
" 'hasn't laughed like that for years' ". (XIX,280,281) Two

things appear to be at work here: a suspicion that some foreign influence is threatening the fundamental unity of their association; a new but unrealized awareness that each may be able to establish and develop a full understanding with someone else. The self-sufficient unity of the pair has been undermined and Philippa is now in a position to act as an individual.

Whereas hitherto hers was a dominating personality, it now undergoes a drastic reversal. This is how the change occurs. Shortly after returning from his trip to Mundham with Nance, Adrian goes out walking with Philippa. They arrive at a disused windmill. After a bit of exploring, Adrian decides that he wants to hoist Philippa through a hole in the ceiling by means of a rope tied under her arms. She balks at this proposal. He insists. She is thrown "into a physical panic". His suggestion has "changed their re-lations — it destroyed her ascendancy, it brought things down to brute force, *it turned her into a woman.*" (XXI,320. Italics mine.) But Adrian is not to be thwarted by her pleading:

His face as he listened to her darkened to a kind of savage fury. Its despotic and imperious lines emphasized themselves to a degree that was really terrifying.

'You won't?' he cried, 'you won't, you won't?' And seizing her roughly by the shoulder he actually began twisting the rope round her body.

She resisted desperately, pushing him away with all the strength of her arms. In the struggle between them, which soon became a dangerous one, her hand thrusting back his head unintentionally drew blood with its delicate finger-nails from his upper lip. The blood trickled into his mouth and, maddened by the taste of it, he let her go and seizing the end of the rope, struck her with it across the breast. This blow seemed to bewilder her. She ceased all resistance. She became docile and passive in his hands.

. . . .

They stood looking at each other in startled silence and then, quite suddenly, the girl moved forward and flung her arms round his neck.

'I love you!' she murmured in a voice unlike any he had heard her use before. 'I love you! I love you!' (XXI,321-2)

What we have just witnessed is the disintegration of a personality. Unwittingly Adrian has taken as complete possession of Philippa as Brand did of Linda; only the consequences are much more dramatic because he has conquered not merely her body but her very spirit. Yet Adrian remains ignorant of this great change in his companion as is evident from an episode which takes place soon after they leave the windmill. Passing a short distance from Dyke House where Rachel now lives alone, Adrian challenges Philippa to prove that she is "like a boy" by displaying courage enough to enter that dark and ominous dwelling. Philippa answers him: " 'I'm not a boy, I'm a woman.' " (XXI, 329) She never deviates from this newly discovered ideal of womanly love. Although she does enter the house, she flees it in terror leaving Adrian to find Rachel's corpse a short while later.

Certain events now become inevitable. As in all tragedy, the latent germ of the ultimate catastrophe is to be found in the essential strength of the protagonist. The intense power of Adrian's character which compels others to meet and accept him on his own terms coils back upon himself. Baltazar, Nance, and Philippa have felt this compulsion and have loved him but they have torn him from his sense of single purpose: they have rent the unique integrity of his mind with its two chief preoccupations, his book and his son. In speaking about both to those who love him he has propagated the negative influence of the former but lost the positive presence of the latter. He once acknowledges this loss in a desperate appeal: " 'Oh, God, . . . give me back my son and you may take everything – my book, my pride, my brain – everything! everything!' " (XXI, 330)

In *Rodmoor* there is no God, at least not one whose Presence makes Itself felt. It is obvious, for instance, that Hamish Traherne, the local vicar, is an ineffectual man whose well-intended but useless spiritual guidance seems to do little else than bolster the self-delusions of naive girls and old women. His most praiseworthy virtue would appear to be solicitude for his pet white rat Ricoletto. Nevertheless, Adrian's plea is answered, not by any force outside himself, but by that same perverse mental necessity which has complicated all of his dealings with others. He precipitates events by urging Nance to marry him. Although she agrees, she "could not help feeling that there was something blind, childish, selfish, unchivalrous, — something even reckless and sinister — about this proposal . . . ." (XXIII,353) Soon Philippa learns of their plans and, in Adrian's presence, begs Nance to permit him to spend the last day before their marriage with her. After a long but inconclusive argument, Philippa leaves, not however without a parting sally directed at Adrian: "'I leave her to you!'" she cries; and then asks, "'*And what will Baptiste do . . .?*'" (XXIV,391) Her last words bring no immediate reaction from Adrian; yet there can be no doubt about their suggestive power. Immediately after this disturbing encounter, Nance discloses the details of Linda's pregnancy to him. He is adamant in his desire to settle the matter with Brand immediately. The interview which takes place at Oakguard shortly afterwards reveals Adrian's shaken mind. No sooner has Brand finished his convincing polemic against compulsory marriage than Adrian attacks him with his walking-stick, beating the man into unconsciousness. Nance manages to restrain him until servants, summoned by her screams, remove Brand from the room. Only then does she become fully aware of the extent of Adrian's madness. He mistakes her for Philippa and, in his confusion, accuses her of taking Baptiste from him. He

then attempts to strangle her but Nance succeeds in
breaking away at the last moment. We are later informed
that Adrian has been committed to that same Asylum near
Mundham which had so fascinated him just over a month
earlier.

In much criticism of fiction, the device of detailed
story-summary is seldom necessary; more often it is a
concession to lazy readers. In the case of the above
paragraph, however, I feel that brief *résumé* does convey
some of the urgency implicit in the closely knit causal
patterns of the original. Adrian Sorio *must* become insane;
Nance Herrick *must* be thwarted. But what of Philippa?
And what of Baptiste? The former appears defeated in her
love and the latter seems as remote as ever. Matters are
not yet resolved. At this point in the narrative we have
little confidence in Nance's ability to alleviate Adrian's
condition by sending for his son, nor are we deceived by
the party held by a group of his friends to celebrate his
seemingly rapid recovery. Indeed the two chapters
(XXV-XXVI) following the one describing Adrian's total
breakdown serve to heighten the suspense of *Rodmoor* by
diffusing a false air of optimism and levity. As elsewhere in
this novel the contrast between the violent and the
peaceful, the rapid and the slow, is used to great
advantage.

The last chapter of *Rodmoor* strikes the final balance.
On hearing the news of Adrian's improvement, Philippa
determines to visit him at the Asylum before anyone else.
She feels that she alone can provide the restorative he
needs, that she of all his acquaintance is best able to
understand him. She takes the train to Mundham. When
she arrives at the Asylum, she not only succeeds in gaining
an interview with Adrian but also receives permission for
them to leave the premises for a short walk. They wander
down "close to the river's edge. A small barge, with its

long guiding-pole lying across it, lay moored to the bank. Without a moment's delay . . . Adrian jumped into the barge and seized the pole. 'Come!' he said quietly." (XXVII,454) Soon the barge is being swept down the river towards the North Sea while its occupants fall into a trance-like state of lethargic contemplation: Philippa, musing on her dark, possessive joy, and Adrian, imagining the ultimate repose of Nothingness. This state continues until their barge strikes a bridge near Rodmoor. Here Adrian leaps out, declaring that he must be alone. He rushes towards the sea and, looking out over it, experiences that moment of visionary truth wherein the actual and ideal are united in his cry: " 'Baptiste!' " He then turns away from the water's edge and attempts to speak: " 'Tell Nance that I — that I —' His words died into a choking murmur and he fell heavily on his face on the sand." (XXVII,458) He is dead when Philippa finds him. In a frenzy of possessiveness, she binds his body to hers with a cord she is wearing and staggers into the waves where the tide carries their bodies out to sea.

Adrian's death is not suicidal; Philippa's is. There is something very satisfactory about this ending. Earlier, when discussing the method of *Rodmoor*, I wrote of process-as-meaning; this is the technique which determines the outcome of the novel. The conflict which tears Adrian's loyalties between the life-affirming ideal of his son and life-negating influence of his book is responsible for all of his difficulties. Like Hamlet, he is never sure — of anything. His affairs with Nance and Philippa reflect his mental indecision; he remains uncertain until death removes his power of choice. And thus we come to the germinal concept in *Rodmoor*: the freedom of the individual to exert his will without the coercion of any external power. Both Nance and Philippa abandon their essential freedom, the former in deference to a conventional code of morality which gives purpose and direction to her actions, the latter in submission to a man whose personality becomes the object of her worship. Other characters in the novel experience similar degrees of freedom according to their own capacities. Nevertheless, this is not an abstract novel of ideas; its power lies in the exactitude with which it portrays the workings of the human mind beset by a myriad of choices and influences. That Adrian could at any moment have acted differently can never be doubted, but that he did not is what matters. The plot of *Rodmoor* is such that the artistic inevitability of the events described is coupled with the complete psychological freedom of the characters involved.

Had Powys been content to structure the entire novel around Adrian's dilemma, had he been satisfied with depicting the interaction between one man and his society, he might have achieved a *tour de force*; however he did not limit his subject sufficiently. There is too much honesty in this novel, too little is rejected. Its author is aware that the idea of individual freedom is almost a metaphysical platitude and he is determined to show that even the most radical attempt at personal liberty is heavily compromised by the effects of natural and elemental phenomena upon the human mind. Representative of these uncontrollable forces are Rodmoor and the Sea.

The village is never given a very detailed description — a few shops, a fishing-wharf, and scattered houses seem to be its general features — but it does have a very strong hold on the minds of its inhabitants, at least of the ones treated in the novel. Even before its introduction to the reader, its name has been associated with Adrian's perverse imaginings. (I,9-10, 19-22) Nance's first impressions of the locality are not promising:

The Spring was certainly not so far advanced in Rodmoor as it was in London. Nance felt as though some alien influence were at work here, reducing to enforced sterility the natural movements of living and growing things. The trees were stunted, the marigolds in the wet ditches pallid and tarnished. The leaves of the poplars, as they shook in the gusty wind, seemed to her like hundreds and hundreds of tiny dead hands — the hands of ghostly babies beseeching whatever power called them forth to give them more life or to return them to the shadows. (II,28)

The "alien influence" felt by Nance does not seem to be confined to Nature. The village doctor, Fingal Raughty, notes interestingly " 'that there exists in this part of the coast a definite tradition of malformed skulls. They recur in nearly all the old families. Brand Renshaw is a splendid example.' " (V,63-64) This is indeed environmental conditioning! Whatever the mysterious power is that pervades the atmosphere, it exerts its influence with inexorable intent. Even the Vicar is aware of its insidious presence and cautions Nance that " 'the Rodmoor air has something about it, something that makes it difficult for those who come under its influence to remain quite simple and natural . . . . Rodmoor isn't the place to come to unless you have a double share of sound nerves, or a bottomless fund of natural goodness . . . . ' " (XII,158) While the village itself remains a vague embodiment of invisible forces, the word "Rodmoor" assumes the nature of a magic-phrase, an incantation which seems to hover over the movement and speeches of the characters; the simple fishing village on the North Sea ceases to exist, Rodmoor becomes a mental atmosphere.

Closely allied with but not identical to the function of Rodmoor is that of the sea. Its sound is omnipresent, the beating of the waves forming a constant background to the events of the story.

To those in the vicinity, whom Nature or some ill-usage of destiny had made morbidly sensitive to that particular sound, there was perhaps something harder to bear in its placid reiterated rhythm under these halcyon influences than when, in rougher weather, it broke into fury. The sound grew in intensity as it diminished in volume and with the *beat, beat, beat,* of its eternal refrain, sharpened and brought nearer in the silence of the hot August noons there came to such nervously sensitive ears as were on the alert to receive it, an increasingly disturbing resemblance to the sistole and diastole, the inbreathing and outbreathing of some huge, half-human heart. (XIX,265)

The power of this sea is passive, its patient continuity mocking the fretful urgency of human action. Characters respond differently to its presence: Brand and Philippa see it as an accomplice in their plans, he in the seduction of Linda, she in her possession of Adrian; Nance simply dislikes it; Adrian, as in other things, vacillates in his attitudes toward it. The villagers, with indifferent accept-ance, know that beneath its waves lie other coastal townships which, like their own, have slowly but neces-sarily been subject to its constant encroachment. The sound of its waves constantly recalls people to the fact of its presence; its meaning remains unknown to them.

Although in the sea and Rodmoor Powys has created two powerful — at times awesome — counterparts to the actions of men, he has failed to subordinate them to the central lines of his story. Both of these creations are too massive to serve as simple commentary on the futility of human endeavour; they become heavy with overtones of determinism and obtrude roughly into Powys's carefully balanced portrayal of the psychology of free-will. What should have remained as the setting for this novel, has taken on the aspect of another duality, land and sea, engaged in an elemental dialogue.

Powys has overstated his case. From an analysis of Adrian's predicament, it becomes apparent that the con-cept of free-will is endorsed and supported without reserve; but, at the same time, complete personal freedom is seen as a near impossibility because of the pressure of life's contingencies. Powys stresses these unknowable, ungovernable aspects to such an extent as to over-balance his principal argument, and, in so doing, destroys the aesthetic unity of this book. *Rodmoor* fails through excess, not want.

Were I asked to justify the space I have given to an examination of Powys's first two novels, I would affirm that conclusions are often more valuable than introductions. The novels which have been under discussion were published within a year of each other; together they evince characteristics of style and content which may be taken tentatively as forming a general basis for Powys's method as novelist. Their very dedications, the one to Thomas Hardy, the other to the "Spirit of Emily Brontë", indicate two quite different lines of approach. *Wood and Stone* is earth-bound: great blocks of descriptive writing emphasize natural settings; accounts of village customs and institutions attempt to convey local colour; strong affinities between the characters and their environment suggest a world of predominantly physical dimensions. *Rodmoor*, as we have seen, is significantly different. Like *Wuthering Heights*, it presents a weird, rarefied atmosphere, where characters move in the half-light between sanity and madness. The subject matter is metaphysical and the treatment of it psychological. At the centre of the novel struggles a tormented mind imparting to the whole an essentially mental texture.

Rodmoor is much superior to *Wood and Stone*. Although some descriptive passages occur, they are usually sparse, with hard, concrete details and, more importantly, they are not static but are used to advance the narrative. Movement, development, and change originate from within events and characters rather than from the arbitrary impositions of the author. So, too, a great deal of what is spoken seems firm and individual: dialogue frequently reveals personality. In this dramatic context events and situations form strong causal patterns. Characters are permitted to show themselves in immediate interaction with specific circumstances. In almost all of these factors *Rodmoor* differs from *Wood and Stone.* In the latter novel, as I have noted earlier, Powys tells us everything through long descriptions and personal commentary. Very little is left to the characters who often disappoint the reader by their failure to perform in the elaborate settings so carefully prepared for them.

And yet there are similarities which, I believe, give a very clear indication of Powys's early practice as a novelist. One of the most striking resemblances between *Wood and Stone* and *Rodmoor* is in the handling of time. Both books relate events in the context of the seasonal movement from Spring to Autumn. Character change appears to correspond somewhat to this seasonal pattern; for instance both Gladys and Linda are virgins in the Spring and prospective mothers in the Autumn. This relationship seems less one of symbolism than of affinity; it also functions as a convenient device for fixing the chronology of the story. Time is also distance, and journeys either on foot or by train are used to provide a limited period for characters to think. Random objects may suggest certain areas of thought to the traveller, or, heedless of the passing moment, he may speculate about the past and future. In both cases, time becomes a mental state bound only by the extremes of the distances traversed. Powys's early treatment of psychological time is crude and rudimentary: what does stand out, however, is his tendency to associate physical movement with intellectual activity.

Powys's characters think better not only on their feet but also when alone. They enjoy solitary strolls over fields especially during the early morning or late evening. If accompanied, they are likely to remain taciturn much of the time. We do not often find people in groups and when we do they will inevitably be in pairs. Individuality is everywhere emphasized: persons maintain their essential uniqueness at all costs and resent the infringements of others. Their conversations tend to be one-sided and a character will speak at someone rather than to him. Although the theme is never articulated, an awareness of the inadequacy of language seems implicit — more so in *Rodmoor* than in *Wood and Stone*. The difficulty of communicating with one's fellows is made all the more evident by the enthusiastic verbosity of some characters: it rarely achieves its ends and oftentimes reverses its intended effect.

These various techniques — psychological time, character isolation, verbal impasse — point to the dominant interest of the author. Powys sees the essential loneliness of the individual and attempts to depict it. To do so he banishes the common occupations of life and concentrates on mental activity: what his characters think is much more important than what they do. The matter of these novels is speculative or reflective.

Once he has chosen the minds of men and women as his subject, the novelist is presented with innumerable possibilities: he may investigate psychological states from within or without; he may examine intellectual or emotional activity; he may note both introverted and extroverted mental processes. The author may avail himself of each of these methods separately or he may use them all in a complex of analytic creation. His final selection and emphasis will determine the tenor of his book. It is here that Powys both triumphs and blunders in his first two novels. *All* activity is interesting to him, *all* must be examined by him. Two important qualities of his characterization owe their success to this all-inclusiveness: the ability to find in every person, even the most repulsive, some sympathetic aspect or redeeming feature; the habit of deflating pomposity, self-righteousness, or intellectualism by some trivial turn of phrase or by revealing a slight mental quirk. The defect in this method occurs when Powys's zeal to probe and expose becomes uncontrolled. At such times he appears unable to sketch in a peripheral character; rather he must plunge to the very centre of the man's mind, trying to extract the essence of his personality. This technique can result in too many characters being portrayed too deeply. The balance of the work is destroyed: we are either tantalized by the single appearance of a person who excites a great deal of interest, or overwhelmed by the minute analysis of someone who bores us. Although more obvious in *Wood and Stone*, Powys's same *penchant* for excessively detailed characterization reveals itself in the full presentation of many of the minor figures in *Rodmoor*.

Of the various facets of human experience, Powys has selected the psychological as his subject. Although in theory this choice can provide an unlimited scope for the writer, it must in fact be severely restricted if it is to be manageable. *Wood and Stone* failed to exclude enough: it tried to encompass political and economic influences, religious and secular moralities, industrial and aesthetic principles – all exerting their diverse pressures upon persons from different levels of society. Little wonder the novel is such a *pot-pourri*. The case is quite different with regard to *Rodmoor* where almost everything extraneous to the central argument of the book is omitted; yet in its exposition of the psychology of those few inhabitants of Rodmoor this novel shows much greater scope than its predecessor. The clue to this paradox lies in the word perspective: Powys's first novel has virtually none, his

second a great deal. A dual relationship is involved here —
the relative distance between objects (persons or ideas) in
the novel and between the author and his novel.

In the former instance — the relative distance between
objects — emphasis through selection indicates the
importance we are to attach to certain characters and
ideas. Without this distancing, the effect of the novel
becomes blurred, its direction indefinite. Multiple subjects
require constant adjustments of perspective if they are to
remain clear. The equal distribution of importance to
every aspect in *Wood and Stone* gives it a flat, even
surface. Depth, on the other hand, typifies the texture of
Rodmoor. Here objects have been made precise by
techniques of comparison and contrast, action centres
about particular characters, episodes are arranged to achieve
specific ends; in other words, a perspective in which the
proportioning of parts contributes order to the whole has
been established. While dealing with fewer subjects than
the first novel, the second has more scope because it gives
dimension to its material. Thus, perspective eventually
creates a hierarchy of values.

In order to make distinctions among the implied
judgements in a novel, another factor must be considered:
the writer's intention. This may be indicated explicitly or
implicitly in the text, depending on the relative distance
between the author and his novel. Determining this
distance can be extremely perplexing in some cases, but
with regard to Powys's early writing it is comparatively
simple. Neither of his first two novels is *avant-garde* in
technique; both have something of the comfortable intimacy of much nineteenth century fiction. Powys stands
close behind his characters, pointing out their mistakes or
applauding their fortune. We are invited to share his fears
and hopes or to disagree with his generalizations. We are
also required to accept his summations of situations which

we did not witness. This sort of camaraderie is rather unpopular in the eye of the contemporary reader but that in itself does not prove it worthless. It becomes offensive only when it detracts from the unity of the whole, as it does in *Wood and Stone,* by taking, for example, the form of unnecessary digression or of irrelevant comment. Powys's voice can however aid the accomplishment of his design by operating as a point of contact between reader and novel. This is evident in *Rodmoor* where complexities of mental activity merge with elemental forces. The author's voice is ready to indicate direction and regulate bias, not in the form of interfering manipulation but as a suggestive pressure. He achieves this end by incorporating his own presence in the general narrative not only in the first person but also through his selection and emphasis of detail. Whether or not this convention pleases the reader matters little; what does matter is whether or not it works in the particular context of these novels. It manifestly does not in *Wood and Stone* but it does in *Rodmoor.* In the latter novel, Powys increases the scope of his subject matter by indicating the open-endedness of his material. His voice, directly or indirectly, is a continual caution to us to avoid drawing either an easy moral or a facile conclusion from the book. The intensity of presentation offsets the moments of reflection and the narrative gains rather than loses coherence through the author's presence.

Thus far in my attempt to deduce Powys's practice as novelist from his first two books of fiction, I have confined myself for the most part to considerations of the "how" as opposed to the "what" of the novels. However, even the most scintillating techniques are empty if not informed by some idea or vision of reality. Just what that "reality" is depends on the author's point of view; if his technique communicates his particular reality to the reader then it must, to some degree, succeed. Powys is at a distinct disadvantage here because he seems to be very uncertain about the nature of reality. When reduced to thematic terms, his first two novels offer us a view of life which avoids cynicism but raises a constant doubt as to the value of any human endeavour. Scepticism is the dominant attitude: it fluctuates in its interests and allows for every contingency; it generates a basic distrust with regard to any dogmatic position, even its own; it renders final judgements impossible. A principle of dualism is found at the core of every question and reality presents itself as a multiplicity of balanced conflicts. Few opinions are seen as indisputably correct, and, orthodox distinctions, such as those between good and evil, seem irrelevant. Since no fixed pattern of ideas or single system of beliefs dictates their subject matter, the meaning of these novels rests in themselves.

We have seen in *Wood and Stone* that Powys's inability to decide about the respective value of anything has caused the meaning of that novel to be vague. His awareness of the multiplicity of life and of natural phenomena should be an asset to his production of fiction but it becomes a liability as long as it remains unshaped and undirected. In this regard, *Rodmoor* is a marked advance. In the second novel, Powys has taken his themes of life and death, of nature and art, sex and idealism, society and the individual, and given them an order. He has weighed one side of each dualism against the other until he has reached a sort of implicit judgement, not with regard to standards of right or wrong, but, as to the essential form of reality – namely, a perpetual state of unresolvable tension among various interrelated persons and things. We recognize this as the same form which determines the shape and structure of the novels whose meaning lies in the process of revelation achieved through a speculative examination of this same reality. Hence we come to the thematic weakness in *Wood and Stone* and in *Rodmoor*. Their significance is locked in themselves. Each is trying to work in an inward flowing pattern from the more superficial aspects of life to its very essence. Such thematic movement must be paralleled by a similar development in technique. Powys was not master enough of his craft to carry this off in his first two novels. They both lack that unity of vision which is necessary before any number of diverse, interesting ideas become fused into the symmetry of art.

Although these novels did not achieve thematic unity, they do indicate, nevertheless, certain fundamental attitudes towards man, his activities, and his world. Nature, both in its animate and inanimate aspects, is seen as self-contained in its being and growth; it may be in or out of harmony with human action. The people who move about in this natural world engage in certain occupations but with little sense of dedication or enthusiasm − doctors fail to practise medicine, clergymen ignore religious duties, craftsmen and clerks never seem to be at work, and so on. Society is composed of individuals, each intent on defining his or her own personality in order to give some personal meaning to life. The preoccupations of these men and women are for the most part metaphysical or psychological; they are hardly ever concerned with the practicalities of daily life. The world of *Wood and Stone* and *Rodmoor* is essentially egocentric: the final critic and judge in all matters is the individual human consciousness.

[1] J.C. Powys, *Wood and Stone,* New York: G. Arnold Shaw, 1915. Parenthetical references are to the novel under discussion unless otherwise stated.

[2] Quincunx's interest in Dolores seems to be at least partially sexual. He is initially attracted to her by "the electric stir produced by beauty and sex [which] can only reach a culmination when the medium of its appearaance approximates to the extreme limit of fragility and helplessness." (XXV,660) This characteristic of "fragility and helplessness" is common to both Dolores and Lacrima (XIII,292), only more strikingly so in the former.

[3] A rather similar idea is treated in a story by Oliver Onions: see "Benlian," *Widdershins,* London: Chatto & Windus, 1968, pp. 153-80. First published in 1911.

[4] There are approximately eighty-five different place names, not including adjectival forms, in *Wood and Stone.*

[5] J.C. Powys, *Rodmoor,* New York: G. Arnold Shaw, 1916. London: Macdonald, 1973 (same pagination).

[6] An early example of one of these "arranged" manoeuvres can be noted in II, 34. Other annoying instances are VII, 94; XVIII, 244-6. It is in their cumulative frequency rather than in their singular occurrences that these pairings become so tiresome.

[7] *cf.* Walter Pater, "Sebastian Van Storck," *Imaginary Portraits,* London: Macmillan, 1920, pp. 81-115.

[8] See, for example, Pater's comments on *La Gioconda* in his essay "Leonardo Da Vinci" included in *The Renaissance.* (Walter Pater, *The Renaissance,* London: Macmillan, 1920.)

[9] Other examples more effective in context point to the same incestuous dependence. See IV, 55; XIX, 267-72.

[10] See also III, 46; IV, 50; VIII, 110, 112; XIX, 281; XXI, 320.

II

Powys's third novel *Ducdame* begins with the assumption that "Some of the most significant encounters in the world occur between two persons one of whom is asleep or dead." (1.1)[1] The statement in itself may or may not be true, but its implications that the dead are as accessible to personal contact as the living introduces a new aspect into Powys's fiction. Although there was some speculation about the activities of the dead in *Wood and Stone* and about their power over the living in *Rodmoor*, it remained undeveloped. In *Ducdame*, however, the dead are the constant companions of the living. Their presence takes the form of an ancestral assembly of the different Squires of Ashover from the time of Lord Roger of Ashover, the Crusader, to that of Squire John Ashover, the most recent to join the company.

Their various monuments and inscriptions are first described when Rook Ashover, the present head of the House, and his brother Lexie pay a nocturnal visit to the local church. Rook has thwarted his ancestors not only by having failed to father an heir but also by establishing a deliberate impediment to that end, namely, the acquisition of a mistress who is unable to have children. Since Lexie is a childless bachelor with an advanced terminal disease, the family name faces extinction. This situation provides the basis for all the action in *Ducdame*: characters exert their energies either to further or oppose the continuance of the

Ashover lineage.

The most radical in his opposition is William Hastings. As the local Vicar, he should be the guardian of those buried within his church; however, he is quite the opposite. Just as the behaviour of these dead fails to conform to Christian patterns, so too do Hastings' ideas deviate from theological orthodoxy. He has abandoned religion for metaphysics and is working on a "Book of Annihilation" which explains "the original secret of Life-Destruction; the great anti-vital energy, the death energy!" He feels that his knowledge is much more than "a mere metaphysical theory": "It is just as much an organic force, an actual magnetic force, as radium or electricity." His book is especially connected with the dead Ashovers, and to definite purpose. He states his views clearly:

'Ever since I came to this place I have been conscious of the power the dead have to preserve something of themselves alive in the world! Old families, like these Ashovers, have this power. . . . Now do you know what I am doing? I am thwarting these dead! *I am driving them back.* . . . There'll be no more Ashovers born into Fromeside. Rook and Lexie are the last!' (X, 145)

These words are addressed to Ann Wentworth Gore, Lord Poynings' daughter, variously referred to as Cousin Ann or Lady Ann, and soon to become Rook Ashover's wife. Her role in *Ducdame* is diametrically opposed to that of William Hastings: she welcomes the life-instinct, seduces Rook, marries him, and eventually bears his child. At first glance, the relationship appears rather straightforward with Ann, the life-principle, victorious and Hastings, the death-urge, vanquished. Were this the case, the "Book of Annihilation" would be just so much rubbish and the Vicar a madman. However, it is not quite this easy to dismiss what is obviously, as we shall see, one of the major concerns of *Ducdame* and, recalling Adrian's book in *Rodmoor*, what would seem to be one of Powys's constant themes.

What are we to think of this strange, dark book written
by a country parson out of the bitterness of an obsessed
mind? When first introducing Hastings, Powys speculates:
"Is there, perhaps, a power of destruction in human
thought capable of projecting its magnetism beyond its
own realm of immaterial ideas?" (IV,45) The author has
tried to answer his own question through his treatment of
Hastings and his book. If we are to understand the answer
we must come to know the man and the context of his
writings in so far as they are given to us.

At various times during the narrative, certain facts are
revealed about the Vicar's past. We learn that he was the
son of a London cobbler, an abnormally sensitive child
who was brought up in comparative poverty; that he was a
"little unhappy boy at school, persecuted by his companions and hating all the world, but able to *think the
whole world away* and to sink back, back, far back, into
the comfortable arms of the infinite Nothingness!" (XIV,
210) He has unwisely married Nell, a young neurotic girl,
whose immature conduct soon disgusts him. He reacts
awkwardly to her passionate nature and their marriage
becomes a sterile contract of fear and coldness. William
Hastings is old beyond his thirty-five years, a short,
paunchy man with a suave, detached air. And yet, his calm
exterior is easily shattered when his book is made the
subject of casual, after-dinner conversation, or when he is
reminded of slights received in his youth from the
indifferent rich. (X,139-41; XVIII,288-9, 293-4) A very
definite picture begins to emerge and it is not difficult to
see a shy, frightened boy hiding behind the guise of this
clergyman-philosopher. Hastings has used his intelligence
to rationalize his childish means of escaping from unpleasantness into a sophisticated philosophy of nihilism: however, he is still trying "to *think the whole world away*" and

is as much on the defensive about it as he ever was.

This much is quite evident about the man, but what about his book? Powys has given his character ample justification for being the way he is, but he is not really interested in establishing the importance of environmental conditioning: Hastings' past is only significant in so far as it has formed those attitudes which have resulted in a life-long dedication to the most extreme goals of misanthropy. What remains uppermost in the novel is the power which Hastings supposedly places in his book. Does this power actually exist and, if it does, how does it operate? Do we see its presence in *Ducdame*?

At the core of Hastings' thought is a conviction that two primordial forces — the death-urge and the life-urge — are engaged in a ceaseless struggle. Until now, the life-force has had the better of the contest and, although never able to conquer death fully, has perpetuated itself as the creative principle of the universe — which may be thought of as God, the sex-instinct, or vegetative propagation. Hastings has discovered the nature of this creative-principle (we are never told exactly what it is) and has set himself up as the champion of its opposite. He hopes to achieve the extermination of life not by simple destruction, which is positive action and as such creative, but by the perverse logic of passive malignant thought. As far as we are told, the Book of Annihilation would seem to contain the whole of Hastings' withering system with adequate directions for implementing the process. Once this negative power has been understood "Man shall say, 'Let there be Darkness!' and there shall be Darkness." (X,143-7, XVIII, 286-94)

Unlike Adrian Sorio, whose similar book was never completed, Hastings finishes his life's work. As the time of Lady Ann's confinement draws nearer, the Vicar's desire to stop the birth becomes more and more intense. His mind grows increasingly unsettled until, in a state of delirium, he ceases to think of his writings in any rational context. He is now convinced that his nihilistic power has passed into the very substance of the book and determines that, if the Ashover name is to become extinct, the book must be carried by Lady Ann to the church where it can be placed under the stones which cover the Ashover crypt. He succeeds in persuading Ann to take the book which she clasps to her pregnant body; she hurries towards the church but, on the way, passes a bonfire — it is autumn and the sexton is burning weeds. Ann impulsively throws the book into the fire and it is quickly destroyed.

What we have witnessed is the transformation of a *quasi* Nietzschean-Platonic philosophy into an elemental form of black-magic. Did the book contain any real power? Had it not been burnt, would it have prevented the birth of another Ashover? We can never know. Were this the sum-total of occult activities in *Ducdame* we might content ourselves with some intellectually satisfying explanation of these happenings. But Powys has introduced yet another point of view from which we can judge the Vicar's negative preoccupations. And here we come to the second factor which distinguishes this book from its predecessors. Contraposed to Hastings' black magic is the white magic of Betsy Cooper and her magic crystal. This old crone, who is obviously the fictional descendant of Witch-Bessie of *Wood and Stone*, lives in a caravan with two grotesquely misshapen dwarfs whom she calls her "partners". They are actually her grandchildren, the progeny of the illegitimate union between her daughter Nancy and Rook's father. Thus, Betsy is closely associated with the Ashover family. Like Rook's, her ancestry, although not quite so illustrious, has its roots deep in the history of Dorset. As well as finding her relationship with the Ashovers useful for a bit of petty blackmailing, she appears to have gained particular foreknowledge about their affairs from it.

The first of her prophecies, which concerns us more immediately, has to do with William Hastings' Book of Annihilation and the delivery of Ann's child. Shortly before her visit to the Vicarage, whence as we have seen she is cajoled into carrying away the Book, she meets Betsy Cooper. Lady Ann has neither sympathy with superstition nor patience with paupers; she brushes aside Betsy's entreaties for a hearing. As she walks away, Betsy yells after her: " Till book be burned no child'll be borned!'," (XXIV,408) These words are the ones which echo later in Ann's mind when she walks by the fire. In itself, this macabre outcry would carry little weight but seen in the light of Betsy's second prediction it assumes greater importance. Earlier in the story, while visiting the caravan to pay ten pounds in blackmail, Rook sees a vision of himself in the crystal globe: he is dead, lying in a coffin, and his mistress, Netta Page, is looking down at him. The scene comforts rather than disturbs him. Later, however, a more alarming episode appears in the ball: Betsy sees Hastings in the act of killing Rook. This is the piece of information which the old woman tries to impart to Ann. The final and most dramatic of Betsy's fore-warnings is given to Rook after Ann's labour has begun and he is walking aimlessly, awaiting the birth of his child. He encounters Betsy in the churchyard where she is digging about in search of her daughter's unmarked grave; she becomes frenzied by his appearance, urges him in vatic tones to return home in order to avoid his own death, and bewails the inattention with which her words have been heard by all she has tried to caution — amongst them the servants at Ashover House and Rook's mother. (XXV, 429-430; also XVII, 262-5; XXIV, 406-9) It almost goes without saying that Hastings does eventually murder Rook.

We can see a balancing and paralleling of forces in these

operations of white and black magic. The exponents of
both are concerned with the dead, but in quite different
ways. To Hastings the dead are the enemy, a form of
race-consciousness, whose very dust, gathering century
upon century, gives proof of the continuity of the
life-urge; for Betsy Cooper the dead have an immediate
presence and her response to them is positive. She devotes
all her energies to the preservation of life – we find her
seeking her daughter's grave in order to mark it and
honour the life which once was; she has respect for the past
Ashovers because of rather than in spite of their tendency
to have mistresses as well as wives, to have bastards as well
as legitimate offspring. Although the black philosophy of
Hastings leads to madness and murder, it falls far short of
its goals for Rook's death has only added one more voice
to the powerful chorus of dead Ashovers.

We have seen something of the inception and method of
Hastings' nihilism, springing, as it does, from personal
deprivation and advancing through individual ratio-
cination: it has no existence apart from the Vicar's mind
or his book which is, after all, only an extension of his
thought. But what of Betsy Cooper's prognostications?
They seem non-rational and impersonal; while their immediate source is her crystal globe they would appear to have a
more mysterious, more remote origin. After seeing his
death in the crystal, Rook asks Betsy where she got it. Her
answer is worth quoting in full:

'From Cimmery Land, Squire,' she answered quietly. 'And that be
the land where folks do live like unborn babies. They don't see
nothink, nor hear nothink, in thik place, except what be like the smoke
of this 'ere pipe [which she is smoking] ; and when them folks do talk
'mid theyselves it be like the turning of Miller Cory's girt wheel –
mum, mum, mum – where us can hear the drumming of wonderful
green water and where millstone be all moss-mumbled and wheel
be all hart's-tongue ferns! 'Tis real wet rain, what's finer than corpse

dust, them folks do live under; and they tell I it be wonderful strange to
see 'un walk and talk * * * mum * * * mum * * * mum * * * and
thik mist all slivery and dimsy round 'un.' (XV,II,264)[2]

Rook finds this picture very attractive; he thinks of it as
"some Elysian Fourth Dimension" of which he had had
intimations but never completely realized for himself.[3]
Within weeks he has an even more direct experience of this
other-world. He is walking along a deserted country lane.
It is a hot day and Rook is very upset: he is worried about
the women he has met and the misery he has caused them;
he is perplexed by his destiny and his place in the universe.
At the peak of his agitation, he feels the distinction
between the real and the imaginary blur. It is at this point
that he meets a young man on horseback whom he has no
difficulty in recognizing as his son. Rook tries to make the
boy understand his problems but fails to articulate his
ideas clearly. Yet the son seems to possess an instinctive
grasp of the very essence of his father's plight: he
commiserates with him, his gentle presence rather than his
few words affording Rook great comfort. After smiling at
his father with a "penetrating sweetness . . . which diffused
itself through every fibre of the man's body", he murmurs
" 'Good-bye, Daddy!' " and rides away. What remains in
Rook's mind "as an ineffaceable reality" is his son's face,
"so unmistakeably resembling his own but with a beauty
and power in it beyond anything he had ever approached."
(XIX,307-10) During the whole of this apparition, all
natural colour had vanished leaving everything uniformly
grey; immediately after the boy's departure, things returned to normality. As Rook regains his equilibrium, he
decides that the occurrence was the product of his frenzied
fancy. But was it? We remember Betsy's description of
Cimmery Land "where folks do live like unborn babes"
and that one of its particular qualities was greyness. At this
time Rook's son is a six month old foetus: does he possess

a pre-natal personality existing perhaps in some dimly obscure fourth dimension? Does Rook visit this region through a species of imaginary empathy or is a momentary spell cast upon terrestrial existence which reverses the order of time and continuity? The event is shaded in ambiguity, neither confirmed nor denied.

Just a few moments before he is murdered, Rook experiences a repetition of this phenomenon, with slight variations. This time his son's presence is more nebulous, of shorter duration and less comforting. There is greater finality in the spirit's disappearance and Rook is left with the conviction that his wife has just given birth to a son. (XXV,433-4) Whether actual or imagined − the second appearance like the first is *rationally* rejected by Rook − these two happenings have profound effects on Rook's thinking. The first meeting provides him with a solution to his life-long problem of indifference and indecision. His philosophy has been that of a sceptic who doubts not only the value of things external to himself but also the worth of his innermost attitudes. By the time he encounters his son, Rook has become the victim of the very ironic stance which he assumed to give piquancy to his dryly rationalized defeatism. Just a little over six months earlier, he had flaunted his ancestors by using the infatuation of Hastings' wife Nell as an excuse for deliberately mocking them: he had taken bitter enjoyment in making love to her in the church which housed their bones. Nell mistakenly took his actions as signs of genuine affection and still pursues him. He feels nothing towards her but is tormented by the disappearance of his mistress, who, he fails to realize, has been misguided by Ann into thinking that Rook is repressing his desire for a son out of consideration for her. All three of these women − Nell, Netta, Ann − have drawn from Rook responses which have forced him to compromise his emotional integrity. Nor have these

complications endeared him to his mother, whose mania
for an heir to the Ashover name has been a constant
judgement and condemnation of his actions. The various
pressures of intellectual, emotional, and moral commit-
ments have become overwhelming: he feels an acute loss of
personal freedom and an equally strong need for reciprocal
companionship. (At this stage, his is very like Adrian
Sorio's final desperation.)

He began to feel as if from henceforth to the day of his death he were
destined to be deprived of all separate individual reality, destined to
become a mere husk or shell, in the centre of which was nothing that
could assert itself, or sink down into itself, but only something that
had to reflect, reflect, reflect the thoughts of a completely alien
person. (XIX, 306; see also XIX, 297-312)

Rook's first meeting with his son resolves these difficulties by giving meaning to the seemingly haphazard and
purposeless events of his past. He sees his child as an
absolute, as containing the beauty and sweetness of life in an
unalloyed intensity. He is aware of and compares their
resemblant identities, finding himself lacking in the face of
such self-possession. Like Adrian before him, he sees in his
son something which diminishes present suffering in the
promise of a richer future. Rook learns the lesson of
acceptance: " 'No one is worthy to live' ", he cries out to
the boy, " 'Who doesn't know that all Life asks of us is to
be recognized and loved!' " (XIX, 310)

This revelation of what has been missing in his philosophy is more easily understood than implemented. As the
vision fades, so too does most of Rook's conviction.
Nevertheless, his mind is more at rest than it has been for
some time. He never succeeds in coming to any genuine
understanding with his wife nor is he able to suppress his
emotional involvement with other women, but he does
manage to become moderately reconciled to his fate as the
months pass. When the hour of his son's birth arrives, it

finds Rook in one of his most receptive moods. His mistress has returned from London, not to stay with her former protector, however, but to make peace with everyone before finally leaving to resume the life of religious good works to which she became converted after leaving Ashover House. This and other changes have prepared Rook for his coming role as father and husband: he meets his unborn child the second time and is confirmed in his certainty that a new, more harmonious life lies before him. He experiences "the most primitive emotion of the human race: that immemorial exultation. . . . . the joy that a man child is born into the world!" (XXV,434; see also XXV,432-3)

The Ashover dead have been vindicated. For they have been present all the while watching over this struggle between the powers of life and death. At times they perform choric functions of interpretation and emphasis; at other times they are the silent but irrefutable evidence of an indomitable life-force. We must distinguish these particular dead from abstract concepts of the dead or death as an impersonal fact. What we are concerned with are the actual dust and bones of Rook's ancestors as they exist beneath the stone floor of the family church. There is nothing religious or spiritual about these remains: theirs is the accumulated power of past consciousness projecting itself into present circumstances in order to assure future continuity. This is what Hastings meant by "the very essence of . . . the life force" which he feels emanating from the tombs; this is what Ann feels, after the birth of her child, when she meditates on the victory of the "mouse-coloured dust in Ashover Church". In their role as chorus, the dead Ashovers affirm their encouragement and approval of Rook's sexual union with Ann. Just before he goes to her on Christmas night, he stands out-of-doors in the cold darkness where he twice hears something inexplicable: "A

most uncanny sound, blood-curdling and shocking" which
came "from the invisible heart of the snow-bound hills . . . .
It was louder and more appalling than the cry of any wild
creature. . . . It seemed to come to him through some
heavy, remote intervening substance. The nearest description he seemed able to give of it was that it suggested the
united exultation of a host of people buried underground". (IX,125; also XVIII,294) That is, of course,
exactly what it is. The only other time the dead react in an
audible fashion is at the termination of an embittered
diatribe against life which Hastings has directed at Rook.
The cry seems an answer to the Vicar's arguments, a
counter-challenge positing the supremacy of existence over
annihilation.

There are other occurrences which indicate the open
dimensionality of *Ducdame*. Netta Page is attracted to a
portrait of Sir Robert Ashover, the Cavalier, which hangs
in Ashover House. She feels that there is a bond of
sympathy between them. Late in the book,she has a vision
of his face looking in at her bedroom window; she is
reassured by this visitation and speculates about it:

How strange it was, she thought, . . . that the mind of a person dead
and buried more than two hundred years should still retain its power
to influence and to console! Was it that something actually survived,
of such a person's subtler, more sensitive consciousness, among the
places where it had moved in its lifetime? Or was there, behind all
the dream stuff of the whole tragic scene, some imperishable cistern
or reservoir of superhuman pity into which these nobler, these more
imaginative responses sank, as the years moved round, adding always
something to this great protest? (XXII,378)[4]

Netta does not have the ability to answer these
questions but her thoughts add to the cumulative impression this novel gives us of a world without bounds, of a
universe where man's consciousness is the germ of creation.

Although there are obvious thematic similarities between this book and *Rodmoor*, certain other features are
more exactly related to *Wood and Stone*. The setting is
again Dorset, though this time in a different and less
sharply defined area; the action is motivated by concerns
which are ultimately social rather than individual; characterization is achieved to a great extent through implied
or explicit contrastings of pairs and by depicting a
relatively wide range of figures. The two last mentioned
deserve special notice: to state that *Ducdame* is motivated
by social concerns could be quite misleading unless strictly
qualified, and the same caution must be exercised when
discussing Powys's methods of characterization. In the first
instance, I am using the word social to indicate the *milieu*
of the events described and the order given them in that
context. In that sense, this novel may be structured almost
exclusively around the psychological preoccupations of
very particular persons while, at the same time, retaining as
its final objective a comprehensive interest in the fate of
the Ashover family. And it is this subservience of the
specific to the general which determines the positioning of
the characters in relation to the whole and to one another.

In order to define and arrange these people Powys uses,
as one of his chief devices, a rather weak form of surface
irony. I have already mentioned examples of this in
passing: the *Reverend* Hastings' nihilism, and Rook's death
just as he is about to embrace life fully. There are others
such as Nell, the clergyman's wife, finding pleasure in
extra-marital involvements while Netta Page, at best a
respectable prostitute, discovers fulfilment in religion.
However, the most emphasized of these ironies is that
which unites and separates Rook from his brother Lexie.
As in *Wood and Stone* James and Luke Andersen were
parts of a duality, so too are the brothers in *Ducdame*,
only in the latter the distinctions between the two are

more subtly blended and less rigid. Rook Ashover is by far
the most complete and sympathetic person we have yet
encountered. He is realized through changes of personality
into a complex human being; his stand on the side of
thanatos might be better described as an inclination. Lexie,
on the other hand, is more clearly like Luke, a fervent
advocate of life and living. But here also we note a
difference: Lexie possesses a certain mental hardness, the
small cynicism of a sick man who feels deprived of natural
enjoyments. Nevertheless, he continues an avid disciple of
eros, flirting with whom he can, and rebuking Rook for his
moral scrupulosity. His attitude towards life is like his
behaviour with girls: he enjoys them "for what they are . . .
without making such a devil of a fuss about it". This same
matter-of-factness allows him to make love to Nell on
several occasions, the most dramatic being during a visit to
a travelling circus. On this last occasion, which takes place
about a month after Rook's murder, Lexie draws the circle
of irony to a close. Exactly one year has passed since the
brothers met in the church-yard; then they had discussed
Lexie's death and arrangements for his burial, now the
situation is reversed with Rook underground and Lexie
still retaining a tenuous grip on life.

My discussion thus far has emphasized three essential
aspects of *Ducdame*: the dead, magic, and open dimensionality. Because of their final inscrutability these considerations lure the novelist towards regions where all things are
indefinite and precise delineation impossible; they tempt
him towards sensationalism on the one extreme and
philosophic disquisition on the other. Only rarely are they
happily integrated by the imaginative genius of a Dante or
a Shakespeare. Powys's third novel is not informed by
genius: it ranks no more with *Hamlet* or *Macbeth* than it
does with the *The Divine Comedy*. How and why does a

book with such profound interests fall so short of literary
achievement? Condemnation rests of course in the word
"literary" when by it we mean that sense of balance,
consistency, clearness, and design which we have come to
expect in truly successful writing. These necessary qualities
are manifestly wanting in *Ducdame*.

A fundamental weakness is evident in the great uneven-
ness with which characters are presented. Powys's handling of the Ashover brothers is a damning example. Lexie is
indispensable to the plot as it is constructed, the opposite
of the fraternal duality, and the final articulation of that
uncompromising energy which is the novel's *raison d'être*.
His personality is strongly evoked in dialogue and admir-
ably presented in numerous scenes; but the very force with
which he is actualized causes a general structural imbalance. He splinters the focal concentration which should be
on his brother alone. For *Ducdame* is really the story of
Rook's personal development in and adaptation to an
evolving social ethos. Lexie obtrudes into this scheme,
thereby detracting from the novel's full impact on the
reader; and yet he is so definitely fixed in a secondary
position that he cannot carry the burden of thematic
responsibility implicit to his role: he is in this novel but
not of it.

Powys's failure to resolve the relationship between the
two brothers is, in the final analysis, his failure to unify
the novel as a whole. The final scenes of the book reveal
the discrepancy between what might have been a strong
but is actually a weak conclusion. Lexie's visit to the
circus, referred to above, should perform two functions:
(i) complete the artistically circular patterns of time and
circumstance, factually and ironically; (ii) break the
thematically centripetal coils which have bound Rook to
the hard exigencies of personal chance and, in so doing,
release centrifugal impulses of creative energy. Symbolic-

ally conceived and dramatically executed, the interlude nevertheless fails: a brief examination of its key action — Lexie's ride on the merry-go-round — and of the novel's penultimate and final paragraphs will show why. In the first instance:

> The noise in the young man's ears was deafening; and as he listened to it, giving himself up to the motion, his mind began wandering off to other sounds of a less artificial character that were at that moment rising up toward the cloud-covered sky from his native Frome-side.
>
> He thought of the way the branches were creaking even now among the Scotch firs on Heron's Ridge. He imagined the grunt of a badger as it trotted in the moaning wind across Titty's Ring. He heard the cattle stirring drowsily in their bartons. He heard the splash of a perch in Saunders' Hole and the cry of a stray mallard drifting across the marshes toward Comber's End. Out of the heart of that brazen clamour he seemed to be listening to the tiny German clock ticking the hour in his mother's bedroom. He even fancied he could hear the quiet breathing in its guarded cradle of the small head of his House, the young new Squire of Ashover. And then suddenly, as in his fantasy he counted up these unnoticed sounds of the night, it seemed to him that he could actually catch the whirring of owl wings hovering about his elm tree in the churchyard, as they had done in the moonlight, just a year ago, when he met his brother at that place. (XXV,454)

These are vivid images, conveying in their immediacy the very "grunt" and "splash" of the animal world, the ticking of the mechanical , the close warm intimacy of the human, the whisper of the supernatural; but, and the "but" is emphatic, they are the images of Lexie's mind, counted "in his fantasy". Within this mental framework, each sound and object recalls a similar sound or object from the opening chapter of the novel — the seemingly haphazard selection here is carefully deliberate. The weight and continuity of consciousness has shifted from Rook to Lexie: the artistic circle is neatly closed and the thematic

one deftly broken. The animate, inanimate, and spiritual
are realized, ordered, and perpetuated by the creativity of
man's imagination.

Now let us look at our second example which also
involves Lexie:

> He, the life amorist, the worshipper of the sun and the sweet air
> and the grain-bearing earth, was up to his knees at that moment in
> waters deeper and colder than the waters of the Frome.
>
> But even there, though his face in the darkness had the injured,
> bewildered look of an outraged child, he held the dead man tightly,
> protectively against his heart. He did not budge an inch from the
> integrity of his nature. But his love, like a spear driven into the bed
> of a swollen river, stood up erect and defiant, visible through the
> driving mist to all such as might come that way, a signpost in the
> night, a signal, a token, a witness that would at least outlast his own
> days, even though it did not outlast the Scotch firs on Heron's Ridge
> or the linden tree and the cedar tree on the lawn of Ashover House.
> (XXV,457-8)

There is no need to comment on the triteness of "up to his
knees" and "an outraged child" or on the forced sequence
of metaphor and simile: they are self-evident. More
important is the inadequate statement of intention, the
anti-climactic vagueness which characterizes these sentences. The ambiguity undermines and cancels the movement
of the novel; it denies the fraternal shift of consciousness
and, in so doing, destroys the validity of human creativity.
The phallic embodied as it is in a destructive instrument is
doubly ambiguous because, whether a homosexual or
generative emblem, it is ultimately sterile. We are left
with a few trees and little hope of their reproduction:
nature is alien and temporal, neither a substitute for nor an
extension of man.

Powys has given *Ducdame* two endings: the first one
which should complete the thematic and artistic shape of
the novel fails because the moribund Lexie is symbolically

unfit and contextually unprepared to assume Rook's revelation; the second ending shows Powys's dissatisfaction with the first. Both failures demonstrate how much more than simple presentation of character is involved in the unachieved depiction of the brothers' relationship. It is not that the argument of the novel is left unresolved — that would be perfectly acceptable — but rather that the unfolding of the argument is unclear. The final lines of *Ducdame* determine our attitude to the book as a whole: we read without believing, understand without responding.

This arbitrary ambivalence in organization is of such major consequence as to render pointless any discussion of minor defects. These, in any case, are not subtle: Powys's prose is frequently as awkward as that last quoted; other characters than Lexie are inadequately realized, among them Nell and Netta; ironies are inconclusive and episodes often under- or over-developed. From a literary standpoint, the most laudable passages in *Ducdame* are descriptive (we have already noted Powys's mastery of this form in the earlier novels). Here, frozen winter scenes are given emotional force through their impact on Rook and Netta; summer fertility is harmonized with Ann's advancing pregnancy into a convincing symbol of life-abundance. (VII;XXI) Although less static than similar descriptions in *Wood and Stone*, these are not as successfully integrated into the novel's dynamic texture as those in *Rodmoor*. In short, no sum of its merits can redeem *Ducdame's* basic flaw: namely, the imperfect public embodiment of an intensely personal vision.

And yet, *Ducdame* remains a fascinating work, a novel not so much "of ideas" as of emotional cerebralism. In Rook, Powys shows us modern man, sceptical and uncertain, fumbling towards an understanding of his beginning and his end. His search is personal, neither illuminated from within by religious conviction nor assisted from without by social convention. Symbolically isolated by aristocratic eccentricity, Rook is an Adam-figure whose prophylactic foreknowledge cannot secure him against his essential humanity. In his progenitive capacity, he is responsible for the life and by necessity for the death of his son. The process is circular (surely the name Ashover is a pun): Rook's dilemma is every man's inheritance.

But *Ducdame* attempts more than a confrontation of birth and death; it encompasses those elusive aspects of life's chaos which are often called chance, good, evil, and the unknown; it suggests that they may be distinct, independent forces or merely variants of one mercurial power. These concepts are actualized as the workings of black-white magic, the dead, and the fourth dimension. There is no question of an allegoric alignment of each abstraction with a fictional counterpart, but, nevertheless, the general equation is quite obvious. Hastings' anti-vital drives are indirectly responsible for Rook's murder; evil and ill-fortune merge into death; Betsy's attempts to do good are both confirmed (Ann's child is born) and contravened (Rook dies) by chance. The separate components blend into the unknown otherness of the fourth dimension. It is at this stage of mystic sublimation that Powys's rhetorical devices are unable to express the subtleties of his vision. His arguments remain nebulous, unsubstantiated by the cumbersome details of a melo-dramatic love-story.

I do not claim that *Ducdame* is a successful novel — indeed Powys himself often seems caught within the fool's circle of his own creation.[5] Nevertheless, the book demands our serious consideration. While having neither the lyrical intensity nor the dramatic compulsion of *Rodmoor*, it explores ideas of greater complexity and depth. It seeks to elucidate the contradictory tendencies of human motivation, to show how one man's thoughts and feelings are interrelated by causal patterns to the desires and frustrations of his fellows. Rook, unlike Adrian, is humane: he is aware of his involvement with people, and, more importantly, is disturbed by his inability to act positively. These primarily social problems are further compounded by his individual predilection for imaginary and occult experiences. *Ducdame* does not resolve these questions – in fact it might justly be said to make them even more obscure – but in its struggle to understand them, it has moved far beyond the sentimental hedonism of *Wood and Stone*, beyond the desperate solipsism of *Rodmoor*. The central vision informing this book is affirmative and, although it may become blurred at times, it strives to comprehend and accept the multiplicity of the human experience.

A clear picture of Powys's evolution as a novelist begins to emerge. He started with a general consideration of the possibilities of the fictional world; he examined the loose relationship of politics to art, lust to love, riches to poverty, work to leisure, and blended these in a texture of philosophical and theological argument; he placed odd or conventional characters in natural settings and balanced them against the social and industrial demands of village life. His judgements were often shallow in *Wood and Stone*, his comparisons unfair to both sides of his thematic duality which, itself, was rather arbitrary and ill-defined. What is relevant to us at this moment, however, is not the book's appalling failure but rather its ambitious comprehensiveness. Its author was willing, but not able.

That Powys himself saw this shows in the drastic limitations he placed on the subject matter of *Rodmoor*. One feels that selection in that novel was guided by a principle of exclusion and, indeed, the essentially negative direction of the tale bears this out. Nevertheless, the

isolation of certain elements for emphasis produces powerfully individual effects in the novel's treatment of psychological behaviour and natural phenomena. Exaggerated,
even grotesque, physical details point metaphorically to
the twisted workings of minds tortured with hope, fear,
and indecision. Powys is definitely on much firmer ground
in this context, with a stronger grasp of his material. But
again there is a sense of want, of something left incomplete. Despite its strength and its superiority over its
predecessor, it is a *cul-de-sac*. Adrian's and Philippa's final
disappearance beneath the waves is the logical extension, a
reductio ad absurdum, of Powys's principle of exclusion.

So, it is not really surprising that Powys's talents as
novelist then lay dormant for nearly ten years. When they
did reassert themselves in *Ducdame,* they came fortified
with a new sense of purpose. Instead of organizing his
material within negative strictures, Powys worked in terms
of a positive vision. Rook, as I have suggested, is closer in
treatment as well as in persuasion to twentieth century
concepts of alienation and isolation; unlike Adrian, who
was socially outcast but personally whole (his book and
son gave him solace), Rook is separated from his fellows
by divisions within himself. It is a valid paradox that the
fragmented personality of the latter should protect him
from the madness produced by the single-mindedness of
the former. *Ducdame's* failings are to be measured in
degrees, not kinds. Rook is inadequate to the total
articulation of the life-experience; Powys needs Lexie to
balance the active powers of existence against Rook's
passive acceptance of them. Much is attempted in this
novel but much more remains to be fulfilled.

Four years later *Wolf Solent*[6] appeared. The 966 pages
of the original two volume edition confirm the promise of
the first three novels. Powys's technique is much surer. He
has fused the dual heroes (James and Luke, Adrian and

Nance, Rook and Lexie) of his past fiction into one man, Wolf Solent. His thinking is also much sharper. The vague (it would be more flattering but much less accurate to say disinterested) plurality of attitudes which held sway in the first novel has been distilled into the uniqueness of a central personality.

Wolf's story seems amazingly simple. He is certainly not a "hero", and even the more recent label of "anti-hero" would add unwarranted lustre to his character. We first meet him on a train speeding from London to the Dorset village of Ramsgard. He has just quit the school -teaching job which had supported him and his mother in London for the past ten years and has accepted an ill-defined post as secretary to Squire Urquhart. His new employer resides at King's Barton, a short distance from Ramsgard and Blacksod. As a child, Wolf lived in this area; so too had his father whose dissolute habits had led to his death in a workhouse.

His occupation, he soon discovers, is to assist the Squire in compiling — Wolf does the actual writing — a libidinous history of the district. In carrying out his related duties, he meets Christie Malakite, a daughter of the old bookseller who supplies much of the unsavoury raw material for the so-called history, and Gerda Torp, whose father is carving a headstone for the Squire's former secretary: Wolf loves the first girl platonically and marries the second. Various domestic complications then arise: his mother comes from London to awaken forgotten memories and antipathies; a new friend is found to be a half-sister; his wife is physically seduced by Bob Weevil, a village butcher, and mentally by Lord Carfax, Wolf's rich cousin; Christie eventually decides to live elsewhere. Wolf makes no effectual protest against these changes in his life; throughout, his energies are directed towards adaptation and resignation. His final state of humiliation is apparently confirmed by his acceptance of a permanent role as cuckold.

The facts of the tale are simple. We have seen that Powys's method usually avoids moments of dramatic confrontation, preferring the anticipation and reflection which can be drawn from them. Thus, it is scarcely surprising that the "action" of *Wolf Solent* – the episodes which link its movement – should be unmomentous. And indeed, we find that the nineteen days selected from the passing year (the book covers a period from March 3rd of one year to the last Saturday in May of the following) are not really of out-standing importance in themselves. They serve principally as devices for grouping characters together – although by no means as crudely as a simple statement implies – and provide uncomplicated chapter -divisions. A glance at the table of contents indicates the unassuming properties of these episodes: "The Blackbird's Song", "The Horse-Fair", "The Tea-Party", "The School Treat" and so on. This very insignificance is noteworthy: the basic monotony underlying Wolf's existence is an essential part of the entire novel's claim to our attention. Rather than encumber his character with a burden of improbabilities and consequently his reader with the restraints of disbelief, Powys encourages our immediate sympathy – which is not the same thing as identification – with Wolf's plight.

There is a prevalent opinion about Powys's early novels that suggests they are "Landscapes with Figures".[7] This is seen as sometimes good, sometimes bad, depending on the literary inclinations of the commentator. Hardy's novels are frequently evoked to provide favourable or unfavourable comparison. Insofar as all such general statements have, within a loose frame of reference, some degree of validity, I would not totally disagree with it – it covers for instance a few of the difficulties we noted in *Wood and Stone* and, to a much lesser extent, the imbalance which mars *Rodmoor*. However, the term is rarely applied to these first novels; it is applied to the later novels which, beginning with *Wolf Solent*, are far too involved in thought and intricate in structure to benefit from any such thumb-nail sketch.

An investigation of nature as conceived and treated in *Wolf Solent* is certainly required. The physical setting of this novel comprises a great variety of things: fields, rivers, hills, marshes, flowers, and wildlife to be sure, but also the smells, sounds, and colours which define these objects. The whole is blended and fused by the winds, the rays of the sun, the light from the moon and stars. We are faced with a multiplicity of influences and effects. Seasonal changes are described with the comprehensiveness demanded by their complexity; even the evanescent shapes of clouds and mists are recorded. (VII,138-9; XV,314-15; XVIII, 388-9; XXV,610-12) All of these manifold impressions are conveyed to us through the feelings and thoughts of Wolf. That is why Powys is notoriously unquotable. Nature in this book is both passive and active; it interacts with Wolf's consciousness while remaining — and it is by no means irreconcilable — a perfectly autonomous creation. It is precisely this intermingling of human perception, a mental activity, with nature, a physical fact, which makes *Wolf Solent* anything but a "Landscape with Figures".

I have chosen two illustrations which — putting aside for the moment their contextual importance — should give us some indication of the deep and intense way Powys uses nature as a fundamental rhythm in this novel. My first example is a "set-piece" and being the simpler serves as a manageable introduction:

It was a during many a lonely walk among the red-berried hedges and old orchards, where the rotting cider-apples lay wasp-eaten in the tangled swathes of grass, that these events worked their wills upon him. Sunday after Sunday, as September gave place to October and October

gave place to November, he would lean upon some lichen-covered gate
and struggle to give intelligible form to these 'worries' of his. Threaded
in and out of such ponderings were a thousand vivid impressions of
those out-of-the-way spots. The peculiar 'personality' of certain
century-old orchards, of which the grey twisted trunks and the rain-
bent grass seemed only the *outward* aspects, grew upon his mind
beyond everything else. How heavily the hart's-tongue ferns drooped
earthward under the scooped hollows of the wet clay-banks! How
heavily the cold raindrops fell – silence falling upon silence – when the
frightened yellow-hammers fled from his approach! He felt at such
times as though they must be composed of very.*old* rain, those shaken
showers; each tremulous globe among them having reflected through
many a slow dawn nothing but yellow leaves, through many a long
night nothing but faint white stars! (XIX,390).[8]

Isn't that a perfect "landscape with figures"? Surely we
can see Wolf pensively reclined against a gate, at one with
his surroundings. Let us look more closely at the paragraph. At once we become aware of movement, of a puls-
ing rhythm of change caught in the chronology of time
passing. Our picture is not a "timeless scene" capturing
autumnal beauty fused with the human spirit. Nor is it
that subliminal moment of stasis when the activity of
living is arrested in a suggestion of eternity. In fact, we
find neither the false peace nor the ultimate sterility
implicit in Keats's "Ode to Autumn" – an obviously
apposite comparison.

The passage is carefully constructed. The first two
sentences emphasize the duration implied by the opening
words – "It was during many a lonely walk . . ." The
alliteratively linked repetitions stretch the imagination
outward towards the monotonous generality of passing
days and months. A profound sense of decay underlies this
description of Wolf's surroundings – our most active word
in these early lines is "rotting". Passive verbs and past
participles – "lay wasp-eaten", "tangled", "gave place to",
"lichen-covered" – contribute a cloying density, a heavy

physical burden of words, which overpower Wolf's cerebral struggle. The natural bounty — hedges, orchards, apples, grass, etc. — lingeringly surveyed in the opening sentences is focussed and given point in the third. Its importance lies, we discover, in the "thousand vivid impressions" made on Wolf's mind. However, the details which particularize this scene are not a selection of *"outward* aspects" but rather a number of inward characteristics that manifest themselves to the dramatically sensitized consciousness of their interpreter.[9] The quality of Wolf's perception might be thought of as the creative difference between a photograph and a painting. Powys has caught the inevitable and organic motion of the imaginative process.

The paragraph pivots on the third sentence. From initial generalities of appearance, it turns in the fourth and fifth (the two exclamatory clauses are really one sentence despite their mechanical separation) to the concrete experience of the immediate instance. We become aware that in the latter half of this passage nature reflects man and not man nature as was true at the beginning. The sixth sentence both summarizes Wolf's relationship with nature and extends the meaning of it beyond the limits of terrestrial phenomena. We are called back to time by the magical synthesis of vision and touch in "each tremulous globe". The languid tempo of seasonal chronology which we noted earlier has altered subtly but momentously. Powys has given to Wolf's interaction with nature a delicate balance of the personal-universal wherein "many a slow dawn" and "many a long night" lead to an etherialized composition of cosmic splendour. We conclude the paragraph with an awareness of worlds and suns, of creations and deaths: the "tremulous globe" has achieved planetary significance.

Such a skilful blending of micro- and macro-cosmic imagery is by no means unique — Shakespeare, Donne, and

Blake did rather well by it — nonetheless, it is remarkably different from a simple "landscape with figures". Even a cursory analysis of this paragraph shows how far removed it is from the "purple passage" and how erroneous it would be to admit its validity solely as a powerful evocation of nature. With complete reciprocity every word describing Wolf or his surroundings reinforces the organic dissolution of both man and season. The psychological and physical are united in a symbiotic bond within which each retains mutual independence. By looking away from his character as well as towards him, Powys has managed to avoid the "pathetic fallacy" with a success which escaped both Hardy and Lawrence. The economy of means Powys uses to charge the multi-leveled dynamism of this paragraph might be best illustrated by the two splashes of brilliant colour —red at the beginning and yellow near the end — whose very incongruity reverberates emphatically against the drab and wasted background.

When we turn to our second example, we realize that the autumnal scene presented relatively few difficulties of interpretation. This excerpt records an early meeting between Wolf and Christie Malakite in the latter's home.

The poignancy of her shyness increased his awareness of the suspense between them; and to loosen the spell he turned his head a little and glanced at the mantelpiece, on which was a china bowl, full of bluebells, late, long-stalked primroses, and pink campions and meadow-orchids. His own mind kept beating itself against the unknown — against that fatal *next moment* which drew to itself the dust-motes of the air, the scent of the wild flowers, the warm wind blowing in through the open window.

'Will she let me make love to her? Will she let me?' was the burden of his thought; and as he stared at that bunch of flowers, especially at one solitary bluebell that hung down over the brim of the white bowl and had gathered a tinge of faint rose-carmine upon its hyacinthine bloom, he felt as though the 'to be or not to be' of that tense moment depended upon chance as inscrutable, as fluctuating, as the light, falling this way, falling that way — light and shadow wavering together — upon that purple-blue at the bowl's edge.

Never had he been more aware of the miracle of flower-petals, of the absolute wonder of this filmy vegetable fabric, so much older, just as it is much more lovely, in the history of our planet than the flesh of beasts or the feathers of birds or the scales of fishes!

The girl's words . . . seemed to melt into that wild-flower bunch she had picked and placed there; and the pallor of the primroses, the perilous, arrowy faintness of their smell, became his desire for her; and the rough earth-mould freedom of the campion-stalks, with their wood-sturdy pinkbuds, became the lucky solitude she had made for him!

'Will she let me make love to her?' The longing to risk the first movement towards his purpose struggled now in his mind with that mysterious restraint, so tenuous and yet so strong, of the girl's obscure embarrassment.

'Did you pick those flowers yesterday?' he broke out suddenly; and he was secretly surprised at the loudness of his own voice.

'The day before', she murmured; and then without closing her mouth, which, with the droop of her under lip, took on an almost vacant look, she frowned a little, as she fixed her steady gaze full upon him.

His own eyes plunged once more into the green-shadowed depths of that midsummer nosegay. Its pale primroses seemed to sway in the wind over their crumpled leaves, as they would have done where she had actually picked them among the wood rubble and the fungus growths of their birthplace. The moist bluebell-stalks, so full of liquid greenness beneath their heavy blooms, seemed to carry his mind straight into the hazel-darkened spaces where she had found them. These also belonged to the embarrassment of that figure beside him. These also, with the cool greenery of the sturdy campions, were the very secret of that 'next moment,' which floated now, with the mocking sun-motes, untouched and virginal in the air about them.

His feeling was like a brimming stream between reedy banks, where a wooden moss-covered dam prevents any spring-flood, but where the water, making its way round the edge of the obstacle, bends the long, submerged grasses before it, as it sweeps forward.

Suddenly he found himself risen from his seat and standing against the mantelpiece! He lifted the flowers to his face; and then, putting down the bowl, he inserted his fingers in it, pressing them down between the stalks into the water. He noticed that the water felt warm to his touch, like the water of a sun-warmed pool; and the fantastic idea came into his head that by making this gesture he was in some occult way invading the very soul of the girl who had arranged them there. Christie may or may not have read his thoughts. At any rate, he now became aware that she was standing beside him, and with deft, swift touches was correcting the rough confusion he had made in her nosegay.

'The bluebell-scent is the one that dominates,' he murmured. 'You smell them, and see if I'm not right!'

As she leaned forward, he allowed his hand to slide caressingly down her side, drawing her slender body, with a scarcely-perceptible pressure, against his own. (X, 234-6)

A man, a woman, a bouquet of flowers; a few spoken words which can hardly be called dialogue; the simple motions of arranging flowers in a bowl — it all sounds very much like something in Virginia Woolf. But we would be mistaken to look in that quarter for the tone or texture of Powys's treatment of this subject. We would be better to examine a few of the personal confrontations in Jane Austen's novels — the meetings for example between Frank Churchill and Emma, the one on the Esplanade between Fanny Price and Henry Crawford, and most especially that in the Wilderness at Sotherton between Edmund Bertram and Mary Crawford — where understatement and indirection allow a passionate sensuality (sexuality would not be too strong a term) to seethe beneath a surface of conventional behaviour. It is exactly this ability to control moments of intense sensuousness that permits Powys to convey the heightened sexual atmosphere surrounding Wolf and Christie. Here the loose patterning of thought, mood, and object into a dramatically revealing context is greater than symbol – although symbolism is of course used; so too the effect achieved is more powerful, and more satisfying, than the semen-drenched extravagances of pornography.

We have witnessed a seduction, an inevitable and effortless procedure which seems as natural as the flowers that are so much a part of it. The situation appears to evolve with the near-classic simplicity of quality cinematography; the climax is reached only after the overtures of love-making have been enacted with the careful deliberate-ness of slow-motion filming. Wolf is cast as the hesitant but determined aggressor. The tenor of his thought is an insistent question: "Will she let me make love to her?" We follow Wolf's reading of Christie's attitude during their encounter; we see her as passive, murmuring, her words melting into the setting; we note Wolf's rising desire like a powerful stream bending in its course the unresisting grass. Our impressions are reinforced by various words which lift us into the dream-like mosaic of this enchanted scene: we feel the "shyness" and "embarrassment" caused by the "inscrutable", "obscure", forces behind these two people; we sense the "solitude" of "hazel-darkened spaces" where "perilous" scents mingle with "the very secret" of an "untouched and virginal" moment in time.

Thus far, our discussion has emphasized Wolf and Christie, specifically their relationship to each other. We have spoken in terms of a seduction and have seen how our impressions were guided by a *pastiche* of words which seem to transmute the human lineaments of this episode into the sacred figures of medieval or renaissance art. Certainly Wolf sees Christie as the undefiled, inviolable lady of the bower. In such an interpretation, the bowl of flowers is decorative, its meaning contained in the meta-phoric and symbolic associations it has with Wolf's thoughts.

There is however one major fallacy in our reading of the passage and, like Christie, we must in the end attempt to set aright "the rough confusion". We have, like so many commentators on Powys's novels, forgotten the author; we have assumed that Wolf and his creator are one and have narrowed our vision to that of the romantic protagonist.[10] Let us re-examine the text neither satisfying ourselves with a hasty *résumé* of impressions nor rendering details according to the stereotyped norms of the conventional love-scene. We must look for more than the puff-ball illusion of a "quality" film-clip *au ralenti*.

We may start by scrutinizing the flowers. While it is true they are wild-flowers, they are now arranged in a bouquet, separated from their natural setting. Wolf fails to note this difference. He associates their scent with "the warm wind blowing in through the open window"; he observes accurately the shapes and colours of the blossoms but forgets their immediate context. Disregarding Christie's comment that the flowers are in the third day of decay, Wolf continues to imagine their living freshness: "The moist bluebell stalks, so full of liquid greeness beneath their heavy blooms, seemed to carry his mind straight into the hazel-darkened spaces where she had found them." It is apparent that Wolf's sensual enjoyment of the floral display is directly related to his awareness of Christie. He sees her, in fact, in terms of the "one solitary bluebell" and his desire is an "arrowy" scent penetrating the freedom of her solitude. A few moments later, "He lifted the flowers to his face; and then, putting down the bowl, he inserted his fingers in it, pressing them down between the stalks into the water." Although Wolf himself vaguely recognizes the strangeness of these gestures, there is no naiveté in the detailed explicitness of Powys's language: the strongly vaginal character of the bowl adequately demonstrates the kind of sexual activity involved here. The prominence given to odours throughout the passage now assumes especial significance, an importance which Powys emphasized and clinches as Wolf's final words; "The bluebell-scent is the one that dominates," lead from contemplation to action.

"But", should you ask, "isn't this interpretation based on the very metaphoric rendering which you claimed was so misleading? Isn't your elucidation of the episode's sexual significance merely an extension of the original cinematic techniques you described?" My answer would be a qualified "Yes", and, were the investigation to finish at this point, such an answer would be totally unsatisfactory. As it is, however, our understanding of the scene's implicit sexuality serves as a means to an end, not an end in itself. What Powys has allowed us to see of Wolf's sub-conscious intentions still depends on a link between the imagery and the man; we have yet to consider the imagery and the woman.

Christie's shyness figures largely in this encounter. Are we, like Wolf, to conclude by inference that she is "untouched and virginal"? If she is chaste, then my reading of the passage is a harsh indictment of Wolf's character. What is the origin of "that mysterious restraint, so tenuous and yet so strong, of the girl's obscure embarrassment"? and why is it "mysterious" or "obscure"? We should also note that Christie remains composed during the interview; Wolf fidgets, moves about, and directs both his outer and his inner eye to the bunch of flowers. Christie, surprisingly enough for someone who is supposedly embarrassed, fixes "her steady gaze full upon him". I have already mentioned Wolf's disregard for the artificial state in which the flowers are preserved and his preference for the imagined beauty of their natural setting. In showing this preference he fails to realise that the "tinge

of faint rose-carmine" on the "hyacinthine bloom" of the
bluebell is the sign of decay and the herald of death — and
we remember Wolf's earlier sense of "the unknown", of
the "fatal *next moment*". This sort of imagery is main-
tained by the near-paradoxical reference to "the wood
rubble and the fungus growths of [the flowers'] birthplace". These are all dimly connected with the secret
shyness of Christie's personality. We are in the presence of
something unhealthy and moribund, something quite
dissociated   from Wolf's overt desire for freshness and
innocence: it is now apparent why the sun motes are said
to be "mocking". Our final indication of what is actually
taking place during this encounter reveals itself in the
closing paragraphs of the passage. Wolf has done a great
deal of idealizing and mentalizing but it is Christie who
initiates the action by moving close to him and "correcting
the rough confusion he had made. . . ."

When we began this discussion, I spoke in terms of
"seduction" and suggested that Jane Austen's handling of
sex might provide a clue to Powys's method of dealing
with it; I spoke of "understatement", "indirection", and
"control". These features seem to me especially well
demonstrated in the excerpt which we are examining.
What through a seeming chaos of thick imagery appears to
be the romantic seduction of a young virgin by a hesitant
young man is in fact exactly the opposite. Powys's manipulation of image, dialogue, character, and movement
manages to suggest a multi-leveled experience which, while
concentrating on both the conscious and subconscious
mind of the protagonist, reveals dark undercurrents of
feminine power in the person of Christie Malakite. Once
we have understood the subtle magnetism she exerts over
Wolf, we can begin to form some estimation of the depth
of sensuality suggested throughout the passage. Christie is
obviously the seductress and Wolf the naive victim. (We

must, however, avoid the assumption that this is a calculated prostitute-client relationship. There are at work here numerous other circumstances untouched in our discussion.) Consequently, we are not surprised to learn, somewhat later in the novel, that Christie may have been incestuously involved with her father.

For our immediate purpose, we need not concern ourselves with either the past or future activities of Wolf and Christie. The main point of this analysis has been to show how Powys achieves dramatic resonance in what might otherwise be thought of as a piece of ornate prosing. His description of the "midsummer nosegay" catches its subject with memorable precision, but it does more; it evokes to tactile immediacy the very breath and texture of the vernal countryside. Using this as his central device, Powys develops his characters around it, their attitudes towards the bouquet either reflecting themselves or transmitting non-verbal messages to each other. Through the flowers, we gain insights into the pair which are much greater than anything actually stated or thought by either. Powys has thus enabled us to know a great deal more about Wolf than seems at first to be possible. We perceive his contemplative sensitivity, his ability to appreciate "the miracle of flower-petals" and to distinguish the scents and shapes of innumerable flora; his idealizing mind which prefers the imagined to the actual; his egocentric *naiveté* which prevents him from accepting the individuality of others as something different from his own; his sexual awkwardness which covers the "fantastic" yearning of a powerfully sensual, unfulfilled human being.

It is this last aspect of Wolf's personality that deserves our particular attention since, after all, we are dealing with a "love-scene". The complexity of the sex-drive in each of us is presented with unswerving honesty. On the conscious level, Wolf protects himself from his totally physical desires by the intensity of his concern with the flowers. Yet, his actions – his animal being – move spontaneously through a ritual of orgiastic significance: he smells and savours the odours, lifts the flowers to his face, then probes with phallic fingers into the warm, wet interior of the bowl. His mind unconsciously filters the violence of this urge which, unknown even to himself, becomes the uncontrolled passion of a sensitive man. " . . . he allowed his hand to slide caressingly down her side, drawing her slender body, with a scarcely-perceptible pressure, against his own." In presenting material with such psychological exactitude, Powys could easily have fallen into one of two traps: the text-book dullness of a case-study, on the one hand, or, on the other, the four-letter word flatness of so much contemporary fiction – Cohen's *Beautiful Losers,* for instance.[11]

What saved Powys and gave him the perfect vehicle for his subject was his comprehensive knowledge of nature. In this passage – throughout the novel for that matter – his ability to impart to the reader a direct sensory appreciation of the green vitality of flowing sap permits him to extend the human experience without repeating it. We are therefore spared the usual redundancy which accompanies almost any creative attempt to deal with the sexual process in no other than its own terms.

Although the sexual is the dominant element in the excerpt, other factors are at work. The scene is a key-revelation of character, hinting as it does at the weaknesses and strengths underlying Christie's and Wolf's friendship. By a method of complete indirection, Powys uses his protagonist's thoughts and impressions to reveal the subtleties of Christie's personality. We glimpse for a moment the illusions, deceptions, and mis-conceptions which usually lie hidden behind a *façade* of conventional behaviour. In the passage's slow prose-rhythms, we observe the harmonic structuring of thought and image, person and speech as an interacting unity. Powys's earlier fiction offers nothing of comparable excellence; nevertheless, in *Wolf Solent*, there are other examples of equal complexity and brilliance. (See VII,139-40; XV,313-14; XVIII,388-90; XXV,610-14)   Nature-description is obviously functioning as an integral working-part of the whole; it is never a mere decoration or stage-property. Powys's technique of co-ordinating Wolf with his natural surroundings is unquestionably one of the basic principles by which this novel is controlled and shaped.[1] [2]

Wolf's impressions of flowers, trees, birds, the wind, and so forth belong to that inner-world of his incommunicable isolation; they belong to that stronghold within his person where he guards his identity, where he finds reason and purpose for his actions. But Wolf has a body as well as a mind. He needs a place to sleep, food to eat, clothes to wear. His corporeal necessities force him into contact with the inn-keeper, the butcher, and indirectly, with that host of people loosely described as "society". The problem of reconciling our inner and outer lives is not new; it bothered Plato, Defoe, Donne, Descartes, Marx, and Sartre as much as it bothered Powys. It is the intransigent paradox at the centre of any discussion of man's essential humanity. Of course the novelist can weight his argument to one side or the other but in so doing he is likely to simplify, compromise, or even falsify his apprehension and consequent presentation of any human situation.[13] Hemingway's aggressive insistence on physical action lies at one extreme and Virginia Woolf's delicate dissection of mental states lies at the other. The balance is difficult, almost impossible, to maintain.

In *Wolf Solent*, Powys has bridged these inner and outer worlds; he has shown us what happens when a sensitive, imaginative, individual becomes involved with the problems, aspirations, fears – in fact with the whole emotional paraphernalia – of those around him. The demands and fluctuations of social intercourse are given added cogency and credibility by the novel's rural setting: we receive an impression of immediacy and the "scale" of life which is so often lacking in fiction set in large urban areas. Nevertheless, life in an English country village seems remote from our own preoccupations. We might think that Powys is escaping from the twentieth century maze, that he is trying to recall the rustic simplicity of *The Mill on the Floss*. Nothing could be further from the truth. As we shall see, the outlook informing *Wolf Solent* is urgently contemporary.

Throughout the book runs an agonizing awareness of economic pressure, of the role played by money in human happiness. Wolf travels to King's Barton in response to an advertised post; when he marries he takes up school-teaching to supplement his income; and much later, he sacrifices his integrity for pecuniary ends. His friends and acquaintances are equally hard-pressed. Mrs. Solent, Wolf's mother, joins her son in King's Barton as his dependent; then her ambition to establish herself as proprietress of a tea-shop develops into an embarrassing financial intrigue as she courts the affluent Mr. Manley for the sake of his wealth and, in the process, precipitates a domestic crisis in her son's home. Upon the death of her step-father, Mattie Smith, Wolf's half-sister, is left the penniless guardian of the orphan Olwen. Stalbridge, a hotel-waiter, loses his job; he becomes a tramp; a poet, Jason Otter, inveigles money for drink. Squire Urquhart is a figure of seedy gentility, dispensing his generosity in niggardly spurts of erratic favouritism.[14]

Not everyone in *Wolf Solent* suffers economic hardship. There are some who seem beyond money-matters – The Reverend T.E. Valley, a confused alcoholic or a wise mystic, depending on which spirit is guiding him; Miss Selena Gault, whose physical ugliness contrasts with her impassioned devotion to the memory of Wolf's father William; John Torp, Wolf's father-in-law, a stone-cutter, whose impenetrable self-possession is as solid and disinterested as the headstones he chisels; and Mr. Round, the half-mad landlord of the Farmers' Rest, obsessed with guilt and suicide. There are still others who maintain a quiet economic stability, who appear satisfied and at ease in their varied circumstances — farmers like Josh Beard from Nevilton, servants like Dimity Stone and Mrs. Martin, the classics-teacher at the local grammar-school, Darnley Otter. This last-mentioned is a complex person, the poet Jason's brother, a man tortured by convention, responsibility, and his sexual attraction to both men and women. Yet he never deviates from his norms of duty or propriety; he eventually marries Mattie Smith. As Wolf's best friend, Darnley represents, among other things, the standard of limited achievement gained through the exercise of self-control, intelligence, patience, and renunciation. He is cautious, managing his life as carefully as his income.

We begin to notice a correspondence between economics and sexuality. The "have-nots" of the first group flounder in both their marital relations and their financial affairs; the uninterested or cautious members of society aim at a sort of sexual coziness attained through various kinds of celibacy or "safe-marriages". A third group of people remains to be examined. Lord Carfax, a cousin of Wolf's mother, is first referred to on the second page of this novel. He is a man of power, a relative of the Squire's and responsible for securing Wolf's secretarial appointment. Mrs. Solent is fond of speaking about "Cousin Carfax" who, during the course of the novel, never seems very far off. In fact, his appearance in the final chapter has much of the *deus ex machina* about it. His opulence

combines with a certain largess of character, each dependent on the other; together they impart an expansive
freedom to his actions. He moves decisively, righting
wrongs, dispensing happiness, providing solutions. Wolf
reflects that "Everything he would like to have done
Carfax had done . . . . His 'lord in London' had recognized
Jason's genius, discovered Gerda's beauty, poured oil and
wine into the wounds of Mr. Stalbridge, added a new
glory to the tea-shop." (XXV,589) We should not be
misled by the good-samaritan image: money, not religion,
is operative. Carfax is known for his "shameless opinions";
and his recognition of Gerda's beauty is hardly platonic.
Generosity and selfishness mingle in an amoral earthiness
which serves as both reason and explanation for his
conduct: " 'I'm all in favour of honest bawdry myself;' "
he tells his nephew, " 'but why sing such a song about it?
Natural or unnatural, it's nature. It's mortal man's one
great solace before he's annihilated! But all this bladder-
headed fuss about it — about such a simple thing — one
way or the other — I don't like it. It's not in my style.' "
(XXV,590)

Wealth . . . freedom . . . style . . . the triad is an
axiomatic proposition of the twentieth century. It reaches
from the frivolities of Oscar Wilde to the extravagances of
Tom Wolfe; it has been institutionalized by Marshal
McLuhan. It is the cornerstone of our greatest modern
mythology (interestingly, Wolf notes that Carfax's face has
"an almost legendary glamour"); its followers are the *élite*
satirized by Waugh in *Decline and Fall*, *Vile Bodies* and
Black Mischief. The myth grows on envy and discontent.
Catherine Morland knew it in its more gentle beginnings;
Emma Bovary was captivated by its intense, romantic phase.
Today it goes unquestioned: the jet-set, the in-group, the
swingers — tomorrow the name will change but the
dream remains the same. Apotheosized in advertisements

and films, the illusion beckons to us with far more insistence than it did in so many of Oliver Onions's stories. Powys understood the myth's insidious attractions. Carfax, a figure of near omnipotence and omniscience, seems, like Falstaff, to inhabit that crepuscular region which divides the human from the immortal. Knocking at the door of myth, he becomes at once the fulfilment of the possible and the refutation of the actual.

In the eyes of his social inferiors, Lord Carfax belongs to an elusive (they fail to see that it is also illusory) world of splendour and power. Bob Weevil, the Blacksod butcher, displays the loose sensuality, the crass mentality of an aspiring *bourgeois*. His dress and behaviour are hollow imitations of the "wealth, freedom, and style" which he envisages as the supreme expressions of personality. His clothing impresses Wolf as "the very top of Blacksod fashion", while his "yellow boots" and "heavy gold watch-chain" seem the suitable complement to a mind which enjoys the impoverished licentiousness of a wall covered with "actresses' photographs". His successful *liaison* with Gerda is a cheap victory over Wolf, a direct extension of his earlier pornographic curiosity about a suggestive picture of the girl.

Lord Carfax and Bob Weevil thus represent, within the framework of *Wolf Solent*, extremes of economic and sexual modernity. Wolf fluctuates between these extremes, buffeted by circumstance. His confrontation of the modern dilemma is by no means heroic: he is not Robinson Crusoe circumventing difficulties with assurance; nor is he Lucky Jim Dixon bumbling fantastically through the cardboard labyrinth of a mock-epic. Wolf Solent is caught in the total condition of twentieth century living. Pressured into uncongenial work by the simple necessity of earning his daily-bread, he is without consolation. The past denies his birthright of freedom or security: the very skull of his father seems to regard him "with nothing but cynical mockery", while his mother's basic nature rejects him with contempt. (XI,249) The future affords no relief: the sterility of a nominal marriage, the drudgery of a monotonous occupation, the frustration of unreciprocated love.

The crisis is familiar . . . and terrifying. Confounded on the personal plane, Wolf is likewise betrayed by the external, impersonal world. He envisages "a countryside covered from sea to sea by thousands of humming aeroplanes"; he foresees a "world, with headlights flashing along cemented highways, and all existence dominated by electricity." (VIII,169) As an average man, an individual powerless against mechanistic advance, faced with the confusing complexity of his experience, Wolf seeks to save what he can of his essential humanity, his sanity, by looking within himself for some immediate response to his present situation.

Wolf's quest for self-knowledge, for a form of integrated personality lies at the centre of this novel. Until his arrival back in Dorset, he had avoided direct involvement with other people or with their doings. He had escaped from life's problems by an extremely sophisticated sort of day-dreaming referred to as his "mythology". This "secret spiritual vice" shares the characteristics of adolescent fantasy. Under its spell, he feels that he is summoning to himself "a subconscious magnetic power" and participating "in some occult cosmic struggle". The arrogant isolation he experiences in "his inner world of hushed Cimmerian ecstasies" protects him from diurnal unpleasantness; yet, it is a self-consuming satisfaction, a form of cerebral masturbation. (IV, 42; I, 8; II, 20; also IX, 169). In its solipsistic convolutions, it rejects rather than adapts to change. It is responsible, on the one hand, for the shapeless imprecision of thought and feeling which underlies all his difficulties with Christie and Gerda; on the other, it is the only source of relief from those very troubles it generates.

Two forces — money and sex — threaten to destroy Wolf's psychic tread-mill of illusion. In a desperate attempt to spare his mother the degradation (a sentiment felt only by Wolf) of obtaining a loan from Mr. Manley, he agrees to resume work on the Squire's book. This he had given up in disgust after about eight months of chronicling the Dorset scandals. His return to Urquhart's employment violates his conscience but, nevertheless, he signs a contract for the receipt of £200 upon completion of the history. His second compromise is sexual. After marrying Gerda, Wolf had resigned himself to a platonic relationship with Christie. He is now offered the chance of spending the night with her, "of holding Christie against his limbs, stripped of her clothes . . . . "The passive integrity of his "mythology" is assaulted violently and is shaken. He realizes that

these two things — to-day's bargain with the Squire and to-morrow's visit to Christie — would be the end of his peace of mind. To these two things had he been brought at last. This was the issue; this was the climax of the mounting wave of his life in Dorset. He had to outrage now — and it was too late to retreat — the very core of his nature! That hidden struggle between some mysterious Good and some mysterious Evil, into which all his ecstasies had merged, how could it go on after this?(XIX,406)

The crisis seems sharply defined: integrity tried, forfeited and lost should be the obvious outcome. However, such is not the case. Wolf soon demurs. " 'Two hundred pounds?' he thought. 'What is that to spoil a whole life? A thin, bare figure held tight for a second * * * what is that to change a person's whole idea of himself?' " (XIX,414) As he continues to rationalize the affair, he fills the gap between act and consequence with further complications.

" 'I can do it!' he thought. 'It isn't over for ever.' And in his necessity he laid hold of those two dark horns of non-existence, from the cold slippery touch of which all flesh shrinks back — the horn of the ages before he was born, the horn of the ages when he would have ceased to be. 'I can plough on,' he said to himself." (XIX,426)

Not surprisingly, we feel slightly cheated. After all, Wolf *has* made his pact with Urquhart and he certainly intends to fulfil his pledge to Christie. Is this merely a simulated climax, a weak device employed by Powys to hold our (waning?) interest? If not, how are we to account for Wolf's easy vacillation during what purports to be a time of intense personal evaluation? The validity of the entire novel hangs in the balance. Approximately two-thirds of it is devoted to the apparent development of Wolf's personality. Should this present threat to his "mythology" prove empty, then all his mental gymnastics have been pointless. The book might well have ended much earlier, when Wolf realized that "If his soul was Christie's, his life must go on being his mother's and Gerda's. There was no other issue." (XI,251) The apparently self-contradictory concept of a static protagonist may be feasible in the *nouveau roman* of Nathalie Sarraute but it is absolutely indefensible in the traditional framework of *Wolf Solent*.

The encounter between our faltering "hero" and Christie offers no solution. In fact, it seems to undermine any suggestion of change in Wolf's nature. As the interval preceding intimate physical contact shortens, Wolf withdraws into his private world.

His mind felt as if it were being torn asunder, so terrible was the swaying of his tight-rope of indecision! On the one hand he knew that in a moment he must draw down upon the bed this hushed, submissive figure, standing thus patient and docile before him. On the other hand, a mounting fear — a fear that had unspeakable awe in it, that had a supernatural shudder in it — held him back. Beat by

beat of his heart it held him back. It tugged at him like a chain fixed
to a post.

. . . .

He reeled awkwardly to one side, and, snatching his hands away
from her, sank down against her pillow. For a second or two the
struggle within him gave him a sensation as if the very core of his
consciousness — that 'hard little crystal' within the nucleus of his
soul — were breaking into two halves! Then he felt as if his whole
being were flowing away in water, whirling away, like a mist of rain,
out upon the night, over the roofs, over the darkened hills! There
came a moment's sinking into nothingness, into a grey gulf of
non-existence; and then it was as if a will within him, that was
beyond thought, gathered itself together in that frozen chaos and
rose upwards . . . .

. . . .

Wolf was honest enough with himself . . . to recognize that there
was, somewhere within him, a furtive upwelling of profound
gratitude to the gods. His life-illusion [i.e. his 'mythology'] *had* been
given back to him! . . . He was still himself. (XX,442,444,447)[15]

Although Wolf has retained his personality, his own
explanation of the process seems hardly satisfactory.
"Well", he thinks, "that was the way things worked out!
Instead of either of the great clear horns of Fate's
dilemma, a sort of blurred and woolly forehead of the wild
goat Chance!" (XX,452)

Let us proceed in our investigation of the token crisis;
but, before doing so, we should remind ourselves of that
essential distance between the author and his creation.
Wolf's muddle is not necessarily Powys's. (The possibility
of just such a confusion must have been apparent to
Conrad, for instance, when, in his great novel of the
token-crisis, he used Marlow to mediate between *Tuan* Jim
and ourselves) Our involvement in Wolf's harassed uncertainty should not prevent us from recognizing the
deliberate organization behind this effect.

Consequence is not easily side-stepped. Wolf soon

completes his writing for the Squire and receives the reward of his labours. The £200 cheque is not cashed immediately; it is kept in a drawer all through the winter. Mrs. Solent has rejected her son's offer in favour of Mr. Manley's; Wolf's action has become meaningless, worthless. When in reply to Gerda's badgering about the money, he states that the issue is "a matter of life and death", the words sound hollow and pathetic. Can we really believe him? He has managed to extricate himself so neatly from previous dilemmas that it is impossible to treat his remark seriously. He then attempts to return the cheque to Urquhart but is foiled at the last moment by his own indecision. Immediately he wonders "whether this crowning defeat over the cheque had really done at last the thing he dreaded! Would he find, when he took up his life again, that his 'mythology' was stone dead . . .?"

Unable to withstand the combined pressures of chance and circumstance, he resigns himself to placing the "spiritual blood-money" at Gerda's disposal. In a desperate effort to shun any personal responsibility for both his actions and omissions, he calls upon his life-illusion. Nothing happens: "That ecstasy, that escape from reality, had gone." He acknowledges "the death of his 'mythology.' "

There follows a period described by mystics as "the dark night of the soul". Wolf feels that Fate is forcing him towards one of two alternatives — a return to spiritual death in London or to actual death through suicide. The latter eventuality appears the more probable. "How did human beings go on living", he asked himself, "when their life-illusion was destroyed? What did they tinker up and patch up inside of them to rub along with, to shuffle through life with, when they lacked that one grand resource?" (XXIII,527) His preoccupations finally bring him to the moment of confrontation. He stands at the

edge of Lenty Pond — a small lake in the vicinity — trying
to reach some conclusion.

He flung his consciousness . . . down into those silent depths. And
then his body — not his mind, but his body — became acquainted with
shivering dread. Was his mind going to issue the final mandate now, at
this very moment? What was his body doing that it revolted like this?
What was his body doing that its foot-soles clung to the mud as if they
had been rooted there? It was not only his flesh that now turned sick
with fear. The very bones within him began screaming — a low, thin,
wire-drawn scream — before what his mind was contemplating. It was
not that life — merely to be alive — had suddenly become so precious.
It was not fear of Nothingness that made his body quake. *It was Lenty
Pond itself*! Yes, what his flesh and bones shrank from was not
eternity. It was immersion in that localized, particular, cubic expanse
of starlit oxygen-hydrogen!

Wolf imagines the discovery of his body and these
thoughts cause him to speculate about people he knows.
He suddenly becomes aware that he is planning to ask
certain questions after he gets back.

Get back? [he thinks.] Get back where? So he wasn't going to utter
that mandate to his panic-stricken body . . . How queer that he had
nothing now left to decide! His future was already there, mapped
out before him. It was only a matter of following the track. Yes!
The track was already there * * * leading back again! All he had to do
was to accept it and follow it from moment to moment, like a
moving hand that threw a shadow over an unfolded map! (XXIII,
542)

We seem back where we started . . . but with a
difference. Wolf's contemplated suicide was, in one sense,
another token-crisis. In another sense, it marks a definite
shift in his personality-pattern. Following his realization
that he is not prepared to die as yet, comes an acceptance
of human activity in all of its monotonous authenticity.
The token-crisis was a necessary counterpart to his
"mythology"; the loss of the one leads to the deflation of

the other. The token-crisis is a part of life — the moment
of revelation and decision, the point of no-return and of
commitment. The irrevocable act which seemed "a matter
of life and death" passes, is absorbed into a larger frame of
reference. Wolf must go on living, no longer relying on an
illusion to give meaning to his life but rather building his
identity according to the incomprehensible rules of natural
adaptation. "And it came over him, by slow degrees like a
cold glimmer of morning under a tossing sea, that the
abiding continuity of his days lay, after all, in his body, in
his skull, in his spine, in his legs, in his clutching
anthropoid-ape arms! Yes! that was all he had left * * * his
vegetable-animal identity, isolated, solitary * * * hovered
over by the margins of strange thoughts." (XXIV,574)

Wolf has lost everything that was once meaningful to
him — Gerda, Christie, his "mythology". In the place of
these, he has only his new awareness of life's unalterable
processes. He therefore determines that he must "set
himself to face in stoical resolution all the years of his life,
as he saw them before him, dusty milestones along a dusty
highway!" His lot will not be easy, but, in accepting it, he
prepares himself to participate as fully as possible in the
richness of human experience. In the significantly entitled
final chapter "Ripeness is All", Powys presents us with a
striking example of the direct interrelation between Wolf
and his environment. Dazed by all that has happened, Wolf
wanders about until he notices a field that "was full to the
very brim of golden buttercups! It was literally a floating
sea of liquid, shining gold!" He feels irresistibly compelled
to enter it.

Back and forth he walked, while the sun, fallen almost horizontal,
made what he walked upon seem unearthly. Buttercup-petals clung
to his legs, clung to the sides of his stick; buttercup-dust covered his
boots. The plenitude of gold that surrounded him began to invade
his mind with strange, far drawn associations.

Up and down he went, pacing that field. He felt as if he were an appointed emissary, guarding some fragment of Saturn's age flung into the midst of Blacksod!

'Enjoying the sweet light of the sun * * * deprived of the sweet light of the sun,' these phrases from Homer rang in his ears and seemed to express the only thing that was important. Carfax taking Gerda upon his knee, Urquhart begging Tilly-Valley for the Sacrament, his mother borrowing from Mr. Manley . . .all these human gestures presented themselves to him now through a golden mist, a mist that made them at once harmless and negligible, compared with the difference between being alive and being dead! (XXV, 610)

In this state of intensified consciousness, categories of "Good and Evil" disappear, the "supernatural itself" vanishes as his "mythology" has vanished: all that is left is his body. He is learning that the contingencies of existing in an unpredictable world are best handled on a day-to-day basis. The past and the future must be forgotten, if the present is to be enjoyed to the utmost. Wolf now understands the hard lesson of his Dorset experience — that "every soul [is] alone". His final acceptance of life's circumstantial pleasures and miseries springs, not from a negative sense of defeat but from a positive act of his will. He leaves the buttercup-field of gold, turns homeward and remembers his wife's unfaithfulness. But who am I, he thinks, "to make pompous moral scenes"? His last thought is one of resolute simplicity: "Well, I shall have a cup of tea." (XXV, 611-14)

In its various forms — from the dim, fleet shadow at the one extreme to the great, ponderous beast at the other, reality has eluded the verbal net of literary critic and philosopher alike. Although the pursuit has led to startling discoveries, strange contradictions, and at times to deadly impasses, the quarry itself remains as nimble as ever. Indeed, Calvin Blick's assertion that " 'Reality is a cipher with many solutions, all of them right ones' " seems in its suggestiveness hauntingly accurate.[16] Hence it should be obvious that any valid assessment of literary realism must discuss aspects rather than fixed principles of reality. This is surely the attitude which allows Auerbach to state on the one hand: "In Flaubert realism becomes impartial, impersonal, and objective"; and on the other: "Nothing happens [in *Madame Bovary*], but that nothing has become a heavy, oppressive, threatening something."[17] Here insight depends on a shifting perception of reality.

Whereas Flaubert describes the great, ponderous beast, Powys follows the dim, fleet shadow. The two novels, *Wolf Solent* and *Madame Bovary*, are thus complementary, representing opposite poles on one scale of human experience. Like Wolf, Emma Bovary lives in a world of dreams; unlike him, she seeks a reality that will correspond to her fantasies. The continual discrepancy she feels between desire and actuality lead her from disappointment to frustration, and finally, to the dark despair of suicide. Such things do happen: the psychological process is brilliantly exact. Nonetheless, suicidal despondency is admittedly rare. At the other end of the scale, we find, equally rare, Wolf's affirmation of positive values worked out through a process of self-redemption and personal salvation. Between these two lies the neutral territory of unresolved compromise; Arnold Bennett's *Old Wives' Tale* is a case in point, reflecting in its artistic drabness the dull uncertainty of its informing attitude.

Powys's achievement in *Wolf Solent* lies in his ability to bring the problems and crises of modern life within the compass of individual, non-specialist, experience; in other words, he assesses the value of an ordinary man's life in a meaningful way. For Wolf's difficulties are both common and contemporary: the sexual and economic pressures which torment him before as well as after his marriage; the social and personal tensions which involve him in his struggle for a significant identity. All of this complexity is resolved in an utterly humane synthesis. There is no suggestion of a higher, impersonal order — be it supernatural or scientific — to which we can turn for support. Our conventions of good and evil, of right and wrong, are simply invalidated. In their place we are offered the powers of imaginative sympathy, of that essentially creative dynamism which vitalizes and restores human personality. (It was, incidentally, this same force that Lawrence so roughly twisted and bent to placate the magnificent but constricted demon of his own unsatisfied energy.)

Wolf Solent points inwards to the reality of the mind. It reveals how the determining fusion of experience and reflection depends on an acutely realized sensibility — in particular, sensibility as a "function of the organs of sense". In this process, the world of everyday experience renews itself in the participating consciousness which perceives it. (It is not surprising that , near the close of the novel, Powys quotes Wordsworth: (XXV,611): [18] there are many similarities between these two writers. Nature, people, and machines are kaleidoscoped together and made personally meaningful by a willed, imaginative act of acceptance. This highly individual, essentially human effort is presented as our one way of coping and growing with the manifold data of modern life. There can be no other solution.

[1] J.C. Powys, *Ducdame*, Garden City, New York: Doubleday, Page & Company, 1925.

[2] I have used asterisks throughout to indicate ellipses found in the text, as distinct from my ellipses shown by dots.

[3] *cf.* Rook "was conscious of a dark, secret pang, as if his nature had suddenly touched some 'fourth dimension' whose superiority to his own level of existence shocked and troubled him." (VI,86); see also XIV,209-10.

[4] For other descriptions of consciousness extended in time and space, see: I,16; VI,85-6; XXI,355-6; XXV,446-7; 457-8.

[5] I refer of course to the novel's title, taken from Shakespeare's *As You Like It*, II, 5, 58-60. In the preliminary pages (p.vii), Powys incorrectly cites scene 6 as the source of Jaques' words.
An interesting aside — particularly in view of Powys's later use of Celtic myth — is a comment by Robert Graves. Footnoting a discussion of Welsh riddles, he writes: "Another form [of introduction] is *dychymig dameg* ('a riddle, a riddle'), which seems to explain the mysterious *ducdame ducdame* in *As You Like It*, which Jaques describes as 'a Greek invocation to call fools into a circle' — perhaps a favourite joke of Shakespeare's Welsh schoolmaster, remembered for its oddity." *The White Goddess* (amended and enlarged ed.), New York: Vintage Books [copyright 1948], p. 18, ftn. 1.

[6] J.C. Powys, *Wolf Solent,* New York: Simon and Schuster, 1929, 2 vols. Throughout my discussion, I refer to the one volume edition published in 1961 by Macdonald, London.

[7] See Douglas Robillard, "Landscape with Figures: The Early Fiction of John Cowper Powys," *Studies in the Literary Imagination*, I, 2 (1968), 51-8; Jocelyn Brooke, "On Re-reading A Glastonbury Romance," *London Magazine*, III, 4 (1956), 44-51.

[8] Autumn receives very similar treatment in Gustave Flaubert's *Novembre*; Powys wrote an introduction to the Frank Jellinek translation of this book (New York: The Roman Press, 1932).

[9] Powys's attitude might be fruitfully compared with Gerard Manley Hopkins's concepts of "inscape" and "instress".

[10] Almost all critics have failed to distinguish between Powys and his characters. Emphasizing a few shared traits, they have found easy solutions and irreconcilable difficulties in this common identity. The only satisfactory discussion I know on this point has come, like so much other excellent work on Powys, from France: see Jean-Jacques Mayoux, "L'extase et la sensualité: John Cowper Powys et Wolf Solent," *Critique* (Paris), XXIV, 252 (mai 1968), 462-74.

[11] I do not wish to denigrate Leonard Cohen's book, only to suggest that his multiple expletives detract from rather than add to the strength of his writing. Few authors can wield the lyric-intensity which helps to save *Lady Chatterley's Lover* from Cohen's sort of sexual overkill.

[12] A book-length study is needed to investigate (perhaps in terms of this co-ordinating principle) the wealth of nature description in *Wolf Solent*.

[13] John Bayley's *The Characters of Love: A Study in the Literature of Personality* (London: Constable, 1960) offers some very pertinent comments on the autonomy of fictional people: Chapters I and V are especially useful. Wayne C. Booth's *The Rhetoric of Fiction* (Chicago & London: The University of Chicago Press, 1961) is also relevant. My own remarks about comprehensive character-presentation are obviously not intended as a judgement on such works as satire, comedy, or allegory, where caricature and bias are deliberately used to obtain calculated effects.

[14] This simple listing of character and occupation raises another *bête-noire* in Powys-criticism: an apparent inability to follow basic plot detail. Both R.M. Lovett and H.S. Hughes in their *History of the Novel in England* (London: Harrap, 1932) and later Lionel Stevenson in his *The English Novel: A Panorama* (Boston: Houghton Mifflin, 1960) confuse Jason and Wolf — the co-authors describe Wolf as "a potential artist who suffers through lack of adequate creative outlet" (p. 441) and Stevenson echoes their words by referring to Wolf again as "a man of creative gifts who is frustrated by lack of outlets for his artistic talent." (pp. 480-1).

[15] This entire episode deserves extended analysis in conjunction with the earlier meeting between Wolf and Christie. (*cf.* above pp. 81-92)

[16] Iris Murdoch, *The Flight from the Enchanter,* London: Chatto & Windus, 1956, p. 305. In her study, *Degrees of Freedom: The Novels of Iris Murdoch* (London: Chatto & Windus, 1965, p. 87), A.S. Byatt notes that Miss Murdoch does not endorse Calvin's statement.

[17] Erich Auerbach's discussion of Flaubert will be found in *Mimesis: The Representation of Reality in Western Literature,* translated by Willard R. Trask, Princeton, N.J.: Princeton University Press, 1953, pp. 482-91.

[18] The lines, with minor alterations, are of course from the "Ode: Intimations of Immortality . . ." IV, 52-4.

III

Within three years of the publication of *Wolf Solent*, *A Glastonbury Romance* appeared.[1] Not only its exceptional length (roughly 450,000 words as compared to *Wolf's* 260,000) distinguishes it from its predecessors; other, more radical differences are apparent. We noted earlier that Powys seemed involved in a process of definition in the first four novels and that in *Wolf Solent* he had finally reduced a chaotic multiplicity of thought and feeling into the very concrete experience of a single, central character. All of this is swept aside in the *Romance*: a list in the preliminary pages numbers no less than forty-seven "principal characters"; its subject matter comprises, to instance a few areas, pagan and Christian religion, Welsh mythology, Communism, labour-management relations, economics, and miracles. Powys characteristically works these topics into the novel's predominantly psychological texture.

He shows us a number of persons involved in a series of thematically interlocking incidents — all with one ideological and geographical centre, Glastonbury. Although these people are united by a common bond, they remain alone as their separate destinies unfold. We thus become aware of the overlapping of private and public life, of manners and morals, as Lionel Trilling might put it. This concern with the community as well as with the individual strikes a new note in Powys's fiction. Hitherto the emphasis was on personal change and development, social *moeurs* being used only for contrast or background. The *Romance*, however, seeks to establish a necessary connection between man and society by suggesting that the two are so interdependent that fulfilment of the one demands total participation in the other.

The opening chapter quickly sets the general frame of reference. The Crow family has gathered in a small Norfolk village for the reading of the late Canon Crow's will. The majority of those assembled have come from or from near Glastonbury. When the terms of the will are announced, everyone is surprised and many angered. Apart from a few small annuities, the bulk of the Canon's fortune – £40,000 – is bequeathed to John Geard of Glastonbury, who had been the old man's secretary and companion during his last years. Before serving the Canon, Geard had preached the Nonconformist gospel in the Glastonbury streets, calling upon the Blood of Christ with such vehemence that he had become known as Bloody Johnny. His evangelical enthusiasm – rising at times to a sort of mystical fervour – seems to have been largely responsible for winning his former employer's admiration. Many of the Crows suspect him of charlatanism, not least Philip, the industrialist, who is momentarily nonplussed by the turn of events. He had been confident of the inheritance which he had earmarked for business development. The implicit conflict between Geard and Philip spills over into one of the novel's most comprehensive themes: the way that money determines the spiritual and material goals of men and women.

Much of this early action is depicted through the personality of John Crow, just arrived from France. He is an adventurer whose rather seedy appearance reinforces numerous hints that he has been living in Paris as a kept man. On learning of his grandfather's death, he hastens to England in the hope, not of obtaining any of the money, but of cajoling Philip into offering him work. When he

discovers that Geard has been the beneficiary, he decides
to set out for Glastonbury, convinced that he can find a
way of inveigling the preacher into somehow supporting
him. Before leaving Norfolk, however, he re-encounters his
cousin Mary, whom he had not seen since childhood. Their
attachment is immediate and violent. They promise to
meet again in Glastonbury.

John Crow's journey to the West Country is very much
a pilgrimage. He travels alone, on foot, sleeping in sheds,
subsisting on buns and tea. He crosses Salisbury Plain with
aching legs and a blistered foot, limping after eight days on
the road. One mile from Stonehenge he is offered a lift
by Owen Evans, who is going first to visit the Ruins and
then on to Glastonbury. Despite his painful limbs, John is
eager to accompany Evans into the stone circle and an easy
companionship soon develops between the two. While the
Welshman speaks with impressive authority about the
origins and purpose of the monoliths, John Crow responds
instinctively to their dark Power. "What . . . [he]
recognized in this great Body of Stones . . . was that they
themselves, just as they were, had become, by the mute
creative action of four thousand years, authentic Divine
Beings. They were so old and great, these Stones, that they
assumed godhead by their inherent natural right, gathered
godhead up, as a lightning conductor gathers up electricity,
and refused to delegate it to any mediator, to any
interpreter, to any priest!" (III,103) His prayer – " 'Stonehenge, you great God! . . . I beg you to make Mary a
happy girl and I beg you to let me live with her in
Norfolk!' " – illustrates the negative outlook which is to
underlie and nullify much of John's Glastonbury
experience.

Both Mary and John dislike the town. The latter
considers it a "dead Ruin" and the former detests its
"sentimentality", commercialism, and "sickening super-

stition": both are compelled by financial necessity to live away from the harsh East-Anglian vitality they prize so much. Their attitude is a definite challenge to many of the assumptions on which the life of the town is founded. Mary is involved in one aspect of this establishment-sham: she is the paid companion of Miss Euphemia Drew who lives at the Abbey House. When the old spinster beseeches Mary to sleep with her, before the girl leaves to reside permanently with John, a morbid array of repressed passions seethes to the surface of conventional behaviour. (XX, 636 - 41) We are given a glimpse of the stagnant waste lying behind a *façade* of genteel manners. But not everyone is content with the *status quo*. Johnny Geard has decided that his newly acquired money should be used to promote the religious history of the town through the establishment of a midsummer pageant which, in its own way, is to rival that of Oberammergau. Irony works on circumstance as John worms his way into Bloody Johnny's confidence and an "easy job" as his secretary. As a confirmed sceptic, John Crow views the pageant as a circus with himself as its manager; he does all he can to turn "the whole Glastonbury Legend into a mockery and a popular farce". (IX,256; XIII,361)

As time passes, he becomes more entangled in preparations for the pageant but continues to disparage the entire affair. Although his shrewd tactics as a public-relations man win Geard's approval, the preacher is fully aware of his secretary's derisive attitude. It happens thus that much of the religious momentum in Glastonbury is generated from a source of disbelief. John Crow never participates in the essential spirit of the town. Aside from the money, his main reason for staying is his cousin Mary. Their love-affair is a strange combination of sexual and mental affinities. John's earliest memories of his affection for Mary are Norfolk ones . They centre around a particular event

which blends the figure of the girl inextricably with that of
another boyhood friend, Tom Barter. This is how John
first describes that memory to Mary:

'I've been wanting all the time to ask you, Mary,. . . whether you
remember that day we couldn't get the boat past the dam — the dam
between the big river and the little river? You said just now that
you'd never been made love to. Why! my dear, I've had a feeling of
longing to see you again all my life since that day I hugged you and
so on in the bottom of that boat. Do you remember that too, the
way the boat leaked, and how fishy it smelt and the way I held
you?' The queer thing was that once more, even as he said these
words, the image of the boy Tom Barter rose up. (I,36)

Mary cannot remember this episode and John decides
later that it was in fact Tom whom he had held in the
boat. Now, Tom lives in Glastonbury where he works for
Philip Crow. John soon discovers that his friend's personality has lost none of its attraction. As they walk
together, he recalls "their vicious play that hot Sunday
afternoon at the bottom of the boat! Vicious with every
sort of East-Anglian sensuality had they both been; and
John was surprised at himself, glancing furtively at Tom's
stolid profile, to find what an intense thrill it still gave
him, what a delicious, voluptuous sensation, to feel himself
weak and soft, where Tom was strong and hard." (IX,264)
Even on the first night he spends with Mary after their
marriage, John is unable to exorcise Tom's spell. He feels
that he has been neglecting his friend; and, as he makes
love to Mary, "his shame about neglecting Tom became
like a bruise, a definite bruise in some back-ledge of his
consciousness." (XX,647-8)

The homosexual bond which unites the two men is
never realized through physical contact; but it is emphatically different from the heterosexual impulses to
which they both respond. In the cousins' case: "Their love
was lust, a healthy, earthy, muddy, weather-washed lust . .

. . They were shamelessly devoid of any Ideal Love."
(IV,125) (This, incidentally, is the sort of relationship
Wolf Solent and Gerda might have enjoyed, had he been
able, at the outset of their acquaintance, to destroy his
illusory world.) For Tom, desire becomes lechery: his
diverse philanderings result in a pair of twins and marriage
to a servant girl — in that order. The mysterious current of
masculine friendship culminates in a final, irreversible
deed. An attempt is made on John's life; Tom rushes in,
takes the blow, and is killed. The effect on John is in
keeping with the parasitic character of his affection:

> . . .he did *not* feel a rush of tender, melting gratitude to his dead
> friend! The truth was he had so long played the feminine role with
> Barter, so long leaned upon him, and relied upon his strength that he
> only felt now as if they had been in some desperate mêlée together,
> where Tom as he always did, had taken the lead; and for that reason
> had got hurt ✳✳✳ had ✳✳✳ got ✳✳✳ in fact ✳✳✳ killed; but when it came
> to making Tom's tragic death a sublime act of sacrifice and of
> sacrifice for him, John dodged that tremendous conclusion with
> shamefully blinking eyelids. (XXIX,1059)

Mary understands the significance of the men's close-
ness. As she tells John: " 'It's you, first and last, that Tom
loved! He came to me when he was in trouble and sad; just
as I went to him when I was unhappy; but in his heart of
hearts it was always you.' " (XXIX,1058) The couple agree
to take Tom's body, his wife, and children back to Norfolk
with them. Their departure from Glastonbury and return
to East-Anglia is clouded by a vague sense of failure.

> 'Come back to us, Tom! Come back to us!' the big river and the
> little river were both calling; and it *was* with Tom that they were
> going back to the place where they would be; but they were carrying
> a corpse with them; not only the corpse of Tom Barter but the
> corpse of their stillborn never-returning opportunity of touching the
> Eternal in the enchanted soil where the Eternal once sank down into
> time! (XXIX, 1062-3)

What is the meaning of John Crow's Glastonbury experience? His sojourn in the town was by no means uneventful, nor was his occupation such that he was left outside the mainstream of activity. Indeed, he was near the centre of everything. Yet, he has obviously missed an irredeemable moment of personal fulfilment. We are given a clear indication of the nature both of the chance and of the lapse. As we have noted, his concern with the legends and history of Glastonbury is superficial. Self-admittedly, he thinks about King Arthur "in a childish and very ignorant way. He had never read the romances." On one of his frequent walks, he stops on Pomparles Bridge over the river Brue to gaze down at the sluggish water. Amidst the refuse which has floated down from Glastonbury, John spies "a dead cat whose distended belly, almost devoid of fur, presented itself, together with two paws and a shapeless head that was one desperate grin of despair, to the mockery of the sunshine." (XIII,357) As he reflects on the suffering this cat must have undergone, he is "struck . . . by a sudden rending and blinding shock". He sees "an object, *resembling a sword*, falling into the mud of the river!" He is absolutely convinced "that he really saw what he felt he saw with his bodily eyes!" "that he knew it was Arthur's sword. . . ." (XIII,361)

The episode throws him into a quandary. He reviews his life in Glastonbury, analysing his motives and purposes, until he brings everything within the circle of his selfish interests. He grows defiant, possessive, prays to Stonehenge, and ridicules Arthur's sword. "A certain chaotic tendency to drift in him – the drifting of the congenital tramp and the recklessness of the anti-social adventurer – had tightened and hardened into a kind of psychic intensity of revolt, of revolt against all the gregarious traditions of the human crowd. " 'There must be destruction' ", he says to himself on entering Glastonbury,

" 'before any fresh wind from the gods can put new life into a place like this!' " (XIII,372)

John's commitment is anti-social. He is touched by the enormity of the Glastonbury tradition but prefers to turn his back on it. His rebellion is that of Milton's Satan — a magnificent act of self-deprivation, yet resounding with the hollow echoes of its own futility. Stonehenge does answer John's early supplication; nevertheless, the reply is ambiguous.

It would be pointless to attempt a full explanation of John Crow's behaviour within the restricted category of his own experience; for his story is only one strand in the complex web of the *Romance's* total statement. Entirely different circumstances become apparent when Glastonbury life is observed from another point of view. That of Owen Evans, the Welsh antiquary who befriended John, presents a sharp contrast. Two things dominate this man: a passionate curiosity about Celtic tradition — he is writing a life of Merlin — and the morbid cravings of a sadistic imagination. The one seems an objective affirmation of spiritual values; the other a subjective negation of personal freedom. Evans believes that an understanding of the occult Welsh myths will eventually relieve him of the obsessions that govern a great part of his life. He is a sensitive man who feels extreme guilt about his sadistic urges and, consequently, blames himself for much of the suffering in the world. Yet, he is unwilling to stop thinking about various acts of cruelty because of the erotic excitement he derives from them. Thus strung up between the poles of masochism and sadism, Evans is alternately tormented by the agonies of remorse and desire. Only the discovery of the grail — not the Christian Cup for which Glastonbury is famous, but the more ancient Cauldron of Celtic myth — can bring salvation. Could he but see it once, he feels that the "madness" would pass; simultaneous with this thought comes the insidious knowledge that he doesn't want to see it. (V,151)[2]

From childhood, Evans has been haunted by the image of "a killing blow delivered by an iron bar". (V,150; also IX,250) He has been tempted to yield to this, to substitute the actual for the imagined, but has refrained because of the consequences. He knows that such a deed could lead to greater temptations, to an escalation of sadistic sensations: "He saw his soul in the form of an unspeakable worm, writhing in pursuit of new and ever new mental victims, drinking new, and ever new innocent blood." Or the act could lead to remorse and a "doom [that] was no crashing annihilation, but a death as slow as the disintegration of certain mineral deposits which under chemical pressure gradually lose their identity and are converted into amorphous dust." (IX,252)

As the sadistic urge mounts, Evans is driven to seek more pronounced ways of expiating for his would-be crimes. He is afforded the opportunity by Johnny Geard's pageant. This spectacle is to consist of three parts, each representing one aspect of Glastonbury lore, opening with a depiction of the Arthurian Cycle, having the Passion of Christ in the middle, and closing with "the ancient Cymric Mythology". Evans is asked to play Christ; he accepts with only one restriction " ' . . . you'll have to make it as real as you can.' " His wish is granted. Bound on the cross with ropes, he experiences such strain that he faints, hae-morrhaging at the mouth. Before losing consciousness, he assumes the accumulated guilt of all the perpetrators and victims of cruelty who have ever lived in Glastonbury.

Kings and Prelates, Saints and Sodomites, Madmen and Monks, Whores and Nuns, People executed and People Imprisoned, together with a woeful procession of common, nameless People upon whose toil and hunger others lived, streamed in a wild torrent of heads and faces and arms and limbs through the tormented consciousness of

Mr. Evans. ... And it was all connected with his deadly, his
irremediable vice. The figures that flooded his brain were all torturers
or victims, every one of them; and as the thing grew and grew upon
him, as he hung there, all the victims flowed into one and became
one, and all the tortureres flowed into one and became one. Then it
came about that between Mr. Evans as the torturer and this one
victim, who yet was all victims, a dialogue arose. ... (XIX, 615-16)

The victim tells Evans that forgiveness for him is
impossible because the sadist knows the meaning of what
he does but does not stop. When Evans replies: " 'Christ
can forgive me. Christ holds eternity in His hand.' " the
voice cries, " 'I *am* Christ!' " (XIX,616) As the victim-
voice continues to accuse him, Evans becomes more
incisive, demanding to know why the Lord wants to
redeem evil-doers in general. Whereupon the Christ-victim
begins to change its tone by dropping its voice so low that
Evans cannot understand it. " 'It is God and He is lying to
me,' " he thinks. "And Mr. Evans hanging there in his great
anguish hardened his heart against the voice. 'We are
alone,' his soul whispered to his body and to the pain
that he was inflicting on his body." (XIX,618)

Nevertheless, Evans himself is an explicit Christ
-figure. He exults in his agony — "extreme pain and
ecstatic triumph embracing each other in dark mystic
copulation." His "triumphant ecstasy" pours down from
him "like a bloody sweat". Identities seem to merge at one
point, when Evans unconsciously shouts Christ's "Eloi,
Eloi, Lama, Sabachthani" just before the blood spills from
his mouth. (XIX,614,615,618) The entire crucifixion
sequence is a brilliant piece of psychological staging on
Evans's part. It not only fails to purge him of his vice, it
aids in its gratification. His sado-masochistic orgy bears
witness to his own Janus-like self-deception. The sexual
thrills of "dark mystic copulation" are those of the sadist,
narrowed to a tight circle of hermaphroditic flagellation.

Unlike John Crow's brush with the Eternal, Evans's experiment in Christianity is without consequence. He fails to find a coherent, personal meaning in his experience on the cross. Since he was unable to allay his vice by playing Jesus, Evans soon turns back to Celtic myth for a solution. Here he is utterly convinced that a form of objective truth exists. He believes that "Glastonbury is the Gwlad-yr-Hav, the Elysian Death-Fields of the Cymric tribes"; and that "Few Glastonbury people realise that they are actually living in *yr Echwyd,* the land of Annwn, the land of twilight and death, where the shores are of Mortuorum Mare, the Sea of the Departed." (XXIII,739) In this place the Fisher Kings sought for "that which exists in the moment of timeless time" when contradictions fuse, for "creation with-out-generation", for "Parthenogenesis and the Self-Birth of Psyche". (XXIII,740)[3] This is essentially what Evans himself is seeking — for a mental state where the warring factions of his personality will be pacified. The quest is futile because it rejects natural law. By wishing to empty himself of all that is individual or personal for the sake of purification, Evans is, in fact, aligning himself with the dead. He is frequently described as "corpse-like" — a characteristic which reveals the anomalous position he holds in society — and would be equally at home in the crowd flowing over London Bridge in that other twentieth century Waste Land.[4]

Everything that Evans says and does is undermined by his morbid obsessions. That this is as true of his interest in Celtic mythology as of anything else seems borne out by the ironic circumstance that the very woman he identifies as the "Grail Messenger" is the one who precipitates the murder which he has been longing to witness. Mad Bet (another in the series of prophetic crones beginning in *Wood and Stone*) has fallen in love with John Crow. The deranged woman is intensely jealous of Mary and decides to keep John to herself by having him killed. When Evans learns that John is to be bludgeoned over the head with an iron bar, he is rent between his sense of humanity – his friendship with John – and the need of satisfying his sadistic curiosity. His wife Cordelia, Johnny Geard's ugly daughter whom he had initially married as a punishment for his perverse nature, guesses that something is amiss. She urges him not to leave their house and in desperation strips her clothes off before him. Despite her grotesque body, her passionate abandon conquers Owen's sadistic craving. Just as their marriage soon after the pageant had surprisingly brought temporary respite from his imaginative hell, so her sexual fullness (she is pregnant) now affirms the power of life over cruelty. It is physical, personal intimacy which, for the moment, saves Owen, not the Grail. When they arrive on the scene, the murder has occurred – Tom Barter of course and not John Crow being the victim. Evans clinically examines the iron bar and Tom's crushed head; then he begins "vomiting with cataclysmic heavings". His sadism has been totally exorcised; but not without one of the foreseen results. The doom of slow, disintegrating death that he feared becomes a reality. This "deadly remorse over his sadistic dreams and fantasies" ages him visibly. His premature decrepitude is balanced by the death of his premature child. Even the Welsh myths appear to have lost most of their vitality; Evans's study of Merlin drags on from day to day to become his life's work. The final clue to the Celtic secret evades him as he searches in vain for "the real meaning of the mystical word Esplumeoir".

Owen Evans's fate emphasizes another, pathetic aspect of the human condition. Throughout his Glastonbury – experience , John Crow retained a strong sense of his own identity, a fierce resilience which enabled him to mock the very force that sustained him. John's loneliness is willed and accepted. In Owen's case, personal control is forfeited through weakness. All of his efforts to establish a meaningful pattern of existence are predestined to fail because they are artificially generated. His concern with myth springs from a need for external support rather than from internal conviction. Regardless of his intentions, Evans is rotten at the sadistic core of his being; as he suspected, there is neither forgiveness nor redemption for him. The birth of the psyche through parthenogenesis is denied him as it was denied Wolf Solent until the latter discovered that wholeness involves the enormous burden of individual responsibility and acceptance. What happens to Evans in no way diminishes the importance of the myth; it simply demonstrates that no idea can be fruitful until it is approached for itself with humility and sympathy. Owen Evans the sadist is destructive to both the spiritual and physical good of Glastonbury.

To Sam Dekker, the Vicar's twenty-five year old son, the way of denial is the way of salvation. His refusal to enter a theological college is prompted by his stubborn desire to come to personally satisfying terms with Christianity. His ideal is clearly stated in a conversation with John Crow.

> 'I'm not saying I've ever practised or *could* practise what I'm talking about. . . . All I'm saying is that there's no life that frees anyone so completely from unhappiness as does the mystic life. If you give up *possession,* if you give up trying to possess what attracts you, a lovely, thrilling happiness flows through you and you feel you're in touch with the secret of everything.' (VII,206)

His self-conversion to Christ, when it does happen, has a dramatic effect on the lives of his friends. Most deeply affected is Nell, William Zoyland's wife, whose love for Sam has been reciprocated in the mutual pleasure of physical and emotional union. On the day she decides to tell him that she bears his child, he chooses to renounce her. She is stunned and assumes that he no longer loves her. She cannot understand his motive for rejecting her. "It was the strength of his passion for her that made the issue between her and Christ so deadly clear to him. . . . In his mind at that moment there seemed to be only two alternatives; possessing Nell, or being possessed by Christ. A month-old conception, a year-old love, what were these beside the ecstasy, the blind exultation of sharing the sufferings of a God?" (XVI,469)[5]

Sam soon learns that the path to mystic bliss is not smooth. The responsibility he feels to Nell and their future child conflicts with his relationship to Christ. The happiness he had anticipated has vanished. Nell begs him to return to her but he can't. " 'Christ has got me by the throat, by the hair of my head,' " he tells her. " 'If you made me come to you tonight He would pull me back to Him. I can't escape from Him! He's going to hold me tighter and tighter all my life.' . . . 'You don't know Him, Nell. He's a lover, I tell you – a lover. . . .' (XVII,537-8)

As an interim solution to his problem, Sam suggests that Nell leave Whitelake Cottage to come and live with him and his father at the Rectory. The Vicar is outraged. A simple, orthodox priest, he had been secretly pleased by his son's success with beautiful Nell; but lately had himself come under the spell of her "lovely breasts". Hence, his violent disapproval of the proposed arrangement springs as much from the frustration of repressed drives as from a religious man's sense of propriety. The matter is dropped and Nell – her husband continuing away at work – lives at the Cottage with a servant until shortly after her baby is born. The child's christening turns into an orgy as William, home for the event, mocks the ceremony, seduces Nell's sister-in-law, gets drunk with her, pours whisky into the christening cup, and finally throws the cup into the river. Mat Dekker breathes this sexually-charged atmosphere.

Nell calls to him for sympathetic assistance but finds "devotion burning beneath his bushy eyebrows. . . . The point had come . . . when he must either tear the priest's mask from him and cover that bowed head with more than religious consolation, or get away from her ∗∗∗ leave her ∗∗∗ get home to his son ∗∗∗ to his aquarium ∗∗∗ to his dead wife — to his God." (XXVI, 863) His immediate departure is a short-lived answer to his dilemma. In less than a few hours, Nell, disgusted with her husband's conduct, seeks sanctuary for herself and the baby within the walls of the Vicarage.

The situation grows tense as the months pass. Sam's commitment to Christ excludes everyone else. With his father urging him to petition for Nell's divorce and Nell's own increasing dissatisfaction with the *ménage à trois*, he decides that he must break completely with the two of them. His announcement brings out the Vicar's voyeuristic lust. " 'You shan't sneak off like this!. . . Leaving your wench ∗∗∗ and your child ∗∗∗ and everything. Have you no natural feeling at all? You promised me you'd let her alone until she was properly divorced and you were properly married to her ∗∗∗ and what do I find? I find you turning your mother's room . . . into a place to fornicate in!' " (XXVIII,918) Sam is unaware that "the secret urge of this anger was a wild heathen delight at being left alone, alone without a rival, with those suckling breasts" of Nell's. Sex for Mat Dekker is visual and puritan; for Sam it is subsumed into his relentless love of Christ.

After renouncing the domestic comforts of the Rectory, the young mystic takes a sparsely furnished room and supports himself by pushing a wheelbarrow at the municipal factory. Like Raskolnikov in the Siberian prison -camp, Sam is initially ridiculed and suspected by his fellow-workers who nickname him "Holy Sam". The epithet sticks as his religious eccentricity becomes known

throughout the poorer districts of Glastonbury. On one of
his visits to a destitute family, he ponders the problem of
sharing the pain and suffering of others.

'A limit there must be,' thought Sam, 'to the sympathy one   soul
can give to other souls – or all would perish. Absolute sympathy
with suffering would mean death. If Christ had sympathised *to the
limit* with the pain of the world it would have been hard for him to
have lived until the day of his Crucifixion. But what does that mean?
Does it mean drawing back from the hell we stare at? Does it mean
that every soul has a right to forget if it *can* forget? Sympathy with
pain kills happiness. There comes a point when to live at all we *must*
forget!'

His conclusion left him with   a feeling of unutterable weakness,
cowardice, contemptibleness. Submerged in sickening humility he
groaned aloud. (XXVIII,931-2)

A short while later, Sam sees the Grail. His vision is
accompanied by pain "so overwhelming that it was as if the
whole of Sam's consciousness became the hidden darkness
of his inmost organism; and when this darkness was split,
and the whole atmosphere split, and the earth and the air
split, what he felt to be a gigantic spear was struck into his
bowels and struck *from below*." He feels that he has
become "a bleeding mass of darkness".

But when the vision appeared, and it came sailing into the midst
of this bleeding darkness that was Sam's consciousness, healing
everything, changing everything, each detail of what he saw he saw
with a clearness that branded it forever upon his brain. He saw a
globular chalice that had two circular handles. The substance it was
made of was clearer than crystal; and within it there was dark water
streaked with blood, and within the water was a shining fish.
(XXVIII,939)

Sam recognizes the Grail and, unwittingly fulfilling one
of the legendary conditions of the Grail-quest, asks aloud
what sort of fish lies therein. His question is addressed to
Christ.

It rose from his pity; it rose from his new insight into pain; it rose from that blood-stained umbel [umbilical?] cord across the gulf between his own ecstasies and the anguish he had glimpsed. It rose from the quick of his being, where life itself was strangling pity lest pity strangled life in the ultimate contest. It was the final desperate cry of humanity to the crushing, torturing universe that had given it birth. (XXVIII,940)

Sam had once begged Christ for some sign of his presence, for some assurance that the sacrifice was worthwhile. The Grail proves to be an ambiguous confirmation: it attests to the existence of "something" behind the structured appearance of reality but it fails to reveal the nature of that "something". As a private symbol, it gives meaning and purpose to his mystic-journey; as a public symbol, it means nothing. Sam's own analysis points to the same conclusion. " 'What [Christ] has become is a power in ourselves that sets itself up *contra mundum crudelem*, against the whole bloody world! . . . Man buried Him and Man has brought Him out of his Tomb. That's what the Grail means!' " (XXVIII,943) These thoughts are a revision of Sam's earlier conception of Christ when he declared that: " 'I'm considering Him as a God. But I'm considering Him as a God among Other Gods. I'm considering Him as a God who is *against* the cruelty of the great Creator-God.' " (XVI,465; also see XXVIII,956-7,962) The centre of power has been shifted. No longer is the struggle between Christ and God, it has been transferred to the terrestrial plane where it continues between each man and the world around him.

In its development, Sam's religious thinking parallels that of John Crow and Owen Evans. Like them, he experiences a moment of revelation that has been preceded by reflection on pain and suffering. In each case the vision is accompanied by a sense of mental shock and physical discomfort. There ends the similarity. John's vision is turned on the pivot of his own ego, selfishly examined and then rejected; Evans's dual experience on the cross and at the murder-scene dovetails into a single, negative apocalypse. Only Sam, by reducing the ineffable to the practical, reacts positively to his confrontation with the personally Absolute.

On the morning after his vision, he is still trying to assimilate the Grail message into his own humane beliefs. With this in mind he sets out to visit an old man whom he has promised to help — the problem is severe constipation complicated by piles; and the remedy is an enema. Sam is, to say the least, unenthusiastic about the job at hand; "but he was a born naturalist and an unfastidious country-man."

As he struggled with his task, bending over the old gentleman's rear, the tension of his spirit brought back with a rush the miraculous power of the vision he had seen. The two extremes of his experience, the anus of an aged man and the wavering shaft of an Absolute, piercing his own earthly body, mingled and fused together in his consciousness. Holy Sam felt, as he went on with the business, a strange second sight, an inkling, as to some incredible secret, whereby the whole massed weight of the world's tormented flesh was labouring towards some release.

As he kept pinching that rubber tube ... there came over him a singular clairvoyance about the whole nature of the world. ... A sharp pang took him when — in this extremity of clairvoyance — he realised [sic] that his living tortured Christ was now changed to something else. But whatever Sam's priggishness may have been, it was mercilessly honest, and he said to himself: 'If Christ be dead, I still have seen the Grail.' (XXVIII,948)

In man, the excremental and the sublime meet. Vague humanistic doctrines are given precise form in Sam's act. The treatment is beneficial: the old man is purged. What Sam had suspected after seeing the Grail is now affirmed; namely that Christ is *dead* — historically and finally — but that the goodness which he represented can be a vitalizing principle in the life of every man. All the symbolism enforces Sam's interpretation. Purification is brought about by the conjunction of a creative force with inert matter. Some sort of penetration is required because the change must occur from within, superficial contact being, as in John Crow's case, a very uncertain procedure. Both the mystic spear and the lowly enema share, as did the love-spear in *Ducdame*, properties of creation and destruction. The anal passage is particularly fit to be the path to life. Surely this is the "dark mystic copulation" envisaged but misunderstood by Evans on the Cross. The phallic standard of creativity penetrates to the heart of inertia, destroys it, and leaves peace and rest. This is truly "creation without-generation," parthenogenesis — the virgin-birth of individual goodness.

Sam is now free to return to Nell. The Grail is his assurance that the creative power residing in each person is sufficient to combat all of the cruelty, pain, and suffering in the world, not that it will necessarily be victorious but that it can never be totally defeated. Such as it is, the battle is eternal; and Sam believes that he has seen eternity.

'I feel now that my life has really finished itself, accomplished itself somehow; and what I want to do now is just to take it as it is and to give it to anyone, to anything, to whatever comes along, following chance and accident, and not bothering very much ... taking everything as it happens. . . .' (XXVIII,974)

These words are scarcely spoken before their sincerity is rigorously tested. Returning after his long absence to the Vicarage, Sam learns that Nell has willingly reunited herself with her husband. The news which he is able to bear with equanimity completely routs his father. In anger, Mat Dekker orders his son from the house: his mind is obsessed by "frustrated passion. His emotions had smouldered and smouldered till they had become like a lump of darkly burning peat, self-scorched, self-fed, self-consumed." Like Wolf Solent, Sam stands alone but confident: " 'I can endure whatever fate can do to me,' " he thinks, " 'for I have seen the Grail!' " (XXVIII, 984-6)

Very early in the *Romance*, the Vicar and his son are described as "proud and shy and anti-social". Both men undergo considerable stress in the course of the narrative; their systems of values are questioned and, for Sam, altered; the older man survives by imposing the lifetime habits of Christianity on himself, the younger by accepting the Grail's message. In the final chapter, father and son are reconciled as they work together on a barge, rescuing people from the great flood which covers the low-lying portions of Glastonbury. "Water dripped from their drenched clothes. Sweat poured from their tired faces." They transmit an impression of "an exultant happiness". (XXX, 1102)

Significantly, Sam is the first of the major figures we have discussed to participate in the flood. (The stories of John Crow and Owen Evans end in the penultimate chapter.) His own purgation and his aid in giving the enema to another presage the general cleansing at which he also assists. The final happiness he knows is denied both John Crow and Evans because they failed to meet the challenge of their Glastonbury experiences. Sam has responded positively to his environment and to his relationships with various people; he has transformed mystic intuition into altruistic action: in short, he has become socially conscious.

Not everyone in Glastonbury aspires to mysticism or altruism. There are those concerned with the commercial life of the town — shop-keepers, merchants, factory hands, down to Mother Legge who runs the local brothel. Philip

Crow is certainly the most adamant in his desire to raise
Glastonbury to economic prosperity. As an ambitious,
successful industrialist — he owns, among other things, the
Glastonbury Dye-Works — he comes across to the reader
far more convincingly than Mortimer Romer, his proto-
type in *Wood and Stone*. He manages his business with
energy and decision, holding meetings, telephoning associates, travelling frequently and quickly by car or aeroplane; his conversation and thoughts are about strikes,
investment, expansion, and labour; his faith is built on
machinery, science, and economics.[6]

After being deprived of his inheritance by Bloody
Johnny, Philip does all in his power to undermine the
preacher's plans to revive the religious past of the town. He
is even more rankled when Johnny uses the legacy to aid in
the establishment of the Glastonbury Commune, a sort of
co-operative organization which sets up its own municipal
dye-works. Philip's hostility is suspiciously misanthropic.

'Humanity!' he thought. 'As they were two, three, four thousand
years ago, so today! To mould them, to drill them, to dominate them
— it's all too sickeningly easy. . . . How much better to struggle with
machinery against the inertness of blind matter than to try to make
anything of such insects!' (XVIII,550)

. . . .

'How these Christs and Buddhas. . . . ever reached the point of
feeling that it was worth their while to save the human race is more
than I can understand. I don't want to torture anyone . . . but it's
impossible for me to understand this "value of human life" that some
people make so much of.' (XXIV,744)

Although he would, for business purposes, be capable of
cutting off "the heads of all the poor of Glastonbury", his
inhumanity is not in the least sadistic. He is pompously
self-important, unlike his cousin John whose scepticism
prevented illusions of that sort, with a thirst for power and

possession. The zest with which he undertakes industrial developments and the satisfaction he derives from them give him sexual pleasure. The discovery and mining of tin in the Wookey Hole caves, hitherto run by him as a tourist attraction, induce "an excitement that was actually phallic". The causes – quite apart from the obvious symbolism – of this condition are easily apparent. Married to a kind-hearted but silly wife, Philip has not known physical passion since an affair with a boy at school. As a man of consequence, he has observed the proprieties and repressed all homosexual desire. Even though he tries to make his cousin Persephone Spear, whose figure reminds him of a boy's, his mistress – he sleeps with her a few times – he is still practising illicit sex within the accepted convention which allows executives to take a woman to bed with them while away on business. Unfortunately for him, Percy (the abbreviated form is significant) is repelled by male-sex, except for a brief interlude with Will Zoyland, and forms a lesbian friendship.[7] Deprived of an outlet, Philip sublimates his sexuality into industrial enterprise. Thus, his factories, the mine, even his aeroplane express the totality of his personality: both his private and public selves are fulfilled in the objects he possesses and exploits.

Opposition to his works necessarily involves opposition to his person. Early on in the novel, he is respected by the common-man for his position and power; later, his dissatisfaction with Glastonbury workers causes resentment and ill-feeling amongst the townspeople. Although Johnny Geard and the Commune indirectly loosen his hold on the town, three other men are more directly responsible. Dave Spear, Percy's husband, is a Communist-theorist who organizes workers in various parts of Britain. His interpretation of Communism is idealistic and emotional rather than practical and rational: in one impassioned speech, for instance, he declares that he is "the voice of the Future" and prophesies a utopian brotherhood of man.

Red Robinson, a local Party worker, is a very different sort of man. The uneducated son of a charwoman, he has achieved notoriety as an agitator and revolutionist. He has a personal grudge against Philip, who once dismissed him from his job, and plots his downfall. He is the one first to propose the nomination of Johnny Geard for mayor of Glastonbury; he is a principal organizer in the formation of the Commune; and he becomes a capable foreman in one of its factories. His theory of class-structure is summed up in his reply to a question about why the upper-classes are still being treated unfairly by the lower, now that the Commune has been established. (The exaggerated cockney accent adds bluntness and point to the answer.)

'Don't yer see *** will you hupper-classes *never* see *** that you've been just sitting, 'eavy and sife, on the top of us workers? When a man's been lying on 'is fice, hunder the harse of a great bewger all 'is life long, 'tisn't heasy when he's thrown the bewger off to talk sweet to 'im. 'Tisn't heasy to sigh, "Poor rich man, did I 'urt yer when I threw yer bleedin' harse off of my fice?" ' (XXVIII, 969)[8]

Offsetting to some degree Red's violent measures for dealing with capitalists (" 'Set 'em up against a wall and pump some good lead into 'em!' ") is the philosophical anarchist and lawyer Paul Trent. It is he who negotiates the land-purchase which incorporates most of Philip Crow's new factory property into the Commune. His role as legal adviser is a small but important one. He, Dave, and Red form the triumvirate which unseats the industrialist from his position of power. As the co-operative venture prospers, Philip's fortunes fall: his tin-mine is quickly depleted and the road and bridge he was building for the more expeditious transporation of the mineral are left unfinished.

From beginning to end of the *Romance*, Philip Crow's

character is static. The final encounter between himself and
Johnny Geard illustrates the tenacity of his ambition.
He is straddling the wing of his aeroplane with the flood
swirling about his legs when Geard approaches in a small
boat. The latter offers, for reasons we shall be examining
later, to take his place in the water. His consideration of
this proposition becomes an assessment of his whole life:

> 'I suppose the noble thing to do would be to refuse his help. . . . My
> plane's ruined. My bridge is down. My road is sunk. Not an ounce of tin
> in Wookey for the last three weeks. . . . The new dye works — all that
> these demons have left me — a foot deep in water! What have I got to
> live for?'
>   . . . .
>
> 'Begin again,' he thought to himself; 'and to hell with
> mock-heroism! Geard and I are two beasts fighting for our lives. *I
> know it.* He doesn't know it! His soft, crazy idealisms, his
> I-am-the-one-to-give-my-life-for-my-enemy, is simply his handicap in
> our struggle. If the man *does* drown before I get back, it'll only
> prove that he preferred his ideal gestures to life. I prefer *nothing* to
> life.' (XXX,1111)

He changes places with Johnny, secretly confident that
his aeroplane will carry the preacher's weight until he can
return with a larger boat to pick him up. His confidence is
ill-founded; the machine sinks in the mud and Geard
drowns.

With Philip, we move into direct contact with Glastonbury life — albeit only one aspect of that life. He is
representative of the town's modern, progressive element.
His ideals, ambitions, and methods are based on a
pragmatic attitude towards people and objects. He stands
for "Progress" which demands " 'A living wage for every
man who wants to do a good honest day's work. . . . Not
old fairy stories but new factories . . . not fake-miracles
but solid hard work; not fancy toys and mystical gibberish
but smoking chimneys and well-filled larders! Let these visit-

ors, when they come to Glastonbury, find . . . a prosperous, independent community . . . ' " (XII,341; also XXVIII, 888) These are the standards of free-enterprise, the solid bulwark of capitalism. Philip Crow is never aware of the strong under-currents of human feeling and thought which bind the myths and legends of the town into a continuous tradition — a tradition that is alive and meaningful to many people. Consequently, he is never required to reject the vision as John does, suffer under its magnitude like Evans, or enjoy the consolation it brings to Sam. His struggle for material ends is, in a sense, a courageous effort to impose meaning on existence; but it is likewise blind and futile because he is unable to see the multiplicity of variegated life around him. The gestures he makes, for example, to better the lot of his illegitimate daughter are sterile: the girl despises his lack of imagination and derides his doctrine of progress; he, in turn, thinks her a rude, spoilt child, thus excusing his dismissal of her. (XXIII, 724-9; also XXVIII,874-8; XXX,1114) As a disciple of materialism, Philip touches only the physical dimensions of Glastonbury — what the eye can see, the ear can hear, the hand can touch.

For an appreciation, an understanding of the pulsating vitality that flows like metaphysical blood under and behind the streets, shops, houses, and hills of the town, we need the guidance of John Geard. After inheriting the Canon's money, he decides to spend it for the good of Glastonbury. He is taken up by the Communists of the town and promoted as a desirable mayor. In time, he is elected: his money and position are influential in the formation of the Commune. Although consulted by the Councilmen and receiving a salary from them, he is, as a political figure, decidedly *hors de combat*. Yet it is fitting that he should be Mayor; for his interest in the town goes far beyond its commercial prosperity — though it does

indirectly assist in that area. This is how he explains it to
Mat Dekker:

'The Lord ✳✳✳ has ✳✳✳ filled me ✳✳✳ with the power of His Spirit,
my dear, and nothing can stop me from doing His will! I feel His will
pouring through me, my dear, by night and by day. Let the glory go
to whom He pleases! I am but a reed, a miserable pipe, a wretched
conduit, a contemptible sluice. But never mind what I am! Through
me, at this moment of time, the Eternal is breaking through. Yes,
dear, *dear* Sir, for I admire 'ee and respect 'ee, it's breaking through!
I'm going to make Glastonbury the centre of the Religion of all the
West.' (X,287)

There are two parts to his plan. The first, the more
spectacular but also the more transient, is the great
midsummer pageant which is designed to attract the eyes
of the whole world; the second, more enduring project, is the
development of the local chalybeate spring known as
Chalice Well into a religious focal point. It is noteworthy
that he leaves the implementation and details of the
pageant to John Crow while he himself sees to the erection
of an arched entrance to the Well and, much later, of a
chapel-like building nearby.

The pageant, briefly mentioned in connection with John
Crow and Owen Evans, brings to a close the first of the
Romance's two volumes. A quick reading of the book
might suggest that it is so climactic that much of what
comes after is irrelevant. The crowd-scenes alone, including
almost every person mentioned elsewhere in the novel, are
staggering, combining the verbal and mental reactions of
numerous individuals with the total movement of a large,
restless throng; the pageant itself is depicted with a curious
mixture of humorous sympathy for the ineptness of some
of the non-professional actors and of intense anxiety for
the traumatic effect it has on many of the participants.
Throughout most of the spectacle, John Geard remains
apart, looking down on it from the top of the Tor, "with a

silent gratitude, with an up-welling feeling of fulfilment, deep as that fount of red water whose flowing he could detect at the foot of the opposite hill." (XIX,573)[9]

The reference to Chalice Well is telling because of Geard's foundation-belief in the Blood of Christ; in fact, he calls the waters of this spring "the Blood". Far from being the centre of his new religion, the pageant is merely an introduction to it — a form of impressive publicity, notwithstanding its own truly serious purport. Once it is over, Johnny devotes all his energy towards the further-ance of his peculiar creed.

Shortly before the Well is officially opened, he visits it with Tittie Petherton, an old woman dying of cancer. He had twice previously relieved her suffering by his ability to share it with her. (see X,292) On the second occasion he had rushed into a room where she was in agony, "snatched her up in his arms, . . . sank down in a chair with her on his lap, and began, in his own natural voice, that familiar refrain which had won him his nickname. 'Blood of Christ deliver us! Blood of Christ save us! Blood of Christ have mercy upon us!' " (XVI,506) He rocked the woman back and forth until she was asleep. This time, he stands, naked in the spring, facing Tittie who is by its side.

> Now he was neither thinking nor feeling. Now his whole body and soul were absorbed in an *act*. This act was the act of *commanding* the cancer to come out of the woman; commanding it on his own authority; so that the growth in Tittie's side should wither up! (XXIII,707)

His power is operative; the woman seems cured and dozes; but one complication remains.

> Perhaps he wouldn't have succeeded after all if there hadn't come into his head at that moment an actual vision of one tiny living tendril of that murderous octopus under the sleeping woman's flesh. With one terrific upheaval of the whole of his massive frame, its gastric, its pulmonary, its spinal, its phallic force, and even lifting

himself up on tiptoe from the gravel at the bottom of the fount, he plunged that Bleeding Lance of his mind into the half-dead cancer. (XXIII,709)

We immediately recognize the features of this healing process: the mind, the symbolic Lance or spear, the physical, phallic energy. This is obviously another version of Sam's and John Crow's visionary experiences. All three men have come into contact with the same force, a "psychic aura", which surrounds Glastonbury; but only Geard is capable of mastering it. Why this should be so involves the Mayor's total personality. He is an extremely simple, earthy man — as unruffled about breaking wind in public as he is about drinking beer with the poorest of the townspeople. While his strong erotic nature is still stirred by his wife's presence after forty years of marriage, he is equally quick to recognize the sexual appeal of an eighteen year old girl. He carries this same sensual enthusiasm into his religious observances. On Easter morning he kneels in his garden eating from a loaf of bread — "the flesh of his Master" — and gulping down port wine — "His blood". Later the same day, he visits Mark's Court, "an old farmhouse" which, "according to a local tradition unbroken for a thousand years" had witnessed the actual pulverization of King Mark by the Magician Merlin. While there, he is induced to sleep in the very chamber — supposedly haunted — where the magic took place. His night-long vigil in that room illustrates an essential link between himself and Merlin; it also unites pagan and Christian religion in a loose bond. He reflects that "He had been well-advised to ride over to Mark Moor Court on the day of Christ's Resurrection. The old magic monger [Merlin] had vanished with his heathen Grail . . . in the heart of Chalice Hill. Well! He, Bloody Johnny, the new miracle-worker, would show the world, before *he* vanished, that the real Grail still existed in Glastonbury." (XV,455)

He goes on to expand this idea:

> 'Thought is a real thing,' he said to himself. 'It is a live thing. It creates; it destroys; it begets; it projects its living offspring. Like certain forms of physical pain thoughts can take organic shapes. They can live and grow and generate; independently of the person in whose being they originated.
>
> 'For a thousand years the Grail has been attracting thought to itself, because of the magnetism of Christ's Blood. The Grail is now an organic nucleus of creation and destruction. Christ's Blood cries aloud from it by day and by night. Yes, yes, . . . I know now what the Grail is. It is the desire of the generations mingling like water with the Blood of Christ, and caught in a fragment of Substance that is beyond Matter! It is a little nucleus of Eternity, dropped somehow from the outer spaces upon one particular spot!' (XV,457-8)

The passage gives us the key to both Geard's spiritual success and to the central concept behind the *Romance*. One common property can be found in all human endeavour through the ages – thought. It forms a continuity which accumulates over the centuries, a sort of reservoir of mental forces that exists in its own right. (The idea is plainly comparable to Jung's theory of the collective unconscious.) Powys seems to indicate that everyone is influenced by its power – even the Philip Crows who deny its existence – but that very few are able to tap the reservoir at will. When some of man's cumulative thought is concentrated on one object, such as the Grail legend, that object becomes a reality having powers of its own. Thus it happens that thought, being indestructible, confers potential eternity on its embodiment. We are now at the crux of this near-paradox. In a very real sense, each man creates eternity through thought emanations; but, once generated, this everlasting continuum lies outside his conscious command. The reason is simple. Most people are too preoccupied with themselves, too busy sending out reflections of their own

personality or defending their egoism from attack to allow
the approach of totally impersonal, superior power. Philip
Crow, the materialist, is blind to it; Owen Evans, the
introverted sadist, fails to recognize it; John Crow, the
sceptic, rejects it; and Sam Dekker,the altruist, is redeemed
by it. All these men live ego-centric lives. Only John Geard
achieves the attitude of selfless receptivity which enables
him to act as a medium between the psychic and the
physical world. In uniting the power of universal thought
with the lives of individual men and women, he becomes
the completing link in a vast circular process wherein all
human activity is made purposive and beneficial.

His behaviour at the opening of Chalice Well and his
entire religious doctrine are one with his belief in the
power of thought and in the Grail. Before delivering his
inaugural speech, he sits on the ground drunk and "empty
of abstract considerations" . He is "in such peace with
himself that his whole being moved in harmony to the
least stray thought that came into his head." We are told
that he may have deliberately indulged "so as to leave no
shred of fussy vain human self-thought between his
intellect and his world-deep sensations." In the speech
itself he draws on this source of inspiration:

'*Any lie,*' he shouted, 'I tell you, *any lie* as long as a multitude of
souls believes it and presses that belief to the cracking point, *creates
new life*, while the slavery of what is called truth drags us down to
death and to the dead! Lies, magic, illusion — these are names we
give to the ripples on the water of our experience when the Spirit of
Life blows upon it . . . I have myself cured a woman of cancer in
that spring . . . . Miracles are lies; and yet they are happening.
Immortality is a lie; and yet we are attaining it. Christ is a lie; and
yet I am living in Him. It *** is *** given *** unto *** me *** to
tell you that if any man brought a dead body before me *** in the
power of what people call a "lie" I would, even now, here and before
you all, restore that dead one to life!' (XXVII,891-2)

These words are immediately followed by his act of
raising a dead boy to life. (The miracle does not go
unchallenged: the boy suffered from epilepsy and, since
his body had not been seen by a doctor, many people
think that he was simply in a fit.)

Belief in the vital continuity of universal creative
thought is the kernel of Geard's Fifth Gospel which he is
attempting to enunciate just before the flood sweeps over
Glastonbury. He states that the Grail and Christ's Blood
have made Glastonbury a focus of spiritual force, that here
people can touch the central pulse of life, that men and
women can participate in this eternal movement through
physical and sexual union. "It matters not at all from what
cups, or from what goblets, we drink, so long as without
being cruel, we drink up Life." This is the "sole meaning,
purpose, intention, and secret of Christ".
(XXX,1085-6)

Once we understand that Geard is speaking of Life as a
universal essence rather than as a physiological process, his
growing wish to die becomes self-explanatory. As he rows
about looking for flood-victims, he becomes "resolutely
set upon dying". He is certain that "a living Being, who
might, or might not, be the Christ the churches wor-
shipped", would meet him after he died and "would
satisfy to the full the accumulated erotic desires, at once
mystical and sensual, which were the master-craving of his
nature." (XXX,1104) We now see the irony both in Philip
Crow's avowal of his love for life and in his condemnation
of Geard's idealism in taking his place on the submerged
aircraft. Bloody Johnny's drowning is no easy affair; his
body revolts against its end but eventually grows quiet.
"Geard of Glastonbury's will to die enjoyed at last its
premeditated satisfaction":

In calm, inviolable peace Mr. Geard saw his life, saw his death, and
saw also that nameless Object, the fragment of the Absolute, about

which all his days he had been murmuring . . . . He was at peace, too, about what should happen in the future to his new Religion. It was as if he had ceased to belong to our world of looking-glass pantomime wherein we are driven to worship we know not what; and had slipped down among the gods and taken his place among those who cast their own mysterious reflections in the Glastonbury of our bewilderment.

. . . .

In his dying moments, Geard of Glastonbury did actually pass, consciously and peacefully, into those natural elements that he had always treated with a certain careless and unaesthetic aplomb.

He had never been an artistic man. He had never been a fastidious man. He had got pleasure from smelling at dung-hills, from making water in his wife's garden, from snuffing up the sweet sweat of those he loved. He had no cruelty, no culture, no ambition, no breeding, no refinement, no curiosity, no conceit. He believed that there was a borderland of the miraculous round everything that existed and that 'everything that lived was holy.' (XXX, 1117)

The novel does not end immediately with Geard's death. As its title implies, *A Glastonbury Romance* (the indefinite article is noteworthy), is much larger than any of the characters it depicts. Its concern is with a definite group of men and women, to be sure, but it goes beyond them to a consideration of the time and, more particularly, of the place in which they live. Glastonbury itself assumes a personality in the course of the narrative, participating in the novel's action through its living history, its physical dimensions, and its spiritual atmosphere. Scene after scene emphasizes this participation, perhaps none so strikingly as the long dream-sequence which unites the town and its inhabitants in nocturnal communion. (XXIV, 746-60) The vast flood, described in the last chapter, is an agent of general rather than individual destruction. As such, it is very much a cleansing force bringing about that great release towards which Sam Dekker felt the world was struggling.

Although a disciple of Johnny's new religion suggests that it is a judgement against Philip's industrial developments, it is more probably — and properly — directed towards Glastonbury itself. While helping to maintain the novel's aesthetic balance — it is the only imaginable occurrence, short of its counterparts, war, famine, and pestilence, that could successfully supplant Geard — it also restores the natural balance of community living. The Commune has been corrupted by success and the common profit, gained for the most part from pilgrims, is unequally distributed; the new religious movement has been well established but its leader wishes to die. Events have reached a climax: there is a sense of rush and expectancy. The flood comes like a giant enema bearing the purgative, life-giving, salt-water into the interior.

The *Romance* goes even further than depicting elemental influences on the works of man; it makes allowance for cosmic forces, paranatural phenomena, and a dualistic first-cause. (The book's opening two paragraphs are fine examples of the way Powys relates and co-ordinates universal factions with human behaviour.) In those respects, *A Glastonbury Romance* is very much a *roman à thèse*. Nevertheless, while suggesting a multi-leveled universe, it is constantly pointing back to man as the centre of everything. Again and again we are reminded that the human mind is the creative organ giving purpose and meaning to life. The final pages of the book speak of mankind's ideals and beliefs springing from "those strange second thoughts of all the twice-born in the world; the liberated thoughts of men . . . and the brooding thoughts of women." (XXX,1120)[10]

The characters we have examined embody certain aspects of the human condition. The more closely they integrate their lives — as in the cases of Sam Dekker and Johnny Geard — with their total ethos, the more easily do they fulfil their individuality . The process requires the total participation of both mind and body. Hence, the Grail revelation is preceded by reflection on pain (awareness of other people), symbolized by a lance or spear (universal thought penetrating the imagination), and accompanied by phallic or erotic sensation (bodily response to the energizing situation). This "epiphany", to use Joyce's term for the corresponding experience, leads to an exacting consciousness of one's fellow human-beings and results in the giving of oneself to others. Sam's altruism follows from his partial commitment to the vision – partial because he never loses his identity completely; Geard's religion, the abdication of selfhood for the good of others, is the furthest extension of social involvement.

Powys no longer applauds, although he may still admire, personal isolation and stoic endurance. John Crow is more closely related to Wolf Solent than anyone else in the *Romance*; yet, quite apart from his sycophantic attitude to money and love, the very traits he shares with Wolf – loneliness, scepticism, individualism, – stifle his reaction to the Grail-message. Selflessness not selfishness constitutes receptivity.

Weymouth Sands is a Powysian *jeu d'ésprit*. Its plot is a simple construction: a series of love-affairs carried on by persons of varied social standing. These characters are as vividly   presented as any in Dickens, but are relatively shallow when compared to those in the *Romance*. This lessening of psychological analysis determines the balance in the novel and points us back to its title.[11] The physical dimensions of Weymouth – less of the town itself than of the surrounding seascape and countryside – are actively present to the reader; beaches, promontories, downs, and moors achieve a massive solidity denied to the spiritually pregnant but more passive outlines of Glastonbury; the roar of advancing and receding waves provides, as in *Rodmoor*, a background to thought and action.

While characters are grouped according to geographical boundaries, they are united in thematic interdependence. *Weymouth Sands* is about sex, violence, and religion. These topics are boringly familiar, splashed across the covers of paper-back "best-sellers" or ecstatically repeated in countless blurbs. Nevertheless, like Sweeney, who voices one aspect of this triadic fact, we know that "Birth, and copulation, and death" form the bedrock of our experience. Powys's approach to the subject is characteristically unique. Within the convention of what might be loosely termed "an adventure novel", he develops enquiries initiated in the *Romance*. He links "normal" heterosexuality with agression and violence; he examines the relationship of virginity to prostitution; he suggests a more explicit interpretation of parthenogenesis in relation to modern living; nor does he shy away from abortion, lesbianism, homosexuality, and incest, not to mention minor deviations such as adultery, fetishism, or voyeurism. Violence is represented as both personal and impersonal: Jobber Skald plans to murder Cattistock on principles of social responsibility; Dr. Dan Brush conducts experiments in vivisection for the sake of truth; Sippy Ballard prosecutes Gipsy May and her companion Larry Zed in a spirit of civic righteousness. Although Church spires may be appreciated as landmarks, the orthodoxy they embody is passed over in favour of more esoteric insights. Sylvanus Cobbold is a gaunt mystic (an aged, enlightened version of Sam Dekker perhaps) whose prayers to the elemental and inanimate merge with his deeply felt respect for the excremental and spiritual unity of man. Women are his means of contacting his source of religious inspiration; they are drawn to him by his physical magnetism but live with him in a state of supra-sexual harmony. Gipsy May is one of these women. She uses Tarot cards to divine the future, is an adept at palmistry, and reads natural signs. Interest in the occult is not confined to the novel's eccentrics; Powys himself frequently interpolates discussion, argument, or query about the role played in human affairs by psychic forces.

Throughout *Weymouth Sands*, Magnus Muir is our touchstone of normality or, should that state be too difficult to pinpoint, of moderation. He is a self-effacing man of forty-six, dominated by the memory of his dead father. He earns a sparse living by private tutoring and seems especially adept at teaching backward children. This quality brings him into contact with Dogberry Cattistock, the local business magnate, whose son Benny has proven unmanageable. It is ironic that, at the last, Cattistock runs off with Muir's fiancée, Curly Wix. Such, however, is the tutor's lot. He is involved in almost all of the book's conflicts, but remains on their periphery. His hesitancy and cowardice are obvious from the first. He is requested by Mrs. Jerry Cobbold to meet her new companion, Perdita Wane, who is arriving by boat from Guernsey. On his way to the wharf he sees Sylvanus Cobbold being bullied by a policeman. He slinks by unrecognized; later he feels ashamed that he didn't intervene. Nevertheless, he shirks his duty again when he asks Adam Skald, the Jobber, to wait for the girl.

This same congenital weakness governs his emotional life, producing in it a sort of naiveté akin to a pathetic innocence. His love for Curly, a Weymouth shop-girl, is blind to her callousness and egotism. Urged by a conniving mother, who hopes to improve her daughter's social standing through marriage, she leads Magnus on. He interprets her indifference as demureness and rhapsodizes when he is permitted to press her soft breast through the thickness of a jacket and to feel her limbs under her skirt.

Curly has, in fact, been deflowered by Sippy Ballard who has introduced her to "contraceptual devices" and who continues to enjoy her favours. No real conflict exists between the two men since Magnus never understands their real relationship.[1][2] When, at one point, the tutor thinks " 'I shouldn't kill myself if I lost Curly . . . . I should just go on, taking my walks, teaching Latin, reading Greek, talking to Father's spirit,' " he expresses his whole personality. He is essentially an observer, wrapped in an unchanging world.

Jobber Skald and Perdita Wane are, in plot terms, at the centre of this novel. Their story gives narrative movement and some unity to the whole book. Skald is a powerfully physical man who insists on the value of action over intellect. " 'Thinking is bad' ", he tells himself. " 'Nothing is ever done by thinking. So much added to thinking, so much taken from doing.' " His plodding attempt to read *Middlemarch* is a self-congratulatory exercise. When he encounters Perdita he is obsessed by the idea of killing Cattistock, whom he blames for much of the hardship suffered by the local working men. He carries a smooth, large stone in his pocket until the time is right for murder. It comes when the "Dog", as he is known, announces his plans to marry Hortensia Lily, a young widow, whose daughter and father are Skald's special friends. The Jobber is bent on killing Cattistock before his wedding night.

As this time draws near, he becomes more deeply involved with Perdita. She has led a sheltered life on Guernsey and longs for a fuller experience. Her duties as companion to Mrs. Jerry Cobbold are disturbing — there are vague lesbian overtures as Lucinda forces her way into Perdita's room each night. The young girl dislikes her employer's morbid, neurotic temperament and finds the sheer physical power of the Jobber refreshing. She understands his personality completely. She knows that

"He's not a thinker at all," and has the honesty to admit
to herself that " 'He's a bit stupid. In fact he's worse than
stupid. He's pig-headed.' " When he makes arrangements at
an Inn for them to pass their first night together, she
reflects on their relationship: " 'I'm sure I don't know
whether people would call what we feel for each other
'being in love,' or whether it's even passion. I think if he
does take me tonight he'll do it clumsily, awkwardly,
brutally, *and I shall be the same.*' " (X,345) Perdita's
straightforward acceptance of her instincts is at a far
remove from the virginal trepidations of Lacrima Traffio
(*Wood and Stone*) whom she resembles in many ways. Sex
is being handled much more bluntly in this novel.

Nevertheless, by omitting any description of the seduction itself, Powys achieves one of his frequent symbolic
coups. The scene moves directly from the lovers at supper
to the lovers in bed together. The connective sentence
states: "Long after Perdita was sound asleep the Jobber's
mind went whirling on in the same blood-stained circle."
Explicitly referring to Cattistock's murder, the sentence
implicitly links the Jobber's social violence with the sexual
violence of breaking the hymen.(A similar sort of indirection was used to describe the sexual play between Wolf and
Christie.) The next morning, Skald leaves to kill his enemy.
That the murder does not happen is providential; Dogberry
jilts Hortensia and never appears at the Church.

There follows a lacuna in the novel during which time
we learn nothing of the Jobber's or Perdita's actions. Only
later do we discover that the girl had despaired of Skald's
reformation — she had been told he still kept the stone in his
pocket — returned to Guernsey and there had taken sick.
The Jobber has likewise fallen on hard times. He has
ceased doing the odd jobs which earned him his name and
drinks excessively. After recovering from her illness,
Perdita returns to Weymouth and Magnus takes her to the

Inn where the lovers had slept. Skald is there, the two are reunited, and Perdita gives Magnus the stone which the Jobber had carried for so long. This reconciliation is hardly convincing. It would almost seem as if some simple moral were to be drawn from the lovers' conduct; that through the personal violence of suffering, one can expiate for the wrongs of others and for the wrong in one's self. Whatever the message — if one is intended — it is much too vague to register.

Just as the Jobber's favourite exclamation "by Dum" reveals his basic personality, so does Sylvanus Cobbold's repeated "Caputanus" reveal his. Portrayed as a gibbering fool, the mystic embodies a paradoxical life-wisdom. In this person, Powys extends the meaning of Sam's experience of giving the old man his enema. When Sylvanus prays to the Absolute, he attempts to obliterate all physical self-consciousness by referring to himself as both "caput" and "anus", thus acknowledging the necessity of placing "the lowest function of his body side by side with the highest". Through the continued repetition of these "nonsense- syllables", he receives "a final revelation . . . of what he had often suspected, namely that the Absolute was to be found in the concrete and not in the abstract, in thought dipped in the life-juice, and not in thought gasping in vacuo. But it was in thought, none the less, *in thought first and last*." (XI,402)

Sylvanus is by no means the only one of Powys's characters to arrive at such a conclusion, but he is the first major figure in Powys's fiction to apply this concept directly to the inanimate. His morning ritual involves burying his refuse and saluting his garden tools. Each of these actions is accompanied by a simple "liturgical intonation". His most extreme reverence is shown to an old rope and a discarded oil-painting: the former he apostrophizes as "a very *strong* rope and a very *wise* rope";

and the latter he addresses as "a masterpiece". These rituals are accompanied by the quick movements of "a small, palpitating, quivery, dancing sunbeam" which he has endowed "with a definite personality" and named Trivia. (XI, 386-93). One of the last glimpses we have of Sylvanus depicts him lifting a dung fork from a pile of manure and kissing its prongs. (XIV, 520)

It is not, however, his respect for the inanimate that causes his eventual imprisonment in Brush Home — a nearby mental asylum known locally as Hell's Museum; nor is it his habit of preaching on the Esplanade instead of below on the beach as he has been ordered. Although both these factors contribute to his arrest, it is his custom of having young girls stay with him that precipitates it. They are attracted to him for the sincerity of his personality rather than by anything he says. While with him, they receive little more attention than he gives to his inanimates. Nevertheless, their presence is necessary to his "mystic-sensuous contemplations". He understands their "inarticulate life-worship" and believes that their virginity is more receptive than anything else to the "ultimate forces" behind life:

He never made love to them. He never made promises to them: and when Gipsy May actually shared the same bed with him he scarcely touched her. Their passion was for him; but his passion was for the Eternal Being; only he had found his masculine reason so much of a hindrance in his struggle to attain what he called the Absolute that he was forever seeking to learn from the souls of women, attuned, as they were to strings and to chords which were hidden from him, some secret entrance to the Deathless and the Immortal which as a hermit and as a solitary he had been unable to reach for himself. (VIII, 272)

It would be contrary, however, to his caputanus-nature, were he to restrict his enjoyment of girls to their souls. And indeed, he does experience genuine sexual pleasure as he holds them: "He had long ago acquired that precious power . . . of reducing the intensity of his physical desire to a level that lent itself to the prolongation rather than to the culmination of erotic ecstasy." (XI,380) When he is to be deprived indefinitely of their company by his confinement to the Home, he prays for these girls. His prayer is a stark presentation of the relation of the human to the inanimate:

'Oh earth!' Sylvanus mumbled in a very low voice, but quite audibly, while the dense darkness seemed to be swallowing up both the wind and the rain. 'O divine ether! O sun, that beholdest all things and hearest all things! O Sea, that hath comforted me and sustained me from my youth up! And you O Wordless and Nameless, that dwellest equally in all wisdom and in all folly, guard Olwen and Lily and Lottie and Nelly and Polly and May and Peg, and especially guard Marret.' (XIV,513)

The religious simplicity which runs through Sylvanus's character breaks new ground in Powys's fiction. This approach to reality is rather phenomenalistic; it antedates by a number of years Sartre's more technically regimented conflicts between the "*en soi*" and the "*pour soi*" and also Camus's victims of self-awareness.[13] The coupling of caput and anus epitomizes the mystic's split consciousness. His quest for identity is a continuous dialogue between himself and his perception, and the conversation itself is the meaning of his life. We know Sylvanus Cobbold as the sum of his actions and sensations, at once artless and complex, a paradox of stupidity and wisdom.

Jerry Cobbold has little use for his brother's mysticism and cynically mocks the suggestion of an Absolute behind life and death:

'Behind *** behind *** behind — that's where you tricky mystics always put the secret, as if life had a rainbow-coloured rump like a pet baboon. It makes me sick to hear you, you old blackguard. Peace to all beings! Our only comfort is to rail, since we're not brave

enough to die! Your baboon's arse may be an Aurora Borealis for all
I care, since we shall never see it! The point is, pilgarlic darling, your
jigging monkey-world is a Monsieur sans queue, an arse-less
Monsieur!' (X,328)

Jerry tries to look the baboon full in the face.
He is misanthropic and enjoys the"excremental under-tides
of existence". His attitudes are at odds with his profession
as a clown. (Powys's failure to realize this side of his
character is a serious fault.) Famous throughout Britain
and Europe, he has retired to Weymouth because of his
wife's idiosyncrasies. We are told that he now performs at
a local music- hall where he dances "his dance" and makes
"his grimaces all the winter long". Jerry's real life is not,
however, to be found on the stage or at home with his
wife, but rather at Sark House.

Run by Dr. Girodel, an abortionist — Curly Wix has
made use of his services — the House serves as a meeting
place for Weymouth's sexual vagabonds. There the doctor
plays the role of pimp, lecher, and inn-keeper. His
"discourse on the advantages of prostitution" is a clear
expression of Sark House philosophy:

'Intelligent women need variety and change, just as men do, and
they need the experience of these things without all the fuss and
fume of what is called love. Of course a girl needn't "go on the
street" as we say; and all she has to do, if she gets landed, is to come
— well! come to me . . . . And it doesn't mean that she kills her power
of falling in love. Girls who have been with endless men can fall in love
in the end, just as we can, and when they *do* love, it's real, I tell you;
for all that silly nonsense that virginity creates, the parthenogenesis
of illusion. . . . has been squeezed out of 'em. You *can't* be
disillusioned and remain a virgin; and yet what intelligent girl, until
she's desperately in love, and not always even then, wants to tie
herself to a husband and children. A conventional married woman
grows inured to dullness and boredom; but she *cannot* be disillusioned, because she's not had the experience for that . . . . Whereas

a girl who has had her adventures – a prostitute if you like – can be
a decent friend to a man without all this silliness!' (XVII, 232-3)[14].

That Jerry Cobbold considers Dr. Girodel his best friend
is enough said about the clown's outlook on humanity.
Otherwise he is just a client. His affair with Tossty, a dancer,
is over-shadowed by the girl's lesbian devotion to her sister,
Tissty.[15] Since he is unmoved by "normal sex-appeal",
this is, naturally, quite to his liking. Although he does
possess some redeeming qualities – he has a passion for
music and entrances Perdita with his piano-playing – his
act of committing Sylvanus to the mental home is un-
pardonable.

The mystic is unconcerned about this turn of events –
indeed he forces the hand of authority himself by his
obstinate persistence in preaching on the esplanade. What
does disturb him are the experiments carried out in an
adjoining laboratory where, he had once been told, "They
cut out the brains of live dogs . . . ." He reproaches Dr.
Brush in no uncertain terms:

'I'd like to see that laboratory of yours combed out, raked out,
scoured out, sucked out, vacuum-cleaned, stomach-pumped, dis-
infected, clystered, *gutted*! Don't you see that the mere fact of your
being allowed to do this – for your chatter about giving 'em
anaesthetics is all my eye – it's those nicely-manufactured straps
that hold 'em so still – proves that we've given up trying to touch
the secret of life by being just and righteous and pitiful. Good God!
Given up the whole direction we've been making toward, from the
beginning!' (XIV, 525)

The theme is vivisection, being treated as a major
concern for the first time in Powys's fiction. This book
presents it as the most extreme manifestation of man's
sadistic cravings and associates it loosely with "the clever
cruelties of Modern Science" . Despite the prominence it
receives through repetition, it is never successfully integrated into the novel's total statement. Magnus Muir is

appalled by this "secret horror behind all modern civilization" but does nothing about it beyond encouraging Sylvanus to speak out. As often as not, characters seem to step out of their appointed roles in voicing their disapproval; and no amount of hectoring on Powys's part can atone for these lapses. No matter how great an allowance we make for its sincerity, importance, and urgency, the campaign against vivisection is extraneous to this particular novel.

Powys is much more fortunate in opposing the psychic to the empirical. Here again he advances new ideas. Until now, his concern with the supernatural had taken the form of guarded curiosity, circumspect and hesitant in its findings. *Ducdame*, his most forthright investigation, fails partially because of its ambiguity on this question; *A Glastonbury Romance* certainly recognizes the presence of spirit-forces but does little to define them. In *Weymouth Sands* psychic activity is presented as a fact. Nevertheless, we must distinguish between the word and the process — Powys does not always do so. He can, on the one hand, refer to non-verbal communication (gesture, inflection, accent, appearance, etc.) as "the psychic atmosphere of speech"; and, on the other, draw a simile, in the most offhand fashion, from direct psychic experience: "He now struck a match, which . . . caused the countenance of Dr. Brush to manifest itself like a ghostly countenance at a séance — the cheeks visible at their extreme edges, the bridge of the nose visible, one side of the mouth visible, and one point on the ridge of the forehead visible." (XI,394-5; XII, 435)[16]

Powys mentions a wide range of occult activities: "telepathic waves of magnetism" pass from one house to another; a gathering of people "falls inevitably into a natural rhythm . . . that gives it form and shape as a psychic entity"; words are "animated eidolons that resemble the astral entities hovering over graves"; objects fade "into some remote psychic dimension" and are replaced by the "symbolic projection" of a certain individual; three people travelling in a car are joined by two other "invisible and purely mental passengers". (XII,421,438,442-3; III,65,77) By far the most graphic of Powys's psychic investigations centres around the characters of Gipsy May and her "half-witted" companion, the orphan-boy Larry Zed — the latter is surely one of Powys's most memorable creations. These two cross the borderline between physical and spiritual worlds at will. It seems perfectly natural that a cow should think in Larry's presence, and that a worm should be "aware — in its obscure worm-consciousness —" of relief when taken off a fish-hook. Gipsy May has a "sacred cat", the gift of a "famous Romany Princess", which acts according to occult impulses. Her high regard for the boy is only overshadowed by her devotion to Sylvanus with whom she feels a subtle psychic communion. Her fortune telling is simply another aspect of her personality. The Tarot cards she uses link the past to the future through her mediumship; the present is represented by phallic energy — " 'To make the cards speak truth there must a man's thing near 'em!' " she quotes as she orders Larry to sit on the table. (V,132-42)

All of these phenomena receive the author's full endorsement — even the strange psychic struggle in which Dr. Brush reveals his feminine, homosexual identity to Sylvanus is handled without a trace of irony. (XIV, 527-8)[17] It is obvious that Powys has come to terms with both the paranatural and the spiritualist worlds. His solution to these problems comes from the inclusiveness of his psychological approach. He will not relinquish one aspect of human experience regardless of how fleeting or pointless it may seem. There is room for both caput and anus — the intellectual and the excremental — for the prostitute and the abortionist, for the clown and the murderer. Each personality must be examined and milked of all possible interpretation. Hence the moods and thoughts of people are considered, not only in themselves, but in relation to others. Powys does not limit the power of reflective consciousness to men; he extends it to animals and the inanimate. He thus establishes another dimension outside of the particular but springing up from it. Although the concept is similar to the one developed in the *Romance*, it differs in that it is now seen as a natural and inevitable process which can be described like any other aspect of reality. Powys draws on spiritualist terminology because it also deals with extra-sensory experience; but there is a profound difference between the two approaches. Whereas spiritualism fixes the source of its beliefs outside man, Powys fixes it within him. All of his psychic phenomena rest on the same premise, namely that every individual has the faculty to receive and project some expression of personality. We are novices, Powys suggests, in our knowledge and practice of this power; nevertheless its existence demands recognition.

Weymouth Sands is an interesting but very disappointing book. Its chief defect is familiar: too many characters introduced far too forcibly. The resulting series of "imaginary portraits", to borrow Pater's phrase, is disconcerting. Characterization is begun on the grand scale. Each of the first three chapters is devoted to a single person; subsequent chapters tend to single out yet other figures in the story. We discover eventually that most of these people remain static throughout the novel. The Jobber's redemption is too quick to convince and so is Dr. Brush's; Curly's flight with Cattistock is — for all of Powys's talk about monogamy, chastity, and prostitution — inexplicable; Magnus Muir's entrances and exits smooth out narrative difficulties with annoying precision. Conflicts are similarly initiated and then give a facile resolution. The Punch and Judy show, for instance, which should or could have large symbolic repercussions stands in a no-man's land half-way between decoration and social criticism. Much of this imbalance is caused by an arbitrary time-sequence. Twelve of fifteen chapters — 454 of 567 pages — describe events from a day in January to the twelfth of February; the remainder of the book covers a day in late August and two in mid-November. These intervals are glossed over with a few lines of summary, but the effect is devastating. Changes in character must be accepted without evidence and altered situations taken for granted. There is an obvious sense of haste in the last part of the book, almost as if Powys had lost interest in his material and had decided to tidy up as best he could. I suspect that the reason for this happening has to do with the nature of his subject matter.

Weymouth Sands is very much a novelist's sketchbook. Many of the topics examined in it — vivisection, mental illness, sexual energy — were to be treated extensively and separately in later novels. These themes are brought together in a form of seminal compression, each discussed briefly but cogently. There is a more relaxed sexual honesty as innuendo is replaced by explicit references to erotic activity and its offshoots, such as contraception and abortion. Various aspects of mental and physical violence — hatred, sadism, deception, vivisection, murder, madness — dramatize personal and social tensions. The religious world is expanded to include the inanimate as well as the living. Salvation is implicitly contained in the knowledge that the grossest physical act is on a par with the most esoteric contemplation — and, indeed, that both are inextricably related. All of these considerations merge in a constant stream of psychic vibration which is coextensive with human personality.

These concepts give *Weymouth Sands* a position of major importance in the corpus of Powys's fiction. This novel is an uneasy mixture of the old and the new, pointing towards fresh evaluations and interpretations. Its strength lies in its potential; but promise does not constitute greatness.

[1] J.C. Powys, *A Glastonbury Romance*, New York: Simon & Schuster, 1932. Throughout my discussion, I refer to the 1955 edition published by Macdonald, London.

[2] Although Evans's sadistic thoughts are never detailed in themselves, their causes and effects are fully described. For examples, see III, 108-10; VI, 176-8; IX, 250-3; XXIX, 1003-34, 1053-5.

[3] For a different approach to the *Romance*, see Roland Mathias, "Gwlad-yr-Haf," *Dock Leaves: A John Cowper Powys Number*, VII, 19 (Spring 1956), 20-9. Mathias emphasizes this novel as a record of *tableaux* rather than as one of character and social comment.

[4] Although Powys had little sympathy with Eliot's poetry — see J.C. Powys, "England Revisited," *Scribner's Magazine*, XCVIII, 3 (September 1935), 143 — the two men share many imaginative attitudes toward modern society and the supernatural.

[5] Sam's affair with Nell is one of Powys's most generous portrayals of full, "normal" sex. Chapter XI, "Consummation", is an amazing combination of sensitivity and honesty in its handling of the lovers' relationship.

[6] For instances see I, 49   *passim*; VIII, 230-4; XVIII, 550; XXI, 663-70; XXIV, 741-6; XXVII, 872-3; XXX, 1111-2.

[7] Percy's sexual relations form a fascinating study in themselves. A dedicated Communist herself, she marries one; then she has affairs with Philip and Will Zoyland – even Tom Barter finds her attractive. Her involvement with Angela Beere, hardly more than a romantic adolescent, ends with her sudden, teasing departure to Russia. For various aspects of her personality, see I, 48, 59; VIII, 235-40; XII, 313-18; XVI, 469; XVIII, 544-5; XIX, 601,611-12; XXI, 671-2; XXII, 696-700; XXVI, 849-66; XXVIII, 958;

[8] There is generosity as well as humour in Powys's perceptive delineation of Red's character. As a voice for the socially oppressed, he plays a minor but determining role in the *Romance*. See VI, 170-82; XVI, 479-86; XXIII, 713-22; XXIV, 762-70; XXV, 799-810.

[9] It would be pointless, indeed impossible, to attempt in the short space needed here for my purpose, any detailed analysis of the sixty-six page chapter describing the pageant.

[10] The incantory prose of much of this chapter and, in particular, of its three closing pages has the grandeur of Beethoven's Ninth Symphony. Its long slow rhythms are – as are those of Molly Bloom's final soliloquy – a testament to the ordering power of the human imagination.

[11] J.C. Powys, *Weymouth Sands*, New York: Simon and Schuster, 1934. Fear of libel action – a law suit had been brought against *A Glastonbury Romance* – led to the publication of a much expurgated edition of this book in England under the title of *Jobber Skald* (London: John Lane, 1935). In 1963, Macdonald, London issued the novel anew under the original title. This new edition reproduces the first - even to the inclusion of typographical errors. In a prefatory note to the Macdonald edition, E.R.H. Harvey clarifies these publishing difficulties. My references are to the Macdonald edition.

[12] See IV, 125-30 for a telling instance of Magnus's obtuseness. The episode invites comparison with Tennyson's "Lady of Shalott"; the reiterated "Tirra-lirra" is strikingly evocative.

[13] Sartre's *La Nausée* was published in 1938, *Le Mur* followed in 1939, and the series *Les Chemins de la Liberté* was begun in 1945. Camus published *L'Etranger* in 1942. The existential approach to

fiction has, I believe, remained in the background of British writing, save, for example, in a few of Iris Murdoch's novels and, more obliquely, in William Golding's. Kingsley Amis has imitated a few of its mannerisms but really continues the tradition of Evelyn Waugh and Anthony Powell. The still later application of phenomenological principles to imaginative writing, as exemplified in the work of Nathalie Sarraute, Alain Robbe-Grillet, and Michel Butor, has yet to cross the Channel.

[14] Dr. Girodel and Sark House are surely the forerunners to Dr. Onirifick and his establishment in Henry Miller's *Sexus, The Rosy Crucifixion*, Vol. I. A study of Powys's influence on Miller could do much to reveal qualities often overlooked in both authors.

[15] These two girls are never realized as music-hall performers. They are another part of the wooden theatricals which creak so pitifully in the wings of *Weymouth Sands*.

[16] This aspect of Powys's work has been provocatively covered by G. Wilson Knight in *The Saturnian Quest*, London: Methuen, 1964.

[17] When Dr. Brush abandons vivisection, he seems to escape punishment for his sadistic acts. This is inconsistent with Powys's overall attitude and is never adequately explained.

IV

When *Maiden Castle* was first published in 1936, Powys had already written five novels set in the West Country shires of Dorset and Somerset. His exhaustive treatment of this region might seem to indicate that yet another Wessex novel — this time with Dorchester and its environs as the scene — could have little new to offer us in either matter or presentation. But such is not the case. This, his seventh novel, grows naturally from the seminal character of *Weymouth Sands*. In order to avoid repetition and eventual stagnation, Powys was compelled to introduce new ideas as well as to re-examine old ones, to rework his narrative techniques and develop fresh structural patterns. Certain definite advances attest to the success of his endeavours: an undercurrent of urgency pulses through the whole to convey the immediacy and cogency of its themes; varied levels of mental and physical activity are united in direction and purpose by interrelated symbols, images, and metaphors; characters attain depth and fullness through highly individualized habits of thought, speech, and behaviour.

Its opening pages introduce us to Dorchester where, in his rooms on the top floor of a building in the High Street, Dud No-man wakes, prepares his breakfast, and, above all, speculates. He has recently returned after an absence of ten years to this town where his mother and virgin wife died during an epidemic. He has come on a death-quest, "to solve, if he only might, . . . the meaning of death itself." It is All Souls' Morning, a propitious time to indulge in sombre reflections. Dud thinks about his childhood with his mother, a mysterious woman from Wales, and his step-father, a church-organist of Dorset stock; he thinks about his youthful discovery that his real father's identity is to remain secret, and about his consequent decision to choose for himself a name "that was no-name". His thoughts turn to his bed, which had been his mother's, and to the "grotesque head of heraldic carving" which tops one of its posts. This head "had been the object round which more than anything else the brooding imagination of his childhood, playing with the notions of both good and evil, had constantly hovered." It is still an integral part of his most fantastic reveries. At times, Dud imagines it as the incubus-lover of his wife's corpse; but, more often, associates it with Malory's Questing Beast and with the Welsh words" 'Dor-Marth,' meaning the door of death."[1]

The symbolism here is clearly of a highly personal nature. In its phallic and mythic aspects, it brings Dud's mother Cornelia and his wife Mona into a circle of legendary beings and circumstances; it arranges sexual and intellectual pleasures into the pattern of a perversely introverted mythos. From these elements Dud has woven a fantasy to replace the identity denied him by birth. He has looked wistfully towards his mother's "Cymric ancestors" for a clue to his inheritance, even allowing himself "to play with the idea that his mother's lover was some great Welsh lord who 'deduced his lineage' from the mythical pursuers of the 'Questing Beast'." (III, 134; also III, 114-5, 128-9)

We are not surprised to learn that this man, possessed of such uncommon knowledge and convoluted imaginings, is an historical novelist. The book he has in hand is about Mary Channing who, for poisoning her husband, was burnt in Dorchester's Roman amphitheatre in 1705. Dud feels not only a passionate compulsion to vindicate her name in writing but also an impelling need to include her spirit in his life. (VI, 244, 258-61) His novel is thus another aspect of his death-quest – namely, a concrete attempt to relate himself through the dead to an historical sequence which has public as well as private meaning.

But what of the living and the immediate? The details I have mentioned place Dud No-man in a rather uncompromising light; he appears a necrophile whose cerebral enjoyments more likely repel than attract our sympathies. His is an imaginative world – recalling, perhaps, that of Huysmans or of Villiers de l'Isle Adam –wherein particulars are rendered abstract and distinctions of time and space are blurred. His consciousness is bound by fictions, by the stories he invents about himself and about others.

Almost paradoxically, his tendency to mentalize everything lead him into action. Returning from a visit to the graveyard "where his own dead lay", he sees a small circus situated across the road from the amphitheatre and enters its grounds. His attention is caught by a young performer arguing violently with her employer. Dud is outraged by the scene, feels that the girl is being treated unjustly, and follows her to her caravan. There his erotic imagination is fired by her alluring figure; he compares her favourably with the dead Mona and determines to free her from her ignoble circumstances. There is, however, a major complication: Wizzie Ravelston is the legal property (she is, after a fashion, adopted) of the circus-manager, Ben Urgan, known familiarly as Old Funky. Dud surmounts this obstacle, however, by offering to buy Wizzie's "contract" from the not unwilling Ben. Neither the crude bargaining that ensues nor the final agreement on a price of eighteen pounds compliments Wizzie, who is quite aware that she is being sold as a person, not as a performer. Dud's thoughts as he signs the cheque are fully in keeping with his personality:

From somewhere deep down in his soul a feeling arose as if all this had happened before, ages and ages ago! He *did* meet her eyes now, as he held that pen, and it was as if out of the remote past of that long-historical spot some reincarnated Bronze-Age invader were selecting from among the girl-captives of the older Stone-Age the particular one that appealed to his erratic fancy, the one, out of them all, that no one else would choose! (II, 81).

After this purchase, he continues to interpret Wizzie's enigmatic aloofness in ways most flattering to his peculiar requirements. As a result, he constantly deludes himself. He is convinced, for example, of her virginity until he is told of Lovie, her three-year-old daughter. Dud's ego-centred fabulations are gradually weakened. He begins to observe certain disenchanting features of day-to-day living which seem to question the validity of his own airy inventions. Thus, "as . . . he watched his 'Stone-Age' girl putting on her hat, a hat bought in Durnovaria for five shillings, he felt as though the real reality of things was much more simple and much less pleasant" than he had imagined. (III, 134.) (The chronological sequence – pre-historic, historic, contemporary – should be noted.)

Although Dud is unable to understand someone so different from himself, Powys can and does. Wizzie Ravelston's characterization is one of the major achievements of *Maiden Castle*. Born an orphan, trained in a circus, Wizzie is a convincing combination of earthy sentimentality and naive worldliness. Her language in its harsh ungrammatical directness reflects her environment: she is first heard denouncing her employer's wife as "a money-licking old bitch" who wants her to perform before a "set of damned grinning kids". For amusement she reads "blood-curdling" tales such as *The Adventures of Lily*

Turnstile: Wizzie neither respects nor comprehends Dud's activity as a serious novelist. Her emotional sensitivity is no more refined than her literary taste: her attachment to Dud does not extend much beyond a sense of obligatory, impersonal gratitude. She is thoroughly annoyed by his readiness to accept her illegitimate daughter and considers "the idea of having Lovie hung round her neck, like the albatross in *Gems of Standard Poetry*, the last straw."

Wizzie is ill-suited to act as Dud's mistress. Her whole person responds to circus-life. She imagines herself "back again in tights and spangles – not in the old lavender-coloured ones ... but in fresh, new, beautiful, sky-blue ones, radiant as the supple limbs they covered, as she would balance herself on her old horse's back ... or would leap like a shooting-star, as no girl had ever leapt before through a rainbow-circle of dazzlement and wild applause!" (VII,318) These day-dreams are tainted, however; she remembers "Old Funky, like a maggot in the rose of that life, withering her petals, her stamens, the very calyx of her being, so that only an empty husk was left, and the seed – the seed!" (VII, 285) Although her world was a violent and sordid one, where she had been raped by her trainer and forced to bear his child, it was nonetheless a vital one. She comes to understand this through her sterile experiences with Dud, until at last she can think of her seduction "no longer as a brutal violation, but as something in which, with a wild self-laceration, she could even exult!" (IX, 456) She recognizes Old Funky as a life-force: " 'You taught me my job. You taught me my power. You taught me my life. You re-created my body!' " (IX, 457) Her eventual escape to America is a necessary flight into the future.

It is now obvious why Dud is so unsuccessful in his dealings with Wizzie; they are heading in opposite directions. His death-quest is much more rewarding. The past

and the dead come together in the person of Enoch Quirm
– he refers to himself as Uryen – who, Dud discovers, is
his father. In appearance he resembles "a half-vitalized
corpse, a being that 'but usurped' his life, a semi-mortuous,
an entity only 'half-there'." Dud notes that his body gives
off "a sweetish sickly odour that really did have a faint
resemblance to the smell of a corpse." (I, 55, 56) Uryen is
obsessed with Welsh myth and legend; he frequently visits
Maiden Castle, on the outskirts of Dorchester, where he
feels the presence of occult powers.

On a visit there with Dud, he reveals his belief that he is
the reincarnation of the Supreme Power itself, known as
Uryen. Quoting Sir John Rhys as his authority, he states
"that King Pellam, and Urban of the Black Thorn, and
Yspyddaden the father of Olwen, and Uther Ben the father
of Arthur, are really, every one of them, just local names
for the 'Uryen' in me, as I was incarnated down the ages."
(VI, 254) He bears the sign of *bran* – the crow – on his
breast and makes Dud feel for its outline through a mass of
foul-smelling hair. The Power he embodies has " 'Death in it
as well as life . . . . It is the old magic of the mind, when
driven to bay by the dogs of reality, it turns on the
mathematical law of life and tears it to bits! It's the old
magic of the mind, the secret of which has been so often
lost; till the Welsh, alone among the races, *hid* it instead of
squandering it.' " (VI, 252-3) It is, above all, the power of
mental pain, especially that resulting from sterile love.
" 'Rampant desire unfulfilled – why, there's nothing it
can't do! Stir up sex *till it would put out the sun* and then
keep it sterile! That's the trick. It's the grand trick of all
spiritual life.' " (VI, 252) The fusion of the sexual and
mental into the spiritual reminds us of "caputanus" and
directs us back to the essentially human components of
belief. Uryen himself acknowledges the subjectivity of his
own views:

'Everything's in the mind. Everything's created and destroyed by the mind. It's the mind, it's not any devil's magic, that makes and breaks our mirrors and mirages. All's vision, lad, all, I say *all*; and the mind's the only demiurge. You think it's madness to talk of the old gods of Mai-Dun? You think I ought to be interested in their excavations, and their proofs that human beings lived in this place like hyenas in holes among bones. I tell you, lad, the truth of life's in the imagination, not in ashes and urns! I tell you *we*, I and others like me, are the gods of Mai-dun — the same yesterday, today and forever. There's no one God, lad. Lay *that* up in your heart. Things are as they are because there are so many of us; and as fast as some create, others destroy; and a good thing too . . . .' (VI,249-50)

Uryen's empathetic assimilation of the past involves the bestial as well as the divine aspects of his personality. Dud's early speculation that his father is "the living incarnation of his mother's 'Questing Beast' " not only recalls the carved head-pieces — Uryen gives a second to his son — but is also a grotesque prophesy of the old man's end. Then, his very posture is altered by his identification with the Powers within: "He seemed to grope with his hands, as a beast might do who was standing on his hind legs. He seemed also . . . to be pawing with his feet . . . ." (IX, 469) A few moments later he is heard "fumbling and groping, like an animal without hands"; and finally is seen "moving down the passage, slowly and heavily on all fours." (IX, 470, 471) His physical death, soon after, is meaningless — as Enoch Quirm he is no-one — his real death is the loss of his mythic personality.

And what does Dud think of this mumbo-jumbo? Very little. In fact, he mocks his father's efforts to reveal himself as Uryen:

How natural, how inevitable it seemed to him that he should now plague, torment, and cruelly tantalize his father by keeping him waiting so long for the least word, the least sign, that he cared a fig why he called himself Uryen!

'Call yourself Urogen,' [he thinks.] 'Call yourself Urus; call
yourself "Urban of Hell" *What is it to me*? Tell me the most ghastly,
the most tragic, the most sacred secret of your life, and I'll treat it as
a joke. I'll play with it as an Arab might play with the Sacrament. I'll
tell Wizzie about it to-night and we'll laugh over it till our bed
shakes.' (VI, 244-5)

And yet, only a few minutes later, Dud amazes himself by
discovering "that his words were not his own. He was his
father, arguing with his father . . . . Not only was he
compelled to talk *like* his father, but he began to feel as if
the Powers of Mai-dun were fusing him with his father."
(VI, 249) What is happening is that blending of the mythic
and the historic into the present. Although the levels
contradict — Uryen's Celtic lore and Dud's historic
pre-occupations — they complement each other in the
larger time-continuum.

Having sketched in the three principals of *Maiden
Castle*, we are in a position to distinguish among them.
There are clearly three different viewpoints about time
being examined: Uryen representing the mythic past; Dud
the historic past, and Wizzie the future. Thus, Uryen is
identified with Maiden Castle and its gods, Dud with the
Dorchester of the Romans (Durnovaria) and of Mary
Channing; Wizzie with the movement of circus-life and
with America. These levels are cleverly interrelated by a
number of triadic similarities. Uryen fails as a modern-day
god — his attempts to journalize his beliefs are a
prostitution of his quasi-divinity; Dud's book on Mary
Channing is rejected by the publishers; only Wizzie seems
guaranteed of success. Again, the past, present, and future
are seen in terms of scholarship, art, and action. Uryen
reads voraciously and quotes freely from Welsh literature
and commentaries on it; Dud reads only sparingly but
writes quickly in an attempt to justify the past in terms of
the present; Wizzie reads thrillers but has no literary

understanding. Their interests are reflected in their lives as religion, speculation, and performance: a trilogy of negative, neutral, and positive elements. This, then, is correlated to racial, social and personal *motifs*. Uryen is the voice of racial inheritance, the spirit of a people intent on giving meaning to life; Dud is preoccupied by the injustice of Mary Channing's execution; Wizzie acts. She is the key to the whole *ensemble*. In sexual matters, for instance, she embraces the normal generative process even to the preference of Old Funky's violent potency over Dud's sterile caresses. Uryen is quite right in comparing her to Caridwen, the earth-mother, for, in doing so, he is unconsciously underlining the contemporaneous operation of myth. In this interpretation Old Funky is a manifestation of Saint Derfel, a Welsh semi-divinity of lecherous propensities, Wizzie's horse becomes Derfel's horse, always associated with the Saint, and Wizzie herself becomes victim-goddess. This comparison is supported by Wizzie's memory of her old horse neighing just when she was being seduced. (IX, 432, 457) The mythic becomes the contemporary and closes the time-circle. In the triadic union, all is essential. The achievement of *Maiden Castle* rests with its vision: a synthesis of the great currents of life — the mythic, historic, and personal. Myth must be radically personal, a form of unconscious existence as it were, before it can assume universal significance. The dead and the past may be seen in teleological terms but cannot replace the present and future. Dud abandons his death-quest and accepts the responsibility of caring for Lovie and Nance Quirm, Enoch's widow.

The fusion of these complex triadic levels into a singularly complete mythos of an intensely concrete and immediate nature is in itself a major accomplishment. But there is another side to *Maiden Castle* equally deserving of our attention; namely, the novel's literary environment.

Quite apart from numerous incidental references to Classical, European, Celtic, and English literature, this book makes very interesting use of two particular works — *Hard Times* and *The Mayor of Casterbridge*. We become aware of the latter by allusion and of the former by inference.[2]

In relating Powys to Hardy, I am not writing in terms of comparison or imitation. What happens is a deliberate use of both Hardy and his characters to explore Dud's personality. On one occasion, No-man considers his purchase of Wizzie in the light of Henchard's sale of Susan and thinks how much Nance Quirm reminds him of a figure in Hardy; (VI, 262-3) on another, he notices the trees planted around Max Gate by the novelist himself. (V, 196)[3] Although there is frequent mention of places and buildings familiar to the Mayor — St. Peter's Church, the King's Arms, the Amphitheatre — this is secondary to the personal meanings they have for Dud. They are associated in his mind with the history of the town and, ultimately, with his work as a novelist. The "statue of Thomas Hardy with its profile turned towards the Roman wall" could be said to operate as one of his favourite symbols. By its side he has an experience which, as we shall see, is closely linked with his writing. There, with Wizzie and other friends, he witnesses "the name 'Mona,' in a shaky hand", appear without human intervention on a sheet of paper he is holding to the back of the statue.

This performance bears directly on his process of composition:

The 'aura' of this old Roman-British town, with its layers upon layers of human memories, semihistoric and prehistoric, seemed to have a magical power over Dud's imagination. He began tapping levels in his consciousness that he had not known he possessed.

The moment he sat down at that table [in his room] in front of those old roofs the spirit of the past seemed to obsess him. Sometimes he actually wrote so fast — especially when his more analytical faculties were in abeyance — that it was as if he became a medium, writing, he scarce knew what, under some unknown 'control.' (III, 112; see also III, 113; V, 201)[4]

In psychic terms we might say that Hardy acts as Dud's familiar, revealing the historic continuity of Dorchester. Powys, in turn, plays the viewpoints of these two personalities off against one another, and, in doing so creates a tridimensional perspective of the town through the vision of all three novelists. This, of course, fits in with the total triadic structure of *Maiden Castle* — an internal pattern supported by the book's formal division into three Parts.

As regards *Hard Times*, the case is not dissimilar, though it is handled quite differently. Circuses figure in Powys's fiction from *Wood and Stone* onwards — the most vivid presentation of one being made at the end of *Ducdame* — but Ben Urgan, his wife Grummer, young Popsy, and Wizzie are the first to impress themselves as performers on our attention. Old Funky, "whose bald head was topped by a red wig and whose crooked person was tightly covered by a long, greasy, greenish-black tail coat," is decidedly Dickensian in appearance. In speech he is as distinctive as Mr. Sleary but very unlike him in attitude. He plays the pimp in selling Wizzie to Dud — " 'Her be young, look 'ee, and her be of a 'lurin figure"; soon he is blackmailing him about the legality of the transaction.

'Me Missus have spoke ere now of calling in the Law ... but in course as 'twixt an Ole Ben like me, what means no 'arm, and a chit like *She* what do now bide along of thee's self, 'tis best, and so I tell my Missus when her do carry on about thee's gall and me, 'tis best to *seech* other, 'tis best to come to 'appy 'rangements. The truth be ...that thee and me with 'eads together and a few gold sovereigns to make the poor 'ooman's 'eart rejoice, can settle this 'ere trouble smooth and sweet, without calling in no lawyer, nor no bloomin' jurycourts.' (III, 119)

Whereas "Mr. Sleary's canine philosophy" affirms "that there ith a love in the world" and that "People mutht be amuthed," the Urgan code eventually extorts Dud's entire savings and promises "something to the effect that if he required any further feminine society Popsy had several amiable friends in Dorchester who would be very pleased to 'see' such a liberal gentleman." The parallel is as striking as it is different.

The details which relate the two circuses — the horse-riding in both, the echo of Sissy in Wizzie, Funky's parody of Sleary — have few values in common. Sleary's company is a reservoir of human vitality and kindness in the mechanical world of Gradgrindism; its function in *Hard Times* is social and moral. Powys's circus has in itself little allegorical significance; its members reflect the traditionally shoddy aspects of itinerant living. Their redemptive qualities show forth in sex and art, the two closely united as we have seen. Sissy can leave the circus and carry her warmth abroad; Wizzie must return to it, for her life is her art. Powys is concerned with a more integrated presentation of humanity than Dickens. His emphasis falls on particular men and women whose problems are personal rather than general. The tension between Wizzie, Funky, and Dud is self-creative and self-consuming: its polarities are generation and death.

Both *Hard Times* and *The Mayor of Casterbridge* are evoked in the cause of literary continuity; the former is seen negatively and the latter positively. *Maiden Castle* is in a sense a commentary on the two novels, on the Corn Laws and Benthamism, bringing them up to date in the light of Communism, Fascism, automobiles and aeroplanes. Powys underlines the increasing difficulty of preserving individual standards of thought in a chaotic world of economic pressure and ideological uniformity. Dud's whimsical understatement, occurring as it does after he has lost all his money and received notice that his book has been rejected, sums up the situation: "But unsuccessful novelists . . . don't get on the dole." As in *Wolf Solent*, many of the contemporary themes are explored through the minor characters. Roger Cask is a Communist who watches aeroplanes and preaches Progress; George Cumber is from London, runs a chain of newspapers and advocates free-enterprise; Dunbar Wye is a Fascist. Their arguments and positions support rather than control the story's psychological problems — Thuella Wye's lesbian transports, Jenny Dearth's repressed sexuality, Teucer Wye's Platonic idealism — all examined with the same keen penetration that we noted in *A Glastonbury Romance*.

Throughout this discussion of *Maiden Castle*, I have worked towards the centre of the novel, attempting to show that in its triadic structure of contemporized myth Powys had introduced new techniques and ideas into his fiction. I have avoided unnecessary mention of Powys's always powerful descriptions of setting and atmosphere; so too have I refrained from discussing the fertile insights into social and sexual behaviour which are so much a part of any Powys novel. These aspects of his writing have been and will be considered elsewhere in this study; for the present, they are there in *Maiden Castle* for the reading.

While it is quite obvious that Powys, like Dud, is looking with growing interest towards Wales, he chooses the subject for *Morwyn or The Vengeance of God* from his earlier discussion of vivisection in *Weymouth Sands*. The tale's Welsh setting is nominal — a mere twenty-six pages describe events on the earth's surface; the remaining pages chart the subterranean geography of a hell created by and for sadists. The book is, in fact, a cosmological investigation of the underworld of the human spirit. It is Powys's only novel written in the first person, the story taking the form of a long (322 pp.) letter from a retired Army Captain to his son — the term "epistolary" hardly seems to fit.

In the company of Morwyn, a nineteen year old girl, her father Mr. — — —, a vivisector, and Black Peter, a cocker spaniel, the Captain is tumbled onto the floor of hell by a passing meteor, "a dark star" that drives a huge rocky plateau on which the group is standing deep into the earth. Once there, the shade of Mr. — — —, killed by the fall, meets that of Torquemada; the two become immediately intimate, the former advocating torture for the sake of science and the latter for the sake of religion. A sadistic trio is formed by the Marquis de Sade's arrival; his exaggerated politeness adds ironic piquancy to the situation. As chief spokesman during the first part of their journey, the Marquis explains the nature and purpose of hell. "*We* invented it. This place and what goes on here is the patient creation, little by little, of all the sadists who've ever lived! (I, 65)[5] . . . I must beg you to remember that Hell is not, and never was, a place of punishment. On the contrary it's the only place in the whole cosmos *where people can do just exactly what they like.* " (II,108) There is no suggestion that *L'enfer, c'est les autres* in this concept; the sadists are organized in their pursuit of pleasure. The majority gratify their lust for cruelty by watching, on vast television screens, direct coverage of vivisection being practised in laboratories throughout the world. A few carry on private obsessions, as in the case of a man sculpting on the rock walls of hell "monstrous representations of abominable cruelties inflicted by prehistoric animals upon one another". They communicate telepathically in a language called "leprosid"; their bodies are transparent, however their ghostly clothing does form an opaque covering. When possessed by sadistic cravings, their nerves respond frantically and the effect is grotesque. Here is a typical description:

> To the end of my days I shall remember the ghastly contortion of this wretched Being's face while all the nerves behind its transparent surface, shivering up from where they transferred their frantic desire from senses to brain, twisted, twined, gyrated, and, as you might say, *spasm-ed* outwards, in horrid erectness, like the quivering serpents of the Gorgon's head, till in a silence more terrible than the most frightful sound — the silence of lust drawn out taut and tense to its breaking-point — they became the multiform worm-heads, all spiralling and straining together, of the phantom's response to what was attracting its deathless corruption. (I,68)

Although Powys draws inspiration from Dante, whose name is mentioned frequently, he is even more subtly influenced by the Homer of *The Odyssey* to whom he also refers. The exploratory journey towards the earth's centre is governed by that same sense of inquisitiveness, observation, and reflection which Odysseus shows in "The Book of the Dead". The Captain makes a rather sorry figure beside the Greek hero but, like him, strives to assimilate as much as possible of his experience, especially in so far as it illuminates the relationship between personal choice and impersonal destiny. In hell, he learns that "The System-of-Things goes blindly on with its unscientific evolution of pity and sympathy . . . ." (I,65) This vague cosmic force is supremely indifferent; "its ways are completely non-human"; it defies comparative analysis; only its existence as a generative power affirms its benevolence. (I, 64-5; also V, 291, 295-6) Once again the burden of living is placed squarely on the shoulders of the individual human being. His twin faculty of sexual and imaginative energy must guide him through a life of chance as arbitrary but as unavoidable as Odysseus's return voyage to Ithaca.[6]

Thus , the Captain's lust — a decorous passion strongly felt but never expressed — for Morwyn is an integral aspect of the adventure. ". . . it may well be", he ponders, "that sex-love, divorced from complete union and divorced from any thought of children, is so far from being reprehensible that it is the most potent of all urges in the process of the evolution of a higher race." (I, 53) Although this thought must remind us of Uryen Quirm's ideas about the power of repressed sex, it also recalls Nietzsche's concepts of self-possession through the control and sublimation of desire. The lengths to which the Captain denies himself for Morwyn's sake certainly attest to a growth of his own sentiments of pity and sympathy.

Sexual vitality is balanced by the imaginative strength of Taliesin's personality. In his quest for Merlin, the Welsh poet has often passed through hell. On this journey, he aids the two humans and the dog in their escape from the aggressive vivisectors. Together they sink down a long shaft leading to the very centre of the earth. There they discover an underground sea and on its shore two half-created, intertwining giants who, Taliesin explains, are " 'the twin-gods of Religion and Science . . . I don't myself know which is which; and I think in the end under the washing of this sea they will become one figure with two faces. They're both, as you observe, still in the process of creation. They're the creation of their worshippers and have only a dim half-life. When we first came down here their worshippers were at work on them. The air was full of scientific and religious thoughts.' " (III, 178)[7] Their pursuers soon track them down and all escape seems cut off until Taliesin finds a passage directly under the twin-torsos. This exit leads them still deeper into the earth's heart, to the gravitational core of the world. Merlin lies here in a sort of ante-room to a great chamber containing Cronos and Cybele; they are all asleep, awaiting the birth of a second Golden Age. With bardic wisdom, Taliesin blends Greek, Druidic, and Celtic myth.

He spoke sadly, but very gently; and proceeded . . . to explain to me that Cronos, or Saturn, was a Cretan ruler in the Golden Age when the only worship known was the bloodless worship of the Great Mother. It was in connection he told me with the baskets in which offerings were made to the Great Mother that the cult of the Holy Grail originated, coming to these islands long before Goidel or Brython, and of course aeons before the Christian era. 'Whatever Creative Spirit,' he said, 'is responsible for the existence of our Cosmos, it's clear that *Nothing can come of Nothing.* In other words Nature, through her human children, refines herself and spiritualizes herself, just in proportion as she returns, though enriched of course by the experience of the struggle, to the Saturnian Age from whose wisdom and simplicity we have so lamentably fallen. Those words [Sleep is the bond forged for Cronos] up there must have been engraved by Druidic hands under the influence of voyagers from the Grecian isles.' (III, 184)[8]

The Druids handed this knowledge down to their followers, who preserved it in myths about Annwn (that dark underworld is explored in "Pwyll Prince of Dyfed", the first branch of *The Mabinogion*); later, when alive, Taliesin himself responded to the occult message and, partially conscious of its meaning, recorded it in his poems.[9] Now, he articulates its significance and, in so doing, reveals the object sought after by Owen Evans and Uryen Quirm — Caer Sidi, the "Esplumeoir" of Merlin and the Welsh secret of life. He predicts a slow but inevitable renaissance of the Golden Age through what we recognize as parthenogenesis or "the Self-Birth of Psyche". Nature, the System-of-Things, refines herself through man; creation has again taken the form of purgation.

Throughout these explorations of myth, the vivisectors have not been forgotten and at least one of them accompanies Taliesin and friends into the chamber of Saturnian repose. There Rhadamanthus, the undying judge, sits "mumbling and gibbering to himself while the spittle [runs] down his monstrous beard." His judicial sense is soon called into play when the Captain meets Socrates. The philosopher has left Paradise to avoid speaking with recent arrivals who pester him with their talk of Science and behaviouristic theories. His newly found solitude has been interrupted however by the appearance of Tityos, the Titan condemned to be the eternal prey of vultures, who demands the judgement of Rhadamanthus. Socrates defends the god's erotic vitality as a natural impulse; a young vivisector speaks for the accuser — none other than "that possessive, implacable, *Automaton*, sometimes called Jehovah, sometimes called Jove, who is forever being half-created by the minds of men, and forever falling back into the maggots of decomposition." The debate is a lively one with the vivisector expounding on the importance of scientific knowledge and Socrates emphasizing the heart of man as the final arbiter of right and wrong. The Greek's arguments are charged with emotional conviction; their message is the meaning of *Morwyn*:

'I submit that all the way down the ages evil and dangerous attempts have been made *to shift the pivot of life* to something other than the character of the individual man. The character of the individual man has been held as unimportant, O righteous Judge, in comparison with the State, in comparison with Religion, in comparison with Knowledge. It is held unimportant now in comparison with Scientific Invention. But I submit to this court that everything in the universe is negligible compared with the character of an individual man!' (IV, 264-5)

Socrates carries the day; Tityos is pardoned and weeps with joy. (Powys must have relished this reversal of Homeric destiny.) The tear he sheds is taken by the others as substantial proof that pity and sympathy do guide the mysterious ways of the System-of-Things. The episode has a powerful effect on everyone. Tityos leads Morwyn, Black Peter, Taliesin — rather oddly — and Mr. – – –, whose shade has rejoined the group, off to America where they all plan to campaign against vivisection. Unlike Dr. Brush of Hell's Museum, there seems little probability that

Morwyn's father will be long free of his sadistic obsessions. The Captain is overwhelmed by the loss of the girl whose "youthful breasts were more developed than they had been before we entered Caer Sidi". He falls into a delirious sleep and dreams about the System-of-Things:

How grotesque this vision of my delirium was can be seen in the substitution in my trance of a fish — a common sea fish — for the unknown Power behind the universe! What under heaven had put into my head this grotesque substitution? Certainly nothing I had seen in that ghastly Cimmerian abyss where those monsters clung and tore. I have never set eyes on a mackerel of the sea except dead and bleeding and sold to me for food. But what insanity! Had I seen the System-of-Things sold in the market? Had I caught its eye fixed upon me glazed and white from the slab of a fish-shop? Had I eaten the System-of-Things with bread-crumbs and vinegar? (V,307)

(The passage recalls Sam Dekker's vision of the Grail; it also awakens echoes of Wolf Solent's self-tormenting perceptions.) Emerging from his trance, the Captain finds himself repeating "The vengeance of God!" He is uncertain about the meaning of the phrase and later dismisses it as irrelevant. (V, 308)[10]

Only one other experience awaits the Captain before his return to Wales through a long corridor from the world's centre. Socrates introduces him to Rabelais, who launches into an explanation of sensual and sexual goodness. He declares that "the exquisite delights of our amorous senses" are wrongly forbidden by Science "in the name of 'Eugenics' " and by Religion "in the name of Chastity. All sensual joy ... is permitted ... as long as it isn't cruel ... " He then proceeds to rail against vivisection and the bigots who encourage it. His final words, addressed encouragingly to the Captain, are taken with a slight but important omission, from Bacbuc's farewell speech to the three friends: " ... and may that Intellectual Sphere, whose centre is everywhere and circumference nowhere, [whom we call God,] keep you in His Almighty Protection." (V,320)[1] [1]

For Powys, the "intellectual sphere" is not God but rather the mind of man in all its imaginative, creative possibility. He explores that mind, or at least certain aspects of it, in the allegoric-symbolic manner of his models — Homer, Dante, Rabelais of course, and Milton to whom he turns at times for comparative illustrations. His discoveries are not always complimentary to man: he finds people lacking in integrity, willing to rationalize their sadism as a necessary part of their religious or scientific search for knowledge; he shows the petty selfishness which undermines our altruism and shapes our attitudes towards other people. Looking beyond the individual, he questions our own century and those past, questions social standards of conduct and the values they imply. Although the assessment is not encouraging, neither is it final. On the other side of the scales lies the dual human power of sexual and imaginative energy. This force unites our lowest and highest drives, kindling sex and imagination into the glowing furnace of consciousness where the generative refinement of our personality occurs. The process is never simple nor are the end qualities of pity and sympathy easily achieved. Powys suggests that our return to the Golden Age depends upon our ability to interpret myth as a revelation of man's ultimate as well as his earliest aspirations. Like Robert Graves, he places poetic truth over literal explanation, finding in the former some possibility of harmony for the individual at least, if not for mankind in general.

While *Morwyn* is an invaluable introduction to Powys's mythic and Celtic interests, it fails miserably as a novel. Arguments against vivisection are repeated without any attempt to develop them; the characters of Morwyn and the narrator are thinly drawn as are, more understandably,

those of the dead; the book's themes are outlined in
skeleton form but never fleshed out. Details and events,
although often intriguing in themselves, seem to spring
from the author's whim: there is an overall lack of
organization in concept and execution. These faults are so
apparent they hardly deserve mention. I have the impression that Powys, after the exacting demands of *Maiden
Castle*, surrendered himself to his fancy, allowed his hatred
of vivisection full rein and wrote very much from the top
of his head. His fascination with Welsh myth crept into the
tale however and anchored it firmly in the mainstream of
his creative thought.

The opening pages of *Owen Glendower* have a familiar
ring. A young man seeking his fortune in a foreign country
comes to a river where he is soon caught up in a struggle
for his life; but the castle he sees is Dinas Bran and not
Plessis-les-Tours; his name is not Quentin Durward but
Rhisiart ab Owen. Powys's direct debt to Scott does not
extend much beyond such superficial similarities – his
appropriation of a chapter-head, "The Castle", is hardly
plagiarism. Indirectly, Scott's influence might be seen in
Powys's eye for detail and colour, in his adept presentation
of gesture or action, and in his narrative fluency. These
traits are, however, no more imitations than were his
assimilation of Dickens and Hardy into *Maiden Castle*.
Once again we discover that Powys is working within a
definite literary tradition, using his predecessors purposively, extending their significance as well as advancing
his own development.
    Unlike any of the earlier novels, *Owen Glendower* is
historical, its subject being the fifteenth century Welsh
uprising against Henry IV. Powys has elected to cover only
a few incidents in the revolt, principally during the years
1400-1405, although he does sketch in enough general

background to give his story a flowing chronology. The final chapter which examines the events of a few days in November 1416 is, as we shall see, a fitting end to the novel but is otherwise non-historical.

The Welsh leader, Owen Glendower, is in every way the central figure in the book. Nevertheless, much of the narrative is about Rhisiart ab Owen, a young Oxonian and a native of Hereford, who leaves England for North Wales to join Glendower, his cousin by bastard descent. En route to Owen's Llys or court of Glyndyfrdwy (the name derives from its location in the valley of the river Dee), he travels with Walter Brut the Lollard, a guileless man, and "Yr Crach", the Scab, King of Fornicators and prophet of Saint Derfel. When they meet John ap Hywel, Abbot of Caerleon, and Philip Sparrow, herdsman and ferryman, at the edge of the Dee, a significant quintuple is formed. Each represents a distinct element in the ferment of the period. Rhisiart, sceptic and scholar, returning to the land of his forefathers suggests personal idealism; Master Brut, persecuted in England as a heretic, demonstrates the new spirit of religious independence; Crach Ffinnant bears witness to the superstitions of folk religion while the Abbot embodies the growing militancy of the Church in Wales; Philip Sparrow speaks for the peasants, his crude socialism is a defiant thrust at the crumbling feudal structure of society — his working-class hostility recalls the Glastonbury Communism of Red Robinson whom he closely resembles. These men remind us forcibly of the political conflicts and religious tensions that accompanied the upsurging individualism of the fifteenth century — an individualism that manifested itself collectively as nationalism and personally as free-thinking curiosity.

The Dee is Rhisiart's Rubicon. On its far side he hears the cries of men and women. He crosses the river and attempts to free Mad Huw, a mendicant Friar devoted to the name of King Richard, from being burnt at the stake by the Welsh supporters of Henry Bolingbroke. His courage wins the favour of Tegolin, Huw's virginal disciple; an immediate friendship develops between him and the girl. It is as much for her sake as for any other reason that he commits himself to the service of Owen Glendower. When Rhisiart permits her to touch his sword and tells her his nickname is Gwion Bach, a ritualistic pact is made: their destinies are united.

The novel's first four chapters are obviously introductory. They prepare us for the appearance of Owen himself by intimating the man's complexity as an individual and as a leader. Rhisiart's very early impressions of his cousin — "crafty, grey-headed, portly, full of punctilious fussiness about nice heraldic points, only anxious to be left in peace to his bards and his women" (I, 11)[12] — are quickly altered; "and in place of a rich, idle, selfish 'Glendourdy' he now visualized as the background of all that was going on in these regions an unapproachable, mysterious figure whose power seemed palpable at every turn but whose personality remained evasive and obscure." (II, 68) His attitude to Owen is typical of the novel's total movement from a simple, concrete world to a complex, intangible one. The physical facts of people and objects are frequently set against their imagined, mental characteristics; the violent action of mob-scenes is accompanied by reflections on motive and intention. This effort to interpret the chaotic diversity of experience in terms of pattern and purpose unites the book's thought and action.

The thematic balancing of extremes has necessary stylistic overtones. Detailed descriptions of men, clothing, horses, flowers, and birds create a realistic setting that counterpoints with psychological speculation, character analysis, and idealization. The prose flows, slow, diversified, and relaxed, gathers momentum as tensions build, quickens and breaks at moments of crisis and decision, subsides into lyrical simplicity. The entire novel is constructed on this principle and within it almost every chapter is similarly organized. The movement may inform even a paragraph; Huw's reflections after spending the night in a barn with Rhisiart and Tegolin offer a good example:

All through that short summer darkness he too had slept an untroubled sleep; and when he awoke to whisper his psalms and to extinguish the smouldering wick in the lantern above his head, it seemed to his crazed wits as if the lost King whose return he confused with everything in life that *is* and yet is not, and with everything in death that is not, and yet that *is*, were present with them in that shed. He mingled King Richard with the sound of the river, with the scent of the hay, with the awakening of the swallows, with the cool dawn-airs that stole into their shelter like the forerunners of an exultant host, but above all with those youthful heads lying side by side! The Maid was his, and this young soldier of his King was the Maid's, and therefore *his* too; and the great John Baptist whose day was dawning was carrying them all three forward, forward where the river was flowing, forward where the mists were lifting, forward into a new Valle Crucis, a new Wales, where there were no burnings and no Bolingbrokes, no hearts that would not heal, no loves that could not be satisfied. (III,70)[13]

Owen's Llys, Glyndyfrdwy, is presented less as an architectural solidity than as a domestic atmosphere. There he lives with the Arglwyddes (his Lady) and his children, of whom the youngest is twelve year old Catharine. When Rhisiart and his friends arrive at the court, they are told that Iolo Goch is dying. A Midsummer Day banquet has been prepared for the evening and the old bard has asked if he may be present for the harp-playing of Griffith Llwyd. The performance not only gives point to Welsh aspirations and idealisms, it also epitomizes Powys's own creative process at its best:

At first the Bard played very low and almost timorously; but as he warmed to his task his fingers seemed to gather strength and swiftness and his whole personality seemed to melt into the instrument and become an organic part of it, so that it appeared to Rhisiart as if that little wizened head, small and brittle as a nut under a mass of foliage, were a physical portion of the harp, and as if the harp itself, endowed with a figure-head of its own, were plucking at its own breast and making music of its own heart strings.

. . . .

. . . Lost in his blind inspiration, the player had forgotten the Arglwyddes's command that *the harp only* was to speak. At first with low sounds that seemed hardly human syllables, and then, as he went on, with words that took their meaning as well as their music from the notes that accompanied them, he began a celebration of his Lord's prowess in battle. 'With a broken sword,' he said, 'the son of Griffith Fychan mowed down the enemies of King Richard! With a red flamingo's feather in his helm he flamed through the battle, and the sound of his onslaught was like the sound of the waves of the sea when they roar over sand-dunes! The dead, the dead fight for the son of Griffith Fychan, and the spirits of the air gather about the rush of his onset, like the winds out of their dark pavilions in the track of the hurricane!'

As the man's voice rose in his wild excitement the notes of the harp seemed sometimes to follow, sometimes to lead his utterance; but what Rhisiart, as he listened, found most extraordinary was the way a certain hard, clear, conscious, almost cold *intention* continued to retain in the midst of the wildest excursions of his frenzy the symphonic unity of his performance.

He went back upon himself, he gathered up his earlier motifs, he reverted to those hummings and whisperings, like the vague stirrings in the air of thousands of summer afternoons. He reverted to the screaming of eagles, to the pipings of curlews, to the cawings of rooks.

Into the rhythm of the hooves of Owen's war-horse, into the rush of the flying track of that flamingo feather, into the cleaving of skulls under that broken sword, he tossed the roar of the falling cataracts he had plundered, he flung the wailing of the journeying winds he had invoked.

Rhisiart couldn't follow all the words he used . . . . Nor could he follow all the strange rhythms of the accompaniment. Many of these seemed to him to be conjured up out of the very abysses of prehistoric time. He heard the crashing of ice-floes in the glacial era; he heard the moaning of winds in forests roamed by mammoths; he heard the hissing of the lava in prehistoric volcanoes as it was drowned in the tidal waves of nameless seas.

There came a point when the lad actually couldn't see the form of the man who was playing. A cloud of conjured-up shapes, like the shapes of the first day of creation, blotted him out. The descendant of Einion had ceased to be a harpist in a smoky hall. He had become the beating of immortal wings in a great void! He had become the breath of the ultimate spirit moving on the face of the waters. (VI, 154-7)[14]

The passage breaks off abruptly when Iolo is carried to the fire-side. His last words are whispered to Catharine who announces that Owen must be proclaimed Prince of Wales on September sixteenth of that year (1400). Glendower's close alliance with the English is thus brought to a close when the wisdom of age and the innocence of youth blend in the prophetic moment.

But the song of the harp does much more than set the stage for Iolo Goch's pronouncement. It is an overture to change and action. I have elsewhere described what is happening as "a period of preparation, of initiation. The reader's margin of credibility is being extended in scope but, at the same moment, is being shifted in perspective."[15] While Owen's stature as a soldier is being saluted, other, more occult characteristics are being suggested. Elemental forces of earth, air, fire, and water conspire towards cosmic significance; the bard's human lineaments are transformed into an image of creative energy; Owen's struggle to free Wales is related to the inevitable processes of nature.

We begin to understand that this book is much more than an historical romance. References to Owen as a "wizard" and "magician" suggest personal powers beyond those of a statesman; so too does his resemblance to figures in Welsh myth contribute to his stature. As W.J. Gruffydd points out in his exceptional *Math vab Mathonwy*, the magus plays a determining role in making the mythic personality or, as is frequently the case, the magus and hero are one.[16] Owen shares these characteristics. Standing to speak at the banquet, he reminds Rhisiart of Pryderi:

> His rising was the signal for a great wave of silence to flow over the company. It was like an enchantment. Where each man stood or crouched or sat — *there* he remained. But when he stretched out the silver flagon and dipped his fingers into it a second silence followed the first silence, like a soft volcanic cloud following a tidal wave. . . . (V, 146)

Magic, myth, and cataclysm meet — all manifestations of a power greater than human. Owen himself had been investigating these occult forces by means of "an enormous crystal globe supported on an ebony pedestal" and "a great square board of ancient woodwork, upon which on a white ground, were inscribed a series of astrological symbols . . . ." Both of these objects are kept in a room at Glyndyfrdwy known as the "magician's chamber". Shortly before his proclamation as Prince of Wales, he muses about his plans. He admits that he hopes to accomplish his ends by unnatural means, "as priests and druids and magicians and fortune-tellers go to work, *by meddling with the future!*" Faust-like, he then makes a pact with the "Unknown Spirit of the Universe"; the tenor of his prayer is, however, totally different. He begs not for knowledge but for "the absolute darkness of your impenetrable purpose." With a large battle-axe, he smashes his crystal globe and accepts his destiny or "tynghed". Immediately afterwards

. . . he went to the window, and facing the sunlight, all grandly accoutred and anointed as he was, he became . . . a figure of gleaming gold.

His countenance, however, had suddenly grown strangely stupid and dull, like the drugged and helpless countenance of a sacrificial animal. (XII, 394)

Owen's action brings to a close the domestic serenity of Glyndyfrdwy. He leaves the court to visit Mathrafal, which he considers an ancient seat of the Welsh people where the very dust still harbours the "indestructible" desires of Wales. Among those ruins he feels himself become a medium, "an inanimate mask" for "the wild stream of words that the spirit of the place poured through him!" As the psychic experience intensifies, his control dominates his personality and he momentarily loses consciousness. At that   instant, he transmits "a new war-cry — *Mathrafal*!" Significantly, his words go un-heeded, perhaps even unheard by Rhisiart who is nearby. Owen Glendower's identification with the oldest mythic centre of his people is never understood by his followers, who continue to regard him essentially as a military leader. From Mathrafal, he journeys to Meifod where he asks Broch, the huge, taciturn miller, to join him in driving the English out of Wales: the Revolt has begun.

Roughly half of the novel is used to cover the events from June twenty-third to September sixteenth, 1400. During these months , Owen has changed from a bene-volent, rather homely Baron into a rebellious war-lord. He has abandoned his search for personal knowledge in favour of his accepted *tynghed* — that of Prince of Wales. There is a dramatic change when the story resumes a year and a half later, in February of 1402. In the early period, the pace was for the most part leisurely, the settings peaceful, the characters happy. Now, we are introduced to a world of guerilla-fighting and treachery. Glyndyfrdwy has been burnt and Owen is in temporary quarters at the foot of Snowdon. He is beset by personal doubts and fears about his own motives, remembering his sadistic pleasure in thrusting an enemy with a broken back alive into a hollow tree-trunk. He feels that the English stories about him selling himself to "the Powers of Evil" may be true. Determined "to prove to Christendom that a spirit accused of such a monstrous deed and accusing itself of such a monstrous deed could yet be the liberator of a nation," he has engaged Walter Brut to help him work out "elaborate systems for the Reformation of Welsh Religion and the Revival of Welsh Learning"; a Welsh Parliament is planned and the establishment of Welsh Universities proposed. Conflicting religious and political arguments are always subordinated to the Prince's overall fight for total Welsh independence. His policy of diplomatic expediency extends to his secretary and young daughter of whom he thinks: " 'I *must* have that boy body and soul . . . and I *must* have a Catharine virginal and intact, to use as my grand tribute to destiny!' " (XIII, 453) Broch's aboriginal wisdom detects the confusion in his Master's mind; he speaks of self-knowledge, quoting an old proverb: "Light the candle, and you'll see how dark it is."

But Owen has chosen his fate; his friend's words are robbed of their personal meaning, they become part of the prophetic utterance. A comet passes overhead and the Prince is further alienated from himself: ". . . if the very firmament is going to breed Pendragons", he thinks, "war to the end it is; war and a plunge, through a world on fire, into utter darkness!" This abdication of personal responsibility is supported by the attitudes of others: "He turned from the sky-dragon and began moving among his excited followers . . . . Nobody dared to speak to him, hardly to approach him. With that symbol of his destiny before their eyes he had become a consecrated figure — unearthly, hardly human." (XIII, 474) The cosmic candle has shown Owen alone, isolated against a background of universal blackness.

The tale gathers momentum. Powys handles the battle of Bryn Glas with Shakespearian compression. Both armies are presented in turn before the encounter; dialogue is used tellingly to convey the enemy's arrogance as well as the tense expectation in Owen's camp. The Welsh attack is co-ordinated with the sunrise and, from the first, their victory is apparent. Reflecting on the outcome, Owen is "confirmed more strongly than ever in his monstrous fatalism." He feels "that there were forces on his side, obscure, unfathomable, tremendous, to which, if he only accepted the trivial and casual accidents by which they worked, he might resign himself with impunity." (XVI, 573)[17] In keeping with these feelings, he decides that it "would be a sacrilege against the high invisible Powers that were using him as a medium" to refrain from arranging a marriage between Sir Edmund Mortimer, captured in battle, and his Catharine, who is enamoured of Rhisiart.

In the meantime, he has shifted his base of operations to Tywyn in South Wales, the home of his ally Rhys Ddu or Rhys the Black. There Catharine and Rhisiart, over-shadowed by the gloomy "black figure" of Sir Edmund, make desperate plans to escape to France together. The Prince has become sanguine of complete victory against the English; support is gathering from all areas of Wales and the enemy is weakening. Throughout the narrative runs a constant interplay between individual, personal desires and general abstract ideals. The conflict is summed up in Owen's attitude towards his daughter's happiness:

What he wanted to do was to be honest with Catharine. He wanted to implore her to let him thrust the sacrificial knife into her bosom as he had decided once and for all to thrust it into his own. 'When you consented, child,' he wanted to say to her, 'that I should be proclaimed Prince of Wales you consented to lie down by my side before the altar of our gods; you consented to let them cover both of us with the pall of death.' (XVI,573)

Although no explanation is ever given, the marriage takes place. The sacrificial *motif* dominates all of Owen's thinking: two of his sons have died for the cause, a third lies wounded; friends and relatives are expendable; his own character is being depersonalized as he becomes increasingly committed to his role as a "symbolic victim in a tribal ritual, decked and adorned for sacrifice".

Owen's uncompromising position seems justified as two years of military success follow Catharine's marriage. The court is now established at Harlech where myth and reality mingle in the splendour of this Welsh renaissance. Independence seems guaranteed when the French offer to assist in the struggle against Henry. The prevailing harmony is disturbed however by Hopkin ap Thomas, "the prophetic Bard of Gower", whose poems have a subtle influence on Owen. He tells the Prince that he has had a revelation about a virgin in armour crowning a king and suggests that "it *might* refer to some native Welsh maid". Owen appropriates the prophesy to himself and, although he has hitherto rejected attempts to see into the future, he now permits the Bard's words to guide him. Admitting that he could negotiate a peaceful settlement with the English King, he nevertheless determines on a campaign to London with Tegolin, the Maid of Edeyrnion, at his side. He has ceased to rely on his destiny in this attempt to force the hand of fate. "He had sacrificed himself and his children for Wales," he thinks. "Did the gods of his race intend to reward him with a triumphal entry . . . into Lud's town?" (XVII, 648)[18] Owen is obviously thinking of himself in personal terms. He has momentarily forgotten the stern necessity of his pact with the Spirit of the Unknown.

His self-interest is accompanied by a resurgence of
sexual desire; he registers Tegolin's beauty and is stirred to
possess her. His choice is clear: between physical, temporal
conquest and spiritual, eternal survival. He feels that with
himself as "the medium through which some vast planetary force, that was absolutely irresistible, was pouring
into the girl's form," victory over the English is certain;
yet he knows that he is part of an even greater context in
which the power of his personality alone can transcend his
earthly limitations. Thus far he has been led, almost
unwilling at times, to an acceptance of his role as victim.
He is now aware of the momentous confrontation of his
will by arbitrary chance. As he weighs the possibilities, his
mind fuses ethics, sex, politics and metaphysics into an
imaginative personal psychology:

> 'What I'll do,' he thought, 'shall be without cause, without reason,
> without motive. I'll do it just to prove to myself that I *can* do it. If I
> let her go they'll think I do it because of them. If I take her they'll
> think I do it because of my pride. But they'll be wrong. I'll take her
> because I want her *more than my free will.* But if I don't take her I'll
> prove to myself that my will can do — in a complete void — what it
> chooses — without cause or motive or reason! . . . She and I together
> could do anything. She'd know what love *was* if I took her, and
> there wouldn't be an Englishman left in Wales! And when the
> French came we'd ride through Hereford and Worcester and Oxford
> and over London Bridge, until — playing off the Mortimers against
> the Percies — and no one but I would take off your armour, you
> lovely one! — but that would tilt the balance . . . with her for the
> motive, for the reason, for the cause. But if I *don't* take her — *then*,
> in an absolute void, my will will please itself. It will choose to
> sacrifice everything — everything but its own life; and thus it will
> show the power of its own life!' XVIII,703-704; see also XVIII,
> 710)[19]

He deliberately thwarts his feelings by arranging an
immediate marriage between Tegolin and Rhisiart. Owen
Glendower has become priest as well as victim in his

sacrificial ritual for and to Wales.

Following the departure of Tegolin at the head of his army, Owen remains at Harlech in a strange, lethargic state. He meditates a great deal about his position as Prince of Wales — a title he feels he possesses officially but without the support of the common people. His tacit approval of Crach Ffinnant's murder arouses the wrath of Derfel's disciples who mob the castle. News arrives of defeated Welsh armies and of prisoners taken. Owen is advised to return to the mountain fastnesses of Snowdon where he can be most effective against the English, but his only reply emphasizes the necessity of waiting for French aid to arrive. The war-lord's character is changing rapidly. He has become preoccupied with teleological problems instead of with military strategy. He uses his dead brother's cat Brith as a familiar to contact its owner's spirit for answers to his questions, but the presence directs him to action rather than thought. As he relates psychic and mythic experience to each other, his true identity is revealed to him:

> He felt as if his recent hours in that darkened chamber, wherein he had used the sleeping animal as a link between himself and his brother, had lasted for many years, and that it was as a *revenant* that he came back now, wandering with his naked blade through a generation that had forgotten him. Had he, like Pwyll Pen Annwn, been living for twelve months in some over-world of enchantment? (XIX, 757)

He discovers that everyone treats him "as if he were already discrowned, dethroned, rejected"; as if he were a leper. Deprived of public significance, he turns inward to affirm the value of his own belief in himself as a symbol of the Welsh people. When word comes that the French have landed at Milford Haven, it changes "the temper of his subjects" completely; he becomes "their venerated leader again". His followers' superficial enthusiasm illustrates the disparity that exists between Owen's early qualities as a fighting man and his present position as a symbolic figure.

The campaign to London marks his total transformation. He has ceased "to comb his beard or to trim his hair." In place of "the four black lions" of his native Gwynedd, his golden arms now bear "the mystical red dragon of the old *gwledig* or chief ruler of Britain." He carries an ancient bronze lance and wears a rusty sword supposedly wrought through the magic of Saint Derfel. His golden helmet fastened round with a golden circlet has "an almost Arthurian look". He is tormented by the mistakes he has made — by the attention he paid to Hopkin ap Thomas's prediction about the Maid in Armour, by his contrivance of Catharine's marriage to Edmund, by his reliance on the French. To his fellow soldiers he seems like a "courtly *revenant* from the Round Table" remote from the pillage and slaughter of his advancing army. On one occasion he falls into a trance before a group of tortured prisoners who stare "with wonder at this bare-headed figure on his tall horse, his forked beard flowing down over his breast-plate, his dragon-helm clasped between his motionless hands, and his lance-point resting among the flowers." (XX, 815)

The Welsh advance is stopped at Worcester where Henry has rallied his forces. As Owen and his troops remain camped on nearby Woodbury Hill, the Prince knows that he has been defeated. Yet there is a sense of unreality about these events; they seem superficial, without consequence. What really matters is Owen's conviction that "he and his people *could afford to wait,* could afford to wait till long after his bones were dust and Henry's bones were dust". He remembers two connected prophecies that traced his fate in the stars: the first predicted that "he would fail in arms but triumph in spirit"; the second that the Welsh people would pass over his body to their triumph; "but it will be a triumph in the House of Saturn, not in the House of Mars." (XX, 821-3) At this point,

Owen's story ceases to be history, it has become myth.

We last encounter Owen on Mynydd-y-Gaer. The Welsh army has long ago capitulated to the English and over eleven years have passed since the Prince stood at the gates of Worcester. Owen's disappearance — his *difancoll* — has started strange rumours: some believe he has fled to South Wales or to Herefordshire; others claim he has been dead for four years, that he lies buried in Bangor Cathedral. One of the most bizarre explanations of his disappearance comes from the poor inhabitants of Edeyrnion who hold that their Prince is "playing chess with King Arthur in the heart of Mynydd-y-Gaer". He has already become a legend to his people, his name heard only in its Welsh forms of Owen ap Griffith and Glyn Dŵr. His death is the ritualistic fulfilment of his association with Welsh myth. As a direct descendant of the aboriginal rulers of Wales, "those prehistoric 'Lords of Annwn' ", he knows the "three hiding-places of [his] race that are indestructible and indiscoverable. One is under the mound at Glyndyfrdwy. One is under this fortress. [Mynydd-y-Gaer means Fortress Mountain.] And one is at Mathrafal." The subterranean secret of Wales, sought after by Owen Evans and Uryen Quirm, explored metaphysically by the Captain and Morwyn, and suggested by Rabelais is finally proclaimed:

The very geography of the land and its climatic peculiarities, the very nature of its mountains and rivers, the very falling and lifting of the mists that waver above them, all lend themselves, to a degree unknown in any other earthly region, to what might be called the *mythology of escape*. This is the secret of the land. This is the secret of the people of the land. Other races love and hate, conquer and are conquered. This race avoids and evades, pursues and is pursued. Its soul is forever making a double flight. It flees into a circuitous *Inward*. It retreats into a circuitous *Outward*.

You cannot force it to love you or to hate you. You can only watch it escaping from you. Alone among nations it builds no monuments to its princes, no tombs to its prophets. Its past is its future, for it lives by memories and in advance it recedes. The greatest of its heroes have no graves, for they will come again. Indeed they have not died; they have only disappeared. They have only ceased for a while from hunting and being hunted; ceased for a while from their 'longing' that the world which *is* should be transformed into Annwn — the world which *is not* — and yet was and shall be! (XXI, 889-90)

With his last words, Glyn Dŵr takes his place beside his ancient ancestors of myth. Referring to himself he cries out: "Prince of Powys — Prince of Gwynedd — Prince of Wales . . . Prince of Annwn!" We are told that " 'He was dead before he spoke. *A spirit spoke through him.*' "

All things coalesce — myth, legend, history, politics, religion, nationalism, personality — in this one symbol of the spirit of Wales. Such is the meaning of Owen's self-transformation from a prosperous feudal baron into a sacrificial victim. His life and death affirm the existence of an other-world where the spirit of man can refresh itself in a timeless saturnian sea.

The extraordinary harmony and coherence of *Owen Glendower* result from a delicate balancing of the ideal and the actual, from a blending of the sublime and the excremental, of the human and the animal. With the Joycean flexibility of *Finnegans Wake* (*Ulysses* in contrast presents a rather regimented series of set-pieces), Powys manages not only to write about but also to create myth. His concern with the past is in many ways a concern with archetypal patterns, with paradigms of behaviour and character; his interest in the present is a fascination with particular men and women, with the incongruities and contingencies of human relationships. Both are submitted to a process of cross-fertilization. The resulting hybrid contains the past and present but differs from them in that its own meaning is a unique gesture towards the future.

This, I suppose, is what we mean when we speak of the universality of art, of its appeal to different people in various places and times. And it is this quality which raises *Owen Glendower* above the confines of patriotic or propagandist literature, which satisfies our demand to recognize the particular and the general as co-existent.

Porius, Powys's next novel, continues to explore man's relation to the time-process. The setting is again Glyndyfrdwy, "where Deva spreads her wizard stream"; but the terrain is scarcely recognizable. The year is 499 A.D. and virgin forests still cover the Dee valley. Although based on a few scraps of documented history, the story is largely conjectural, dealing as it does with Arthur's attempt to unify the quarrelling tribes of Edeyrnion against Saxon invaders. Powys convincingly assembles his cast from fact, legend, myth, and imagination. King Arthur is conceived as a perceptive military strategist with an engaging if slightly whimsical personality. He and his "silly courtiers" camp near the newly named village of Corwen in North Wales. Myrddin Wyllt and the enchantress Nineue figure important-ly in the tale as does the Emperor's traitorous nephew Medrawd. Prince Galahaut is briefly but intriguingly portrayed as a self-pitying youth; while the poet Taliessin is depicted as a boy-prodigy working absent-mindedly in his Patron's kitchen. Some native tribes trace their ancestry to Greek or African sources (Arthur himself is said to have had a Roman father and an African mother), still others claim to descend from the survivors of Lost Atlantis. Porius, the book's title-character, shares in this mixed inheritance. Besides being the son of the reigning Brython Prince, he has the blood of the Romans, the forest-people, and the Cewri in his veins.

Although he does not dominate the narrative, his role in the novel is central. His decision to fight with Arthur places him in disfavour with many of his people who fear, in a pact with the Emperor, the loss of their already vanishing tribal identities. He is further alienated by his sceptical attitudes to the religious beliefs of both Pagans and Christians. Schooled in the teachings of Pelagius, he has gone on to develop a personal interpretation of life which in its vital humanism contrasts sharply with the narrow fanaticism of local Christianity as well as with the austere Mithraic practices of his foster-brother Rhun. He is convinced that the human imagination must defy "not only the Bull and the Slayer of the Bull, but the Crucified and the slayer of the Crucified, yea! and all the God-Bearers and all the God-Slayers from the beginning of the world unto this hour! The human imagination must never be robbed of its power *to tell itself other stories* and thus to create a different future." (II, 44)[20] His story-telling faculty is neither naive nor evasive; it performs "miracles" of self-discovery and self-preservation. He knows "Pelagius is right. Man's imagination and not God's will is what creates." (IX, 141)

Porius is about the imagination, what it creates, and the meaning of its creations. Its themes are astoundingly contemporary considering the remoteness of its overt subject. In an age when the cry for relevance in literature is frequently raised, this novel speaks with more than immediate emphasis. Its accents are prophetic. The conflicts depicted during this one week in October 499 (Powys's most compressed time-sequence yet encountered) touch on essential human activity — masculine-feminine attraction in both its sexual and non-sexual extremes; the uneasy relationship between literature and politics, especially in the forms of contemplative study and aggressive fighting; the effects of revolutionary change on a disappearing race and on the birth-pangs of a new nation; the effort required for personal survival in a limiting atrophied society. Powys goes far beyond the solutions proposed in

Wolf Solent and *Owen Glendower*. He resolves the triadic distinctions of *Maiden Castle* through his vision in *Morwyn* to discover the fullness of individual creation. He predicts the succession of Pisces by Aquarius and a "second Golden Age". The dubious magic of the Tarot pack in *Weymouth Sands* is replaced by the portentous sorcery of Myrddin Wyllt who is "the latest incarnation of the god of the Golden Age". Cronos (Myrddin) is a principle of creative continuity. Speaking to Neb ap Digon, his *gwas* or servant-boy, he enunciates the novel's fundamental statement of passive revolution:

Nobody in the world, nobody beyond the world, can be trusted with power, unless perhaps it be our mother the earth; but I doubt whether even she can. The Golden Age can never come again till governments and rulers and kings and emperors and priests and druids and gods and devils learn to un-make themselves as I did, and leave men and women to themselves! And don't *you* be deceived, little one, by this new religion's [Christianity's] talk of "love." I tell you wherever there is what they call "love" there is hatred too and a lust for obedience! What the world wants is more common-sense, more kindness, more indulgence, more leaving people alone. But let them talk! This new Three-in-One with its prisons and its love and its lies will only last two thousand years. The thunderer I begot – and I'd have swallowed him if his mother hadn't given me a stone instead – lasted for ten thousand years. But none of them last for ever. That's the hope of the world. The earth lasts and man lasts, and the animals and birds and fishes last, but gods and governments perish! (XV, 276-7)

The context here does not admit of petty ecological arguments; Powys is writing in terms of millennia, not of decades. He opposes the notions of a spiritual trinity by the assertion of elemental powers – those of earth, air, fire, and water.[21] As Gogfran Derwydd, Druid of the Forest people, states, the real issue of the struggle between the contending forces lies in its religious significance. The confrontation is dramatic and conclusive. Both Druid and

Christian priests die. The former, after being impaled by a
spear, seems to achieve a moment of transcendent awareness denied to the latter who suffers a convulsive stroke
following an impassioned speech — this, presumably,
because the Derwydd's trinitarian beliefs, antedating
Christianity by centuries, embrace physical knowledge
excluded from the priest's narrow doctrine. At the
moment of crisis, Myrddin hides his head in the earth, his
passive resistance drawing on the elemental strength of his
conviction. When he rises, he speaks, his head "swaying a
little from side to side as it uttered its mandates, as if it
were the head of an inanimate automaton or at least of a
deus mortuus, or a 'corpse-god,' risen from its tomb, but
towering now by reason of its height over them all." The
word he utters is *Cymry;*

... and no sooner had it been flung out upon the air by Myrddin
Wyllt's enormous head — that darkly looming head with its great
flapping animal-like ears that was swaying now from side to side,
above spearmen and archers, above horses and riders, as if it were the
decapitated head of Bendigeitvran, the head of the never-dying yet
eternally dead being, whose destined nature it was to be the ghastly
but imperishable medium between the buried past and the new-born
future — than it was caught up in a thundering shout from thousands
of ecstatic throats — Cymry! Cymry! Cymry! Cymry! (XXI, 490)[22]

As always, Powys's logic is imaginative rather than
intellectual. He sets the scene for the conflict between
Myrddin and the priests of the triad to coincide with the
Feast of the Sowing. At this festival, ancient "orgiastic
mysteries" are celebrated to the accompaniment of the
Fisher-King's chant. The main ceremonial act consists of
plunging "a huge seven-times-elongated African
spear . . . carved in certain respects to convey the impression of a colossal and hideous phallus" into Saint Julian's
Fount. On this occasion, the sexual ritual is surrounded by
the bloodshed and screams of battle. Myrddin's mental

energy penetrates the confusion and causes a psychic change which withers the frame of the ranting priest and impels the soldiers to peace. Slaughter and generation are reconciled by an act of the imagination..

If we recall the imaginative ordering of experience revealed to Sam Dekker in the *Romance* and the mystic elementalism of Sylvanus Cobbold in *Weymouth Sands*, we discover that the national unity symbolized by the word "Cymry" is an extension of this "caput-anus" attitude to life. Powys has broadened his conception of personal salvation. It is now apparent that imaginative creation involves society as well as the individual. The secret lies in Myrddin's dual personality as magician and god. He is not only an old man reincarnated through the ages, he is also Cronos embodying the future. Powys is suggesting that men living in time can shape the direction of events by dissolving the contrarieties of life into the harmony of imaginative acceptance. The process of integrating human consciousness with the inscrutable workings of time is emphasized in the characters of Porius and Taliessin. The former indulges in an activity he refers to as "cavoseniargizing":

He used the word as one of his precious sensation-symbols and to serve as a description of those recurrent moments in his life when the gulf between the animal consciousness of his body . . . and the consciousness of his restless soul was temporarily bridged; so that his soul found itself able to follow every curve and ripple of his bodily sensations *and yet remain suspended above them.* (V, 83)[23]

Porius's cavoseniargizing, unlike Wolf Solent's "mythology", uses the immediate matter of experience in its interpretative process, thereby humanizing it. It is rooted in the present, not in the past. It is devoid "of all religious mysticism and . . . of all spiritual illusions." Its subject includes "inanimate elements and inanimate objects"; especially those composed of earth, air, fire and water.

Porius is a man of action; his virility is obvious on and off the battlefield. He thinks as little of deflowering two women — one his wife and the other a giantess — on his wedding day as he does of facing an armed man empty-handed. Because of his intensely physical preoccupations, his cavoseniargizing is a self-reflecting transcendence, providing only short respite from bodily necessity. A more permanent way of overcoming time is through art, particularly poetry. Taliessin's method of versification rejects temporal restrictions. Myrddin Wyllt, an obviously competent judge, thinks that it is

... the enjoyment of a particular essence, an essence to be found not only in things and persons but in historical and mythological events, and that this essence could best be reached by so close and intimate an identification of the poet with the thing alluded to, or with the event described, that it was as if he stripped himself to the skin but retained his bodily senses as he plunged into the thing's essential being and became a conscious part of it, carrying the impressionability of his human senses into something which to the uninitiated might be merely a drop of lifeless water, or a piece of inanimate wood, or some formal grouping of traditional symbols grown fabulous and dim in the remote past. (XIX, 414-15)[24]

Although Taliessin's poetry receives its impetus from the same source as Porius's cavoseniargizing, namely individual sensations, it achieves an altogether different completeness in its final depersonalized objectivity. Powys traces this quality to "the boy-bard's absolute immunity to all the human emotions where sex plays a dominant part". This asexuality characterizes the poet himself who "seemed to have no sex either. He resembled not so much an hermaphroditic idol come to conscious life with the vivid intensity of both its sexes, as an elemental creature entirely devoid of all sex instincts and of both sex organs."

Both Porius and Taliessin represent extremes of behaviour; both play essential roles in their society; both use the same mental powers — the one to accept the principles of personal physical action, the other to understand the harmony of universal being. Together, they attest to the current of imaginative energy which winds like a river of life through the maze of human endeavour.

There are others, however, who would dam up the life-stream: Medrawd seeks to thwart Arthur's plans for a better society by subverting his uncle's allies; Nineue would imprison Myrddin and his magic for selfish ends. Although possessed of a few redeeming qualities — Porius makes allowances for him and assists him to evade capture — Medrawd gains little of the reader's sympathy. He is the direct literary descendant of Hastings in *Ducdame* but is much more insidious. Whereas the Parson, until mad, contented himself with writing about his nihilistic attitudes, Medrawd puts them into practice. He tries to seduce Euronwy, Porius's mother; he later succeeds in debauching Teleri, a half-mad servant; and is eventually caught "scrabbling in the grave of a dead whore, and wreaking his passion upon her corpse". His necrophilia is only one aspect — perhaps the least odious — of his personality. As a traitor to the Emperor's cause, he instigates dissent among the soldiers and contention among the tribal leaders. He states his motives and aims clearly in conversation with Porius:

'In life there's more pain than pleasure, more ugliness than beauty, more lies than truth, more misery than happiness, more cruelty than pity, more illusion than reality. So I have condemned life to die, and I have appointed war its executioner. The twin children of life, Hate-Love and Love-Hate, I have likewise condemned to death with war as their executioner. I am come that the world should have death; and I am strong because death is more powerful than life, higher than life, larger than life, older than life, and deeper than life. It existed before life appeared and it will exist after life has disappeared.' (XXIV, 570)[25]

Nineue is less interested in universal problems. She stands behind the action of the novel where, Delilah-like, she practises tricks of sexual domination. She is reported to have "more power than any woman in this Island", for she controls Myrddin who, in turn, controls Arthur. Her dark beauty combines with "a sort of immaterial eman-ation" as the expression of her "inmost identity". Porius suspects her of knowing a method of cavoseniargizing; and the general public considers her an enchantress. Myrddin is totally infatuated with her. He eventually succumbs to the pressure of her entreaties and reveals the location of "the stone on top of Wyddfa under which he's going to disappear" to await the Age of Aquarius. This he calls his Road to Annwn. Once there "she'll know where to find him when she wants to be loved; . . . she'll fasten the stone down so that no one but she can lift it. And then she'll have him really to herself. She'll go to him whenever she wants his love; and she alone in all the world will know where he is and he'll never be able to come out." (XXV, 593-4)

Imaginative energy is not so easily stopped up. Myrddin's apparent disappearance under the stone is only a ruse to deceive Nineue. He plans, with help from Porius, to escape from y Wyddfa (or *gwyddfa*, translated significantly as "tomb") and to go "to an island in the Sea where he'll be served and tended by the fifty beautiful daughters of the Old Man of the Sea, very young and very lovely young girls, *who never grow up*. . . ."(XXIX, 668)

The book culminates with the joint struggles of the magician and the soldier. When Porius arrives at the peak of y Wyddfa, Nineue has already placed the stone over Myrddin. The enchantress seems filled with supernatural power as the setting sun falls upon her, "turning her body to magnetic gold". Porius feels "his lust gathering within him like uprushing lava." He touches her. "Her whole

figure has become transmuted into flowing gold. And . . .
she now deliberately, heedless of the icy air about her,
exposed one of her breasts. And lo! the sight of it froze his
desire at the source." (XXIX, 674) Porius is attracted "to
fully and largely developed breasts only when their nipples
were abnormally small"; it is Nineue's misfortune to have
"an unusually large nipple in the midst of an unusually
small breast." These details may seem silly and arbitrary,
but they are extremely purposive. Erotic desire is forced to
depend on circumstance or personality; its power can be
completely reduced by the slightest chance influence. In
her final bid to insure Myrddin's captivity, Nineue offers
Porius a temporal age of sexual gold in place of the
magician's permanent Saturnalia of the imagination. Her
defeat is graceful. "For instead of being angry or showing
the least [sense (a typographical error occurs in the text)]
of affront in the presence of the worst insult which
femininity can suffer, this extraordinary woman smiled at
him more indulgently than he had every seen her smile,
and . . . she drew forth from between her unequalled
thighs a small, hard, heavy, pear-shaped lump of iron-ore
and handed it to him." (XXIX, 675) Like the tear of
Tityos, it represents a pledge of understanding. It is a
thunderbolt that had been in Myrddin's body since, as
Cronos, he was struck down. " 'You can give it back to
him now,' " Nineue tells Porius. " 'He has escaped from
the wheel that turns.' "

While Porius wrestles with the stone covering Myrddin,
Nineue rides away. The retreating "metallic strokes" of her
horse's hoofs remind him of "some mineral space-clock,
matching the motion of time's water-clock". The sound
blends with his reflections on cosmic change and on his
sensation of being at "a centre-point in the midst of
appearing and disappearing universes". As he looks down
upon the prone figure of the magician, his thoughts remind

us again of the vast scale on which Powys has conceived
this novel:

He felt as if he stood on an earth-crust that covered a cosmogonic
cavern wherein the bones and ashes and the mouldering dust of gods
and men and beasts and birds and fishes and reptiles had been
gathered into a multitudinous congregated compost, out of which by
the creative energy of Time new life could be eternally spawned;
spawned, it might be for the use of other universes, when this one
had been dissolved. (XXIX, 678)

It is not surprising that Porius in the company of Cronos
should feel himself, in Eliot's phrase, "At the still point of
the turning world." His experience is raised to revelation
when Myrddin, after emerging from the hole, offers him
"an extremely greasy leather bottle" which contains a
"Saturnalian nepenthe". Under its influence

... he fancied he could catch moving up to that mountain-top a
vast, indescribable, multitudinous murmur, groping up, fumbling up,
like a mist among mists, from all the forests and valleys of Ynys
Prydein, the response of innumerable weak and terrified and
unbeautiful and unconsidered and unprotected creatures, for whom
this first-born and first-betrayed of the wily earth, this ancient
accomplice of Time ... was still plotting a second Age of Gold.
(XXIX, 681)

Before falling asleep, he accepts the terrible loneliness of
each individual in a "chance-ruled chaos of souls", but
considers this better than existence in "a world of blind
authority, a world ruled by one Caesar, or one God". He
wakes the following day to find Myrddin gone and himself
magically transported to Harlech. There, reflecting on
what has gone before, he decides: "There are many gods;
and I have served a great one."

Porius is a profoundly religious novel. It strives to
discover some code of behaviour, however tenuous, which

will give meaning to human action. Its bizarre explorations reveal unexpected wealth. In a confused world of disintegrating values runs a thread of purpose — the imagination, creating a future which can be shared on an individual basis. Society, as the sum of its parts, will necessarily benefit from this concentration of positive mental energy. It will also change radically.

Powys is aware — no one is more, perhaps — that men and women have physical and well as cerebral needs, that they must live in close proximity to each other, that there must be some underlying ethical bond to prevent discord. Nevertheless, he is a convinced anarchist who believes that compassion — not love, for that leads to possession and domination — results from an imaginative grasp of each person's essential loneliness and that the kindest attitude to our fellow man is one of noninterference. He is equally aware that our lives are subject to spatial and temporal contingencies which are materially unalterable. Our struggle against these natural restrictions is expressed in aggressive war and organized religion, not to mention minor disputes such as domestic conflict or social ambition. We have come a long way from the simplicities of "the will to power" and "the will to sacrifice" mentioned in *Wood and Stone*. We cannot choose to reject or evade unwanted experience; we must learn to live with it, even accept it. Some form of commitment is now required. In the earlier novels, characters like Wolf and Dud achieve personal compromises with circumstance, but always in exclusive terms. For Porius, decision constitutes involvement. From the novel's inception, he knows that "he had to take, for the first time in his life, full, absolute, solitary personal responsibility for a choice of action that would affect, and affect catastrophically, every person connected with him" (I, 3) In none of Powys's novels are people more concerned with each other than here.

Cavoseniargizing, or some similar feat of mental gymnastics, would formerly have been the high point of self-knowledge – Johnny Geard and Owen Glendower are notable in this regard. *Porius* presupposes self-knowledge, or some approach to it, in its concentration on the violence and tension behind human relationships. Never before has Powys been as free with open discussions of sexuality, politics, militarism, and revolution. The book's emphasis on a matriarchal society seems to forecast such recent developments as the Women's Liberation Front, while its concern with the anarchy of the imagination anticipates and transcends the contemporary fixation on personal freedom advocated popularly by the likes of Charles A. Reich in *The Greening of America* and Jerry Rubin in *Do It!*

There are of course points of contention about this novel; but the context is so large, the range of speculation so far-reaching that minor discrepancies are dwarfed. To allow anachronisms – Arthur's eyes are as gay as those of "a boy steering a canoe" – to destroy the whole is like condemning Stonehenge for a chip in one of its columns. Techniques are often impressionistic rather than photographic (Powys describes his method, in a note on the story's background, as "*representative* rather than historical".); dialogue is fluent and colloquial; invention is fertile and extravagant. These factors contribute to a relaxed immediacy of tone which translates the remoteness of the subject matter and the density of the thematic movement into an urgently needed critique of our modern age. Humour plays an important part in establishing rapport between the reader and someone removed from him by roughly 1500 years. Life is injected, for example, into Porius's father as he urges his son to touch the broken tip of his sword: " 'It must have hit a rock,' " he says. " 'Feel it, for Christ's sake, boy!' " Lot-el-Azziz, the Jewish doctor, conducts an anachronistic ante-natal examination with a quaint show of delicacy. These and other touches ground the novel in an unequivocally human setting.

Porius is in many ways Powys's most comprehensive and successful statement of his life-vision. It surpasses all of his earlier fiction in the daring breadth of its scope. Man is seen in cosmic terms — not simply in relation to the cosmos as was the case in the *Romance* — struggling personally with the abstracts of time and space. On the periphery of this world, we sense the lurking shadows of Blake's Four Zoas. The concept of a single authoritarian god is rejected, although not denied, in favour of a pluralistic set of divinities who take their being in the mind of man. The body, its passions, and reasoning faculties are harmonized by the imposition of an imaginative unity which, in turn, incorporates planetary and cosmic forces into a total synthesis. Again, like Blake, Powys sees all these levels in constant flux and in a continually shifting perspective. There is no ultimate resolution, nor can there ever be.

[1] J.C. Powys, *Maiden Castle*, New York: Simon and Schuster, 1936. Throughout my discussion, I refer to the 1966 edition published by Macdonald, London. For various references to the head, see I, 17; II, 104; III, 114, 115, 121, 134, 141.

[2] No serious attempt has yet been made to place Powys's fiction in a literary perspective, although the need has been recognized. (For example, see Angus Wilson's article, " 'Mythology' in John Cowper Powys's Novels," *A Review of English Literature*, IV, 1 (January, 1963), 9-20. My own brief comments and Dickens and Hardy are necessary for an understanding of the technique of this particular novel, but are scarcely more than an approach to comparative analysis.

[3] Powys, or perhaps purposively Dud, mistakenly remembers the Mayor's name as "Trenchard".

I am puzzled by Malcolm Elwin's approving reference, in his preface to the 1966 edition of *Maiden Castle* (p.8), to Wilson Knight's remark that "we are little aware of Dorchester as a town." While Professor Knight is speaking about "town-life" (*The Saturnian Quest*, p. 51), Mr. Elwin is explicitly concerned with the "vivid evocation of the story's setting" — by no means the same thing. It seems to me that Dorchester, as a solid physical presence, is graphically rendered.

[4] The subject of Dud's novel may have partly originated in *The Mayor of Casterbridge* where, in Chapter XI, an account of Mary Channing's execution is given — her name, however, is not mentioned.

[5] J.C. Powys, *Morwyn or The Vengeance of God*, London: Cassell, 1937. This novel is divided into Parts instead of Chapters; my Roman numerals refer to these divisions.

[6] Powys's debt to Homer is enormous. His life-long readings of the Greek Classics culminated in two particular tributes to their influence: *Homer and the Aether* (1959) and *Atlantis* (1954). Powys carries his classicism easily; unlike Joyce, his writing flows from an unbroken tradition rather than being grafted onto it.

[7] At the centre of this world where the dead waters lie, we find one of the few instances when Powys and Lawrence overlap. See D.H. Lawrence's "The Ship of Death," especially stanzas 18-20.

[8] The phrase "Sleep is the bond forged for Cronos" is from Plutarch. It is quoted and documented by Sir John Rhys in his Introduction to Malory's *Le Morte d'Arthur* (London: Dent, Everyman's Library, 1906; last reprinted 1963, I, xiii-xiv). This detail is significant in view of Dud's reading in *Maiden Castle*.

Powys's belief that all myths originate from the one world-myth of a Matriarchal society has much in common with a similar theory advanced by Robert Graves in *The White Goddess*. The Celtic preoccupations of both suggest that their work deserves some extended comparison.

[9] Many of this Taliesin's remarks appear to be from the "Preideu Annwfyn" in the thirteenth-century Book of Taliesin.

An indispensable source for understanding Powys's later novels is *The Mabinogion*. Although Powys himself preferred Lady Charlotte Guest's translation (London: Dent, Everyman's Library, 1906) because of its additional materials and extensive notes, the present-day reader may find *The Mabinogion* newly translated and introduced by Gwyn Jones and Thomas Jones (London: Dent, Everyman's Library, 1949, last reprinted 1966) a more helpful introduction to the general context of Welsh myth.

[10] This raises a question about the book's title: does the "or" separate two distinct subjects? does it present a choice between Morwyn's attitudes to vivisection and the vengeance of God? or does it imply that Morwyn *is* the vengeance of God? I feel that the last is the most probable. Morwyn embodies the pity and sympathy of the System-of-Things; her virgin-innocence is a rebuttal of sadism.

[11] The bracketed clause is from Rabelais, *Gargantua and Pantagruel*, Bk. V, xlvii. Before condemning *Morwyn* out of hand as a mere tirade against vivisection, the reader would do well to examine J.C. Powys's *Rabelais*, London: The Bodley Head, 1948. In it Powys relates Rabelais to Welsh mythology and to his own thinking.

[12] J.C. Powys, *Owen Glendower*, New York: Simon and Schuster, 1940, 2 vols; reprinted London: John Lane The Bodley Head, 1941, identical pagination.

[13] In connection with Powys's prose style, a word should be said about the auditory power of his writing. Since he spent over thirty years earning his living as a public lecturer, it is hardly surprising that his prose rhythms are even stronger when read aloud. George Steiner

in "Literature and Post-History", *Language and Silence: Essays 1958-1966*, London: Faber and Faber, 1967, p. 415 has written: "What is less generally understood [he is discussing McLuhan's *Gutenburg Galaxy*] is how much of literature — and how much of *modern* literature — was not conceived to be read in private silence; how it was directed towards recitation, the mimesis of the raised voice and the response of the ear. Dickens, Hopkins, Kipling are example of modern writers whose root sensibility was oral, and who tried to adapt essentially oral means to the silence of print." Steiner might certainly have included Powys in this tradition — especially in view of his own familiarity with Powys's work.

[14] Even lengthy quotation fails to convey the cumulative impact of Powys's writing; so many effects rely on a large contextual sweep.

[15] See my article *"Owen Glendower*: The Pursuit of the Fourth Dimension," *The Anglo-Welsh Review*, XVIII, 42 (February 1970), 211. In a recent essay, "The Sacrificial Prince: A Study of *Owen Glendower"* in *Essays on John Cowper Powys* edited by B. Humfrey (Cardiff: University of Wales Press, 1972, pp. 233-61), Roland Mathias rejects a mythic interpretation of the novel. He writes that Powys "chose a subject overtly political in its emphases"; one "concerned with the nature and the making of a *Prince".* The novel's failure to present the political side of Owen's revolt, he argues, undermines any real value it may be said to have. These comments might apply to "ordinary" historical fiction; however, I do not believe Powys was trying to write the sort of book Mr. Mathias would like him to have written.

[16] For a brilliant exposition of interchanging personalities in Welsh myth, see W.J. Gruffydd's *Math vab Mathonwy: An Inquiry into the origins and development of the Fourth Branch of the Mabinogi with the text and a translation.* Cardiff: The University of Wales Press Board, 1928. Gruffydd's scholarship is meticulous, logical, and coherent; his book must be read as a continuous argument.

[17] Comparison with Shakespeare reveals Powys's inventiveness in adapting material to his own purpose. For examples, compare the two Henrys — *Owen Glendower* XX, 855 and *Henry IV, Part II*, III, i, 4-31 — also the nurses — *Owen Glendower*, VII, 207-8 and *Romeo and Juliet*, I, iii, *passim*; II, iv, 153-232.

[18] Powys's use of Joan of Arc's fame seven years before her birth is

another of the novel's attempts to bridge time; another instance occurs (XVII, 663) when Hotspur's words from *Henry IV Part I*, III, i, 99-101 are quoted.

[19] There are suggestions here of existential *angst*, of the Kierkegaardian leap into the unknown. As I noted elsewhere in reference to *Weymouth Sands* (see above p. 131 and n.13, p. 139-40), Powys's philosophy is often as contemporary as his style is traditional, *cf.* p. 201 below.

[20] J.C. Powys, *Porius: A romance of the Dark Ages*, London: Macdonald, 1951.

[21] The title of H.R. Sullivan's unpublished doctoral dissertation, "The Elemental World of John Cowper Powys", (University of Georgia, 1960) unwittingly points to a central aspect of Powys's conception of the universe, one which deserves extended discussion. Unfortunately, Mr. Sullivan makes no mention of the elements in his study, being concerned with what might more properly be termed the "essential" Powys.

[22] Myrddin is also called Pen Annwn, "Head of Hades." He is thus incorporated into the Welsh myth of *Owen Glendower* and of *Morwyn* where, it must be remembered, Annwn is an underworld of the blessed rather than of the damned.

[23] See Angus Wilson's lucid examination of the differences between Porius's "cavoseniargizing" and Wolf's "mythology" in " 'Mythology' in John Cowper Powys's Novels."

[24] Although this interpretation derives in part from Symbolist doctrine — Powys's own poetry was strongly influenced by it — it is nevertheless an interesting observation on the Taliessin poems; so too are the parodies of his poetry included in *Porius*.

[25] The Biblical overtones and evangelical zeal of Medrawd's words contribute to the book's anti-Christ theme; they also show Myrddin Wyllt, referred to as "anti-Christ" by the Christian priest, in truer perspective.

V

The Inmates, published a year after *Porius*, shows little resemblance to its immediate predecessors. Events are supposedly contemporary; the geographical setting is indistinct, although numerous details suggest a possible West-Country location; the plot is relatively uncomplicated. Its subject, however, is familiar to the Powys reader: mental illness. It is prominent in the first six novels where it is often described with an impassioned emphasis that verges on the melodramatic — the suicidal James in *Wood and Stone* and the nihilistic Hastings of *Ducdame* come to mind. Other, more subtle, presentations show complex, convincing cases — Adrian Sorio's brilliantly sustained agony in *Rodmoor* and Mr. Round's tortured conscience in *Wolf Solent* are superb psychological studies. But it is *Weymouth Sands* (already noted as a seminal book) that most clearly anticipates, in Dr. Brush's establishment, *The Inmates*.

Glint Hall, like Hell's Museum, is both an asylum and a vivisection laboratory. Dr. Echetus, the urbane scientist who runs the institution, embodies rationalized sadism; his assistant, Gewlie, represents man's unreflective lust for cruelty. Since both are preoccupied with vivisection, the certified patients are left to the care of attendants and clergymen. Indeed, there is little about Glint to remind the reader of an orthodox mental home: the insane receive minimal short-term treatment and are never cured permanently. A definite purpose underlies this arrangement. In the "Prefatory Note" to *The Inmates* Powys writes:

> What in fact I am trying to do in this wild book is, if I may so put it, to defend the crazy ideas of mad people – in so far, of course, as they don't run to homicide and cruelty – as against the conventional ideas of sane people. I want to show that between all manner of quite different types of patients in a mental institution there is – when you come to these crazy ones' basic philosophies – sufficient mental agreement to constitute what I would like to have the courage to call the "Philosophy of the Demented". In other words, though these unfortunates differ greatly in their aberrations from one another, they really do possess, if we drain off or skim off those details of their manias which are obviously peculiar to the individual, certain dominant attitudes to life, to nature and to the cosmos, which, though contrary to all the accepted notions of the conventional minds who make up the world's judgment, have a deep abiding philosophical truth. But this 'truth,' this Philosophy of the Demented, is naturally under the ban of our authorities in Church and State. And being condemned at the top level it is very noticeable that it is anathema to the underlings, whose personal power and glory depend, of course, as they mount up, on the conventional ideas they have at last, after many rungs of the careerist-ladder, come to embody and represent. (vii)[1]

Powys's argument is a definite extension of his belief in the anarchy of the imagination as developed in *Porius*; only in *The Inmates*, the perspective is being shifted from socio-political behaviour to psycho-philosophical debate. The novel's ostensible narrative pattern is largely displaced by allegorical technique; characters are defined by their points of view rather than by their personalities. Even the protagonist, John Hush, who engineers an unnecessarily complicated plan of escape for the patients – this conspiracy forms the basic plot – is an essentially static figure. Powys, again in the preface, gives us an important clue for an understanding of the allegory:

I like to tell myself that one aspect of the Philosophy of the
Demented is that daring cosmological theory . . . of William James that
we live in a multiverse rather than a universe. Everyone of my
inmates is a symbol of some important aspect of its truth which
seems to me especially alien to the schoolmaster-taught conventional
mind with its passion for unity and oneness. (viii)

Thus, we are introduced to the Zeit-Geist, otherwise
known as the Marquis of the Fourth Dimension or
Professor Zoom of the College of Doom, who articulates
that everything is an illusion "inside another illusion, and
all these double and treble illusions inside bubbles that are
themselves inside other bubbles, and all of them together,
bubbles and illusions, floating on a dream-river in a
dream-world." (XIII, 237-8) Mr. Pantamount, who looks
like a "sage from the lost continent of Atlantis" with his
"ichthyoid eye", proposes that the combined power of the
love-hate relationship can produce an "electric vibration"
or "creative magnetism" with magical powers. (XII, 204)
Yet another is the Commander, who advocates using the
mind to stop from thinking. Only then, he believes, can a
person fully participate in life. "It is by plunging your
minds . . . into what you touch, hear, see, smell and taste,
that you endow poor, patient, humble, passive, enduring
matter, which by itself is nothing, with all its magic
attributes. They are all in you, for you are a multitude.
Every self is a multitude and every self is a mind, and the
plunging of every mind into matter creates a new world."
(VIII, 149)

As specific views are aired throughout the novel, a
general framework of reference is established. Individuality
is to be both cherished and protected at all costs, freedom
must be achieved on either the mental or physical level,
preferably both; suffering and pain of all sorts should be
mitigated or, when possible, abolished. Love is condemned
as an "insucking maternal eye, . . . in the serpentine coils

of its devouring insatiability, swallowing its offspring's freedom to live a life of its own and exciting itself to swallow the more voluptuously as its own pity for the helpless thing's struggles draws forth more maternal saliva to smooth the path to its re-enwombing." (XII, 200) These words are realized in the actions of Nancy Yew who, in a frenzy of possessive love, is accidentally killed while trying to prevent her son from escaping to America with the inmates. Her attitude receives explicit comment: " 'Every living soul has the one right that none can give or take away, one right in the infinite chaos of the innumerable warring worlds among which we are born, one right and one necessity, and that is the right to be free and alone in our thoughts!' " (XVI, 293)

Despite the observations and reflections of John Hush, the book is really a series of tirades and diatribes. One passage, perhaps the most vehemently telling, will serve as an illustration. The speaker is "Katch-as-Kan", described as a "jibber-jabber crazy clown from Outer Cathay . . . and an honest-to-God inmate":

'Nobody knows how many worlds there are — all totally different! *Our* realities, *our* worlds, our *truths*, *our* ideas, *our* impressions, are all different, and we may take it for granted that we are surrounded by millions of completely separate and completely different universes, some of them attainable from our dimension, most of them entirely beyond the scope, not only of our science, our reason, our logic, our intuition, our instinct but of our imagination, too!

'What the generations of mankind are like and what they've been like ever since they first appeared is the generations of the leaves of the forest! . . . We ought to aim at becoming like a cloud of flies, a cloud of gnats, a cloud of midges! Thus and thus alone shall we escape places like this, preachers like this, and the silly solemn stupid humbug of taking for granted that a person is crazy because he doesn't accept the opinion of the hierarchy of ages, the academic poppycock of ages, the traditional abracadabra of a rabble of priests, professors, lawyers, doctors, scientists, politicians, divines, whose

pontifical claptrap and up-se-daisy assumptions are simply the milk
of those old moo-cows of habit, custom, tradition, and vain
repetition, curded by the holy horrors of hoodoos and taboos and
put over on us, ever since man first appeared on the earth, by those
who want to rule.

'How much better to do what I do and become a mob of midges,
that is to say to blow up once for all this self-satisfied idea of
wholeness and integrity and the beauty of a well-stuffed rounded-off
person's person . . . . You say you can make me suffer and can force
me to obey?

'Oh yes! And destiny, fate, necessity, chance, can beat me down
to the ground. But what can they really do to me till they kill me *en
masse* and finish me off *en masse*? They can do nothing! They can do
nothing because I am not one but a *multitude*. And because every
single thing and every single identical life is a multitude of things
and lives!

'No, it's a lie that the universe is one. It's a multitude of
personalities, of gods, of demons, of men, of animals, of midges and
worms, of electrons and atoms! The reality of realities is not One
but Many. And, of this many, nothing is eternal. Everything passes
away! My thought, your thoughts, and the thoughts of every god,
every demon, every insect, every worm, every minutest life that
exists — *all* pass away, *all* "leaves", as the Great Magician says, ' "not
a rack behind"! ' (XIII,241-3)

Katch-as-Kan's pronouncements confirm a growing
trend in Powys's thought. Myrddin Wyllt and Taliessin
spoke about a similar ideology and acted in accordance
with it, Owen Glendower used it as his life-spring into
eternity, Uryen Quirm, Sylvanus Cobbold, and Johnny
Geard made themselves its priests; none the less, it has
never been expressed in such extreme terms. In their
anarchistic formulation, these ideas lead to ultimate
dissent from and total subversion of contemporary social
values. The inmates' revolt asserts the wisdom of insanity
over conventional knowledge. The words of no less a
revolutionary figure than Mao Tse-Tung have disturbing
relevance to our discussion:

A revolution is not a dinner party, or writing an essay, or painting a picture, or doing embroidery; it cannot be so refined, so leisurely and gentle, so temperate, kind, courteous, restrained and magnanimous. A revolution is an insurrection, an act of violence by which one class overthrows another.[2]

And there is plenty of violence in the last chapters of this novel. The sadistic Gewlie is destroyed or, more accurately, disintegrated by the mental powers of Morsimmon Esty, a mystic from Thibet, who, as an observer, accompanied Katch-as-Kan to Glint. Dr. Echetus is shot through the head by Cogent Cuddle, a misguided but likeable Communist; Nancy Yew, already mentioned, falls on "a twisted, sharp-edged six-foot iron stanchion" which breaks her back and crushes her skull. The impetus behind these catastrophic forces is personal at its source but widespread in its effects:

... men are men, and women are women, and their association together through many years has the power of heaping up, day by day, and from thousands upon thousands of microscopic details, such smouldering stock-piles of explosive and even annihilating resentment that once released it seems to tap some Satanic crater that can draw upon the central lava of world-destruction! (XVI, 310)

The images of nuclear armageddon fit the context. Supraphysical powers are epitomized in Morsimmon Esty's magic. Before it, Gewlie undergoes "almost chemical dissolution", as if the Thibetan "had found a crack in the heart of life" and "thrust an atom-bomb into it." (XV, 274) When later, Cogent Cuddle is faced with the problem of disposing of Dr. Echetus's body, Morsimmon Esty reduces it to dust by, what we have been told, is the operation of "some devolutionary cosmic ray that has the power of magnetising people back from human to animal, from animal to vegetable, from vegetable to mineral, and so on down the scale to bodiless gasses and even, perhaps, to atoms and mesons." (XV, 279) By this action "The death of the master of Glint had in fact been lifted out of the sphere of the criminal and tragic into the sphere of the fantastic and miraculous." (XVI, 307)

The final limits of revolutionary doctrine have been reached: murder has been condoned as an imaginative necessity. Magic, a key-word throughout *The Inmates*, sublimates the unnatural into the acceptable as man's thought triumphs over scientific fact. Like Prospero, the novel's presiding god, Powys has created his tempest by infusing the elemental world of earth, air, fire, and water with the psychic resources of the human personality. The book is bound by a network of psychic vibrations as telepathy, thought emanations, and even teleporting play their part. Tenna Sheer, John's girl, is a combination of Ariel and Undine, while John himself has been certified because his search for Undines "and nothing but Undines" has developed into a mania for cutting off feminine curls.[3]

Sex is handled in terms of manias, fixations, and fetishes. Although "completely devoid of every sort of homosexual vibration", (IV,80) John Hush has a "blind sick horror of everything feminine"; his phobia is in fact vaginal, "associated . . . with everything that was soft, with everything *that went in*." (XIV, 247) At one point, he feels "his breasts beginning to grow and their nipples to distend and get longer and longer" until they wave in the air beyond his control. (XIV, 249) The Zeit-Geist's finger is said to be "super-sexual", suggesting "the self-ravishing and self-impregnating sex-organism of some abysmal being in the process of whose eternal spawning the copulating opposites of mind and matter and male and female were as yet undifferentiated." (X, 174) The Commander, paraphrasing Plato, recognizes John and Tenna as a hermaphroditic unit. (VIII, 145-6) Bill Squeeze, a servant-patient, carries a phallic wooden image called Heraclitus in his pocket. Still other inmates maintain a continuous sado-masochistic relationship. Even Father Toby, the Church of England chaplain, has "a tendency to paederasty"; his wife, Ursie Mum, is a virgin. (IV,76;XVI,305)

All this weird sexuality contributes much to the book. The images are singular and provoking, dense in their suggestiveness, encompassing in their subtlety; certainly a "Philosophy of the Demented". Nevertheless, the faults of this quasi-allegory are obvious. It abounds with clichéd speech, repetitions, and pointless exaggerations. Characterization is thin, events are mechanical, arguments often directionless. The resolution is especially unconvincing. As the inmates board a waiting helicopter on the first stage of their trip to America, money, passports, and immigration laws are forgotten. John and Tenna decide not to accompany their fellows; they are suddenly offered permanent sanctuary as performers in a travelling circus. Throughout these scenes, the author's point of view changes frequently. Interjections and digressions are interpolated at random: the dramatic introduction of "nigger"-hating Colonel Cochineal from the Southern States is a memorable instance. It would be tempting to invoke the subject-matter as a justification for this incoherence; but then we remember that Powys, not an inmate, wrote the novel — and the Preface alone is enough to assure us of *his* sanity.

By piercing through the jumble of psychological analysis, philosophical debate, social comment, and political criticism, we discover the tale's overpowering rationale, which I shall call the truth of fantasy. Powys exposes, albeit in chaotic fashion, the moribund condition of our apathetically ordered world. The limitations we impose on ourselves are, he reveals, of our own making. By assenting to the uniformity of convention, we destroy the unique possibilities of individual, creative living. We vacillate between extremes of *"ennui"* and *"angst"*, unable to retain the "Ideal Now". (XI, 182) Only by a freely willed integration of our consciousness with the myriad lives — inanimate as well as animate — around us can we fully realize the "dramatic mask of destiny" which is life. He foresees the need for a radical adjustment of each man's personal attitudes to the challenge of multiversal phenomena, for a philosophical change which, although imaginatively generated and sustained, must have an impact on physical behaviour. Thought, the magic-catalyst, produces revolution, and revolution breeds anarchy, and anarchy brings freedom.

The theme of revolt runs through many of Powys's novels. It appears as a personal defiance of fate by men like Luke Andersen, Rook Ashover, and Wolf Solent, or as the socio-political upheavals of *A Glastonbury Romance*, *Owen Glendower*, and *Porius*. In *The Inmates*, it operates in a deeper philosophical context that includes extreme action as well as ideological commitment. The later novels emphasize the far reaching effects of revolution, bringing magic, psychic, or paranatural phenomena increasingly to the fore. From *Morwyn* onward, allegory, myth, and legend are used as major devices to show man's place within a cosmological framework. Quite unlike Hardy's characters, who are so often dwarfed by the immensity of their surroundings, these individuals are enlarged in proportion to their awareness of expanding dimensions of reality.

The impetus behind an activated consciousness of other worlds is, of course, the creative imagination. Powys makes this abundantly clear in all his fiction. (That the novels themselves are, so to speak, existential proof of imaginative powers is obvious enough to be overlooked.) In exploring various human possibilities, he turned, as we have seen, slowly away from contemporary or "realistic" subjects to historical or allegorical ones. Thus he freed himself from the limitations of immediate plausibility; he replaced the truth of fact by the truth of fantasy. The results were dramatic   but still somewhat restricted.

It is only with *Atlantis*, his twelfth novel, that he finally breaks away from every restraint. Using the *Iliad* and *Odyssey*, as general source-material, he tells the story of Odysseus's last voyage. Although his erudition is impressive, it is never pedantic. The Greek myths are interpreted with disarming familiarity — the sort that comes only after long association. Powysian interpolations and alterations abound: Homeric figures are revived from the dead to play final roles; the original tales are sometimes amplified or extended to fit new situations; various theogonies are blended to establish novel relationships among the gods; and, above all, the personality of an ageing Odysseus is fleshed out with warm, sympathetic insight.

Other details add to the liberated fantasy of *Atlantis*. "Sub-human creatures" both animate and inanimate play important parts in the narrative. The Club of Herakles, instrumental in killing the Nemean lion, belongs to Odysseus. It stands in the corridor leading into "the royal dwelling" where it communicates with the Sixth Pillar, an ancient piece of stone designated by markings on its pediment as "the Son of Hephaistos". Each possesses, like all inanimates, some degree of "emotional consciousness". Around these objects flutter a moth and a fly. They too communicate with each other. The fly is an aggressive, pragmatic male, while the moth is a passive, emotional female. As the novel begins, these creatures are discussing vague rumours reaching them through elemental vibrations of a revolt among the gods. They are also concerned with a more human disturbance threatening Ithaca. Enorches, a priest of the new Orphic religion, is attempting to replace Odysseus's son Telemachos, now a middle-aged contemplative, in the Temple of Athene; the King himself is being pressured to abdicate by a certain Krateros Naubolides who urges a prior claim to the kingship. Since Odysseus appears completely uninterested in these domestic crises, the fly concludes that the old man has begun "to lose his grip upon the sequence of events".

Quite the opposite is true. Odysseus feels himself ill-suited to the sedentary life of a prosperous ruler. He looks to the west, longing for action. " 'The marrow in my bones howls and growls for the random odds of the old great Circus!' " he says. " 'I must, I must taste again the salty taste of real plotting and real planning and real deceiving and real achieving!' " (II, 56)[4] The thought of rejecting "an honoured, peaceful, well-regulated life" makes him wonder: ". . . what's the matter with me that I can't rest by day or night till I've built my ship and hoisted my sail and am steering for an unknown horizon?" His plan is opposed on all sides. Deserted now by Athene, "the great goddess who was his friend", he asserts his determination to embark upon his voyage regardless of the difficulties. " 'The gods with me or the gods against me,' he thought, 'I shall do what I shall do; and what will come of it will be what will come of it!' " (IV, 103)

Although most of the gods are too preoccupied by the cosmic revolt to care much about mortal activity, Atropos, "the wisest and the oldest" of the three Fates, or *Moirai*, decrees that Odysseus must begin his last journey towards "the Isles of the Blessed" by sailing Westward. Over two thirds of *Atlantis* describes the old king's efforts to obtain sufficient sail-cloth, *othonia*, to equip his ship. He is assisted by Nisos Naubolides, his rival's teen-age son, who, we eventually learn, is really his own son. Together they engage the help of the Rabelaisian Zeuks, a farmer, who keeps "the winged dark-skinned horse", Pegasos, and "the black maned" Arion in his stables.

This man — his name an obvious parody — is one of Powys's most light-hearted and engaging creations. Like Myrddin Wyllt, he seems able to change his shape and to hypnotize animals; his physiognomy is excessively "bulbous", yet attractive.

Every single one of the man's features was so to say swollen by the inordinate pressure within it of the particular purpose for which the creativeness of nature had designed it. The forehead of Zeuks seemed bursting with its overpowering plethora of thought. His nose seemed bursting with its abounding zest for smelling. His mouth with its full lips, its strong white teeth, its grandly sensuous curves, seemed to have been created by the insatiable palate and indefatigable tongue within it, a couple that were united in conjugal understanding, the palate as the female to the tongue as the male, for the tasting and enjoying of almost everything that could possibly, conceivably, indeterminably be tasted and enjoyed. (V, 131)

Zeuks is the son of Arcadian Pan. Like a super-Falstaff, he exults in sensual enjoyment with "inconceivable gusto"; his zest becomes palpable as "a burning atmospheric fire-ball of protection" above the heads of those near him. He unhesitatingly supports Odysseus's quest for sail-cloth. The two come to such an immediate understanding that, when the king finally departs, he leaves Zeuks in complete charge of the Island of Ithaca. At the centre of his exuberant philosophy stands "the word *Prokleesis* whose simplest meaning is a 'defiance' or 'challenge.' " This, he says, "is the best clue to life we can have!"

'Whatever else to be alive upon earth, or above earth, or under earth, may mean to those who are landed in it or sunk in it or confronted by it, it is clear that it means a challenge to a battle! O my friends, my friends, we have not got the secret of life, I mean the secret of our *experience of life for ourselves*, till we've defied it to make us cry, "Hold! Enough!" This challenge, this "Prokleesis," is *the secret of life for us."* (VI,183)

Zeuks's challenge is an energetic plea to experience life
as fully and directly as possible. It is, above all, a
consciously controlled, or willed, mental activity. As such,
it is personally generated and sustained. The Orphic priest,
Enorches, denounces such an individualistic approach to
living, and ridicules Zeuks, calling him "Turd of the
World", among other things. In place of a personal
philosophy of life, he would substitute authoritarian
doctrine in the form of dogmatic religion. His gods are
Eros and Dionysos between whom exists a "miraculous
communion" of "Love in Intoxication, and Intoxication in
Love". Although the former brings the joy of "Divine
Lust" and the latter the redemption of "oblivious
ecstasy", both are impersonal and indiscriminate forces.
They offer, in Zeuks's words, "an escape into death in place
of a battle with life."

At this point, we may well feel that Powys's interpretation of the life-death duality has become — no matter
how intriguing the presentation — a rather hackneyed
formula. And this would be so, were it not for a
key-episode in *Atlantis* which seems to synthesize the
polarities. The resolution, or revelation, happens shortly
after Ajax, white-haired and decrepit, arrives at Ithaca in
Princess Nausikaa's ship. Crossing a field with Zeuks, he
sees a statue of Hector adorned in the armour of Achilles.
After acknowledging his companion's parentage, Ajax dies
at Hector's feet. Zeuks then lays the dead man's head
between the statue's knees and thrusts his own head
between Ajax's knees:

Thus were the three figures united, one a corpse, one a work of
art, and one a living creature; and this uniting of life with death, and
of life and death with a graven image of human imagination had a
curious and singular effect: for there came into the already confused
and naturally chaotic mind of Zeuks one of the most powerful
impressions of his whole life. In embracing those dead limbs and in

drawing into the depths of his being the bitter smell of the old hero's scrotum, and the salt, sharp taste of the perspiration-soaked hairs of his motionless thighs, Zeuks completely forgot the dead man's announcement as to his own paternity. What filled his mind now was a sudden doubt about the wisdom of his proudly proclaimed 'Prokleesis' as the best of all possible war-cries for the struggle of living creatures with the mystery of life.

. . . . .

'And since I've got to live out my destiny, whether I challenge it and defy it or simply submit to it, it seems silly to go on making this "prokleesis" of mine the essence of the whole thing. No! I can now see well what the right word for my life-struggle is — not the word "prokleesis," "defiance," but the word *Lanthanomai*, or "I forget," followed by the still simpler word, *Terpomai* or "I enjoy."' (IX, 283-4)

Death, art, and life fuse into an imaginative and sexual illumination. The discovery is accompanied by "the bitter smell" of genitals and "the salt, sharp taste" of sweaty hairs. His experience recalls Odysseus's longing for "the salty taste" of real adventure. By rooting itself in concrete earthiness, his imagination breaks through cerebral obfuscation to the clarity of vision:

'It is,' he told himself, 'as if I were embracing this corpse beneath that famous tree outside the great wall of Ilium; and as if I had been given by the gods the power to suck and draw and drain from the lapsing semen of this dead body such magnetic force into the peristaltic channel of my spirit that a fresh and a new insight into the whole of life radiates through me.' (IX,285)

This image of necrophiliastic fellatio bridges the gap between life and death to affirm the continuity of the human spirit. There is no trace of the morbidity so characteristic of Dud No-man in *Maiden Castle* nor of Medrawd's almost vampirish predilections in *Porius*. Zeuks's decision to forget and to enjoy is an advance on Wolf Solent's more taciturn acceptance and endurance; it also qualifies, perhaps even questions, the wisdom of Rabelais.

Inspiration drawing on sexual and imaginative sources is bound to express itself through generative symbolism. In *Atlantis*, the phallus becomes the central catalytic agent; the creative force assumes more positive proportions than it did in the anal and vaginal imagery of the earlier novels. Our phallic standard is the Club of Herakles which, in turn, relates directly to its owner. Having stood idle in the corridor for seventeen years after the death of Penelope, it testified to the mental inertia and physical sterility of Odysseus's life. Once the King decides to act, he again takes up his Club, carrying it with him constantly. It possesses independent power which, as we shall see, plays a decisive role at the novel's climax.

Here, as in so much of Powys's fiction, thematic conflicts are examined in terms of sex. As always, the emphasis falls on the value of sexual sensation in developing human understanding. Thus, extremes of unreflective physical behaviour are condemned because they lead to a loss of personal consciousness rather than to its expansion. Enorches, so named "because of the enormity of his testicles" and known among his fellows as "the well-hung brother", represents the stultifying effects of unbridled sexuality. His god, Eros, is said to have "mutilated himself so that he can make love to both sexes and be loved by both". Although the hermaphroditic ideal receives Powys's general endorsement, its attainment must be the result of wholly natural contingencies — for example, John Hush and Tenna Sheer form a natural unit.

Even more dangerous than self-inflicted unnaturalness is the imposition of scientific experiment on others. This, we learn, is why the continent of Atlantis was destroyed. Its ruler discovered "the secret of some new magnetic stone that can influence unborn embryos" and which "may have the power of making the embryo bi-sexual." The gods

(Powys thinks of them in the Greek sense as being personifications of natural forces) keep "sex, and birth, the issue of sex, completely under their control" and thereby rule us. Man's biogenetic science — the "Embryo Stone" — threatens to subvert the natural order. The Ruler of Atlantis is himself, or herself, the monstrous androgynous product of rational experimentation. As such, this creature is bereft of all human qualities; it speaks in the "mechanical, automatic, and metallic voice" of science. When finally confronted by Odysseus in the depths of the sea, it enunciates the laws of Atlantis with computeristic inhumanity:

'These laws will, in their own time and in due course, become the law of the whole earth, the law of every country and race and tribe and nation and people. This law will be absolutely and entirely scientific. As it is born of science, so it will grow, century by century and aeon by aeon, more purely scientific. Its one and sole purpose will be science for the sake of science. It will care nothing about such trifling, frivolous, unimportant matters as faith, hope and charity. It will care nothing about the happiness of people, or the comfort of people, or the education of people, still less, if that be possible, about the virtue or the righteousness or the compassion or the pity or the sympathy of people.

'It will use people — that is to say men, women, and children as it uses animals. It will practise upon them and experiment with them, not for their sake, but always purely and solely, as it ought to be, for the only Purpose, the only Religion, the only Object, the only Ideal, the only Patriotism, the only Cause, Reason or Consideration worth anything in the world — *to understand everything that exists in every aspect of its existence.'* (XII'451-2)

Mesmerized by the voice, Odysseus and Nisos are powerless until the Club of Herakles acts of its own volition. Quivering erect, it smashes into the monster's head completely crushing it. Phallic strength destroys scientific determinism.

Although sex must triumph over the perversions of science if essential human qualities are to be preserved, that in itself does not guarantee harmony within the natural order. Balance can be achieved only through a reconciliation of opposites. In *The Inmates*, Powys explores the evil of uncontrolled maternal love; in *Atlantis* he shows the beneficent power of feminine attraction. Odysseus and Princess Nausikaa unite on both emotional and physical levels. Her arrival at Ithaca provides the King with a ship to fulfil his life's ambition (it is doubtful if he would have enlisted enough support among the Islanders to begin his quest); while later aboard ship, her presence gives him the opportunity to affirm himself as a complete sexual being. Odysseus's decision to procreate is stated to Nisos with the relaxed fullness of an integrated personality: " 'Well, my son, what our new Queen and your old Dad have to do now is to plant between us the seed of a new brother for you . . . .' " (XI,404) There can be no doubt as to their success.

While the pair clearly represents an extraordinary balancing of male-female opposites, nowhere is it suggested that necessary differences are ultimately dissolved. In this figuratively hermaphroditic union all dominance is destroyed; yet individuality is retained. Powys seems to think that such an equal arrangement is possible among particular men and women but implies in his discussion of the cosmological conflict against which the story is set that no final resolution of contrarieties is likely. Petraria, Nisos's nurse, speaks of the masculine-feminine duality as "the great 'old battle' "; she insists that the gods' revolt is a feminist plot to overthrow the oppression of Zeus and the Fates themselves. Her words are prophetically pointed, cast into accents worthy of any emotionally charged member of the Women's Liberation Front:

'It is the Revolt of Women! Yes, of the Women-Slaves of the entire universe! Yes, Nisos, nothing less than that, the revolt of all Females in the cosmos against the tyranny of all Males in the cosmos! Themis, the goddess of Custom and Habit and Tradition, has always been unfair to us women, always trying to force us back into slavery to men whenever we've tried to escape. And, as with Themis, so with the Fates. They too are against us. They too want to hold us down to the laws, ways, manners, morals, usages, privileges, conventions, institutions, organizations, founded upon male stupidity and bigotry!' (III,80)

. . . .

'[After the Revolution] men will sink back once more into what was their position when the world began, that is to say into complete inferiority to women; so that from that moment onwards their proper use and value and status in the world will be as it was in the Golden Age under the Rule of Kronos; that is to say as merely the breeding animals that we women use at our free will and pleasure, so that we can bear a sufficient number of girl-children who will in their turn become the rulers of the earth!' (V,142)

Hers is an extreme point of view, as radical in its extensions as Enorches's. Powys does look back to a matriarchal society, but always in terms of the female principle which he sees as the dual embodiment of the "actively competent and divinely creative" and of the "incompetent and divinely passive" woman. Again, a balance is struck. Fullness of life is to be experienced in an egalitarian society: the Age of Gold is a paradox of homogeneous individualism.

We are never informed about the outcome of the struggle among the gods — and for good reason. As long as multiversal forces exist there will be continuous action and reaction; a dialectic that defies synthesis. Powys seems to envisage the attainment of personal wholeness, however. When Odysseus, his ambitions satisfied, eventually lands at "a place called Manhattan", he decides to burn his ship and to remain among the "Red-Skins". Since the old King lives out his last years according to his own desires,

scarcely heeding the cosmic war, we may infer that a
laissez-faire approach to life's problems is the most successful; or, to quote Zeuks, we must learn "to forget" and
"to enjoy".

The message of *Atlantis* is an explicit formulation of
Powys's earlier arguments about the anarchy of the
imagination. Revolution and peace co-exist as an expression of the human condition. Dualities can never be
destroyed completely; at best they can be transcended by
an imaginatively willed response on the part of each
individual. Sex is a key to the process of self-revelation,
activating our minds as well as our bodies. The resultant
integration of human powers shapes our personality, en-
larges our understanding of others, confers the capacity for
self-fulfilment. Although we might find it difficult to
retain such Atlantean wisdom, we should nevertheless (to
quote from a very different writer).

> . . . still be proud
> Just to peep at Atlantis
> In poetic vision . . . . [5]

The Brazen Head, Powys's thirteenth novel, returns us
to England and to the West-country. But all has been
transformed. We enter a magical world of marvels and
miracles far stranger than anything explored in his previous
fiction. The year is 1272; the landscape is thinly pop-
ulated, save for the dominating presence of three castles —
the Fortress of Roque, Cone Castle, and Lost Towers.
These are situated respectively to the West, South, and
North; to the East stands unimposing Bumset Priory. There
Roger Bacon, a happy prisoner, works to perfect "a
mechanical Head capable of uttering oracles". Although
introduced to us as one of Bacon's "world-changing
inventions", the Head is nowhere described as scientific;
rather, it is referred to as an act of worship, as one of his
"magical creations". Once, when threatened with des-

truction, it is preserved not by "the protective magic ... of its creator" but by "something ... in the Head itself, just as if by some inexplicable chance the creative energy in the Friar had overreached its proper scientific limits, and had created a being capable, not only of personifying its own identity, but of escaping altogether from the control of its creator." (XIII, 188) Powys is obviously dealing with something much greater than a piece of machinery. Indeed, we discover that the Brazen Head's preternatural characteristics tie in with themes of parthenogenesis, Aristotelian *"energeia-akinesis"*, and apocalyptic humanism.[6]

Briefly examined in context, each of these concepts reveals an approach to understanding the principle forces behind the sensory world. The Head, although mechanically complete, is lifeless. "What it wants", the Friar decides, "is the inspiration of Virginity." He induces the Jewish servant-girl, Ghosta (her name reverberates), to straddle the Head, pressing it against her naked flesh, while he repeats "the sounds of an ancient invocation, the exact meaning of which has been lost to the world for two thousand years". During this ritual, the girl experiences "a weird erotic ecstasy"; she retains her maidenhead while "drawing from the inmost depths of herself a dew-drop of living creation". Thus, the Head is activated by the vicarious sexual union of Bacon and Ghosta – definite parthenogenetic creation; it becomes a cerebral force, given "that unique power of revelation, of illumination, of ultimate vision, that virgins alone possess!" This vitalizing process rises from "a force within us, which we feel by an overpowering instinct to be as much outside God as it is outside the Devil." It is, in fact, the power of "an absolutely new revelation, a revelation that may change the entire world".

Roger Bacon's belief in parthenogenesis is explained in

terms of Aristotle's theory of energy which contends "that since matter is eternal in its inherent essence and is capable, in itself and by its own secret energy, of renewing the universe, and of bringing into existence an everlasting recurrence of the multiple forms we see around us, we are driven by our reason to assume that the cosmos is eternal." Friar Bacon has learnt to tap this creative centre of being, "the actual essence of the substance of the earth". Because *energeia-akinesis* is eternal, it is spoken of as "the Fourth God": the Head is its prophet. We can now see how Powys has related the Christian tradition, with its accompanying doctrine of Christ's virgin-birth, to Bacon's use of Ghosta – another Jewish maid – as an instrument through which the Fourth God manifests itself. (" '. . . I behaved to you as the angel, on Annunciation Day, behaved to our Lady,' " he tells the girl.) Unlike Christ, however, the Brazen Head, being the psychic child of Earth, contains an "imprisoned demonic power" as well as oracular benevolence. This dualism precludes equating it with Christ, but does support Bacon's own belief that the Head is "a rival creation to Adam and Eve". Such a position does indeed constitute a new revelation, one outside good and evil.[7]

As the symbol of a wholly human apocalypse, the Head is exceptionally fitting. It is the "child of the *essence* as well as of *the being*" of Bacon's soul, "a man-created machine" brought to life by the parthenogenetic union of man and woman; its power flows from the elemental energy of brute matter; yet it functions on a totally cerebral plane to communicate earth wisdom to man. Here we catch a hint of that prophetic voice – rarely quiet in Powys's later fiction – which, in *Atlantis*, foresees the dangers of biogenetic permutation; now it suggests man's development of computer-techniques, especially in the field of cybernetics.

Although possessing the dual nature of its origins, the

Head is intended to be a positive, constructive power rather than a harmful one — its oracles are to be "very helpful" at both the personal and national level. The activating process of parthenogenesis seems to suggest that properly controlled sex can contribute to our mental well-being. The oracle is thus embodied in a head which, at one point, is equated with the rational soul of man. But there is another side to man — his physical, animal nature. This non-human force, if not directed upwards — sublimated to the mental plane — may be directed downwards towards a negative, destructive pole.

Powys has allowed for such a negative perversion in Peter Peregrinus, a "great student of magnetism" and long-time acquaintance of Roger Bacon. Originally from Maricourt in Picardy, he comes to England attracted by the fame of the Brazen Head. He carries "his newly formulated, newly invented, newly tested magnet" in a velvet bag pressed closely against his genitals. This lodestone is the result of twenty years' experimentation; its main purpose is "the deliberate manipulation of his own sexual force . . . for the domination of the souls and wills and minds of other entities". It operates by depriving man of his reason, reducing him to an animal; it could apparently be fatal were its power unleashed fully. Peregrinus is uncertain of its absolute effect but is sure that he could become a dominant force "behind the scenes" and destroy so much of the present order that he could create a different one. In this he is like Roger Bacon: both seek a "new revelation". Unlike the Friar, however, who is working on a humanist level outside good and evil, Peter thinks of himself as Antichrist: his doctrine smacks of Atlantean perversity:

'What I would do then,' he told himself, 'the moment I had got the world entirely under my control, would be to build up an absolutely different kind of world altogether. I would have no more of this hypocritical humbug about "love" — as if it were possible for any child of the elements, born of earth, air, water and fire, to fight for anything, to achieve anything, to become anything, except by the assertion of his separate, distinctive, individual, and unique self — and what I would aim at in *my* world, in my Antichrist world, in my super-scientific world, would be to create a new race of beings altogether, creatures as superior to what mankind is now as man is superior to beasts, birds, and fishes!' (XVI,243)

Both Peter Peregrinus and Roger Bacon are playing at God; the former's attempt is nevertheless much more dangerous than the latter's. The one would destroy humanity — both its qualities and defects — to substitute a non-human structure, while the other merely wishes to assist man within his natural framework. Ironically, the two men are using the same natural human power to arrive at opposing goals. Bacon himself admits that without Peter's "inspiration" he could never have invented the Brazen Head; and elsewhere the Friar's "authentic inventive genius" is contrasted with Peregrinus's "extremely exalted imagination."

Since the lodestone is shown in operation a number of times while the Head is not, we might infer that sexual activity is stronger than intellectual concepts. Considered on a short-term basis, our conclusion would not be totally incorrect. Bacon's ideas are speculative and ideological, far-reaching and long-range; they belong, we are told, to the realm of philosophy, not science. The stone is adapted to producing immediate results; it is practical and spectacular in its effects. We see its power transform Sir Mort, the habitually passive, bemused Lord of Roque, into a frenzied animal who hurls himself at a horse's "privy parts", saying: " 'I am a beast. Man is no more. Your own beasthood learn to adore!' " Just prior to this exhibition, Peter had experimented with Roger Bacon, giving him a "magnetic shock" which had knocked him unconscious. It is only in the final confrontation of the lodestone with the Brazen Head that the relation between the two is defined and finally resolved. At the book's conclusion the two forces clash: the Head utters its sole – incomplete – oracle: " 'Time *was*', it said. 'Time *is*', it said. 'And time *will* — — — —' " The lodestone assumes its total sexuality as it transmutes itself, its inventor, and his sex-companion Lilith into a "single fiery ball" which falls upon the Head; "and neither it nor what destroyed it was ever seen again". Both are annihilated: their powers are equal.

Our knowledge that Peter's magnet draws "like to like" points to the exact meaning of these events. The Head and lodestone are similar in having powers beyond those "in harmony with Nature"; they have no place in this world; consequently they neutralize each other. Albertus Magnus, who alone of those present catches "the full significance" of the final scenes, comments that " 'Sex is the maddest force there is. ... Sex is the greatest pleasure and the greatest pain in life . . . .' " The Brazen Head was Friar Bacon's attempt to cerebralize the pleasure; the lodestone Peregrinus's effort to actualize the pain. We are left with an affirmation of certain basic life-values advocated in most of Powys's writing. The words are Roger Bacon's (he had by this time grown indifferent to his creation): " 'As long as we are considerate to other people,' he said, 'and as kind and sympathetic towards them as our circumstances permit, we have all got to live to ourselves, for ourselves, in ourselves and by ourselves.' " (XXII, 340-1)[8]

The *Brazen Head* is the product of Powys's maturity. It incorporates almost all of his earlier concerns from the basic dualism of man and nature to the extremes of his anarchistic speculations. There are numerous Biblical allusions, Celtic references, psychic and magic inter- pretations, elemental and excremental images; varieties of

both mental and physical sadism are investigated as well as
forms of imaginative and actual sex. Sundry comments on
the new revelation and parthenogenesis seem to parallel
many of Yeats's concerns — the 2000 year cycle Bacon
ponders reminds us of "The Second Coming" while the
virgin-god relationship recalls "Leda and the Swan" and
"The Mother of God".[9] They also reflect the more
esoteric aspects of the revolutionary ideas advanced in
Porius and *The Inmates*.

Many of the characters seem little more than symbols
of human attitudes. Sir Mort of Roque's philosophy
embodies man's ability to unify his personality by relating
astral travel to elemental forces in an act described as
"intercourse with the cosmic multiplicity". (He is in fact
what Porius may have become.) Baron Maldung — the
name is appropriate — his Lady Lilt, and their daughter,
Lilith, of Lost Towers represent the "sad, mad, and
absurdly fantastic" mentality of sadists; their end is in
keeping with their crimes: they die violently and their
castle is destroyed by the lodestone's power (like attracts
like). Boncor of Cone is a neutral, ineffectual figure,
willing to assist in a good cause but uncertain of the means
to take; he seems to play the part of life's bystanders,
eager to talk but unable to act. Bonaventura is portrayed
as a religious fanatic, anxious about financial affairs,
scrupulous in matters of superficial morality, but inwardly
confused and filled with hatred. He is the cause of Bacon's
imprisonment and labels the Friar a heretic. And thus we
could continue down to old Dod Pole, another in the line
of radical socialists which includes Red Robinson of the
Romance and Philip Sparrow in *Owen Glendower*.

Among the more complete characters are the young son
and daughter of Sir Mort — Lil-Umbra, a sensitive
fifteen-year-old, and John, the eighteen-year-old disciple of
Roger Bacon. The latter is endearing in his sexual ardour;

he explains in answer to a question about girls:

'O I adore them! I worship them! I embrace – in my mind of course, or in my imagination – every single one of them I meet! Off, off, off, off I slip their pretty clothes! And oh! so quickly I'm hugging them! But that's the worst of it, for it's the whole of the best of it, and the end of it! For I have an ecstasy at once, and all my soul rushes out, and all my seed is gone, in a minute, and I've no strength left to ravish them and take their divine maidenheads!' (X, 141)

Some of his sexual fantasies are sadistic: he imagines "something different from the male organ of generation being thrust into a female's womb" or "a fiery rod being thrust into a man's anus." The catastrophic events concluding the novel purge him of these images through their apocalyptic impact. He sees the horrors of religious and scientific hypocrisy: by rejecting them both he consolidates his own personality.

Unfortunately the thematic success of this novel is seriously compromised by inconsistent details and a major fault in the plot-structure. These difficulties involve Peregrinus and his lodestone. Chapters I to XVIII proceed flawlessly, building a careful mosaic of interrelated, balanced details. In Chapter XV Peter visits Bacon and works the power of the lodestone; in Chapter XVI he again appears, this time at Roque, where he magnetizes Sir Mort. But in Chapter XIX Peregrinus is *again* introduced to the reader. He is in France, has yet to reach England, and is wandering through a bleak, symbolic wasteland peopled by gnomic figures. His character is totally malevolent, incongruous with that described in the preceding chapters. From this point on there are a number of weak attempts made to reconcile this shift in characterization but they are unconvincing. The lodestone is variously mentioned as being six inches long, one foot long, and seven inches long. Since, apart from the plot discrepancy, the fault is chiefly one of emphasis, general relationships remain unaltered and viable. There is no absolute contradiction. Nevertheless this very definite confusion in the story's chronology and in the development of Peter's character mars what might otherwise have been Powys's most artistically satisfying novel.

All or Nothing is an apt title for Powys's last published novel: dualism is a constant theme in all his fiction. He repeatedly examines the polarities of life and death, pleasure and pain, sex and chastity, good and evil. Man, the biological embodiment of these extremities, is physically and mentally able to create or destroy. The tension of personal choice in these matters can be devastating, breaking the individual under its inexorable pressure; but it may also be constructive, leading to a fresh vision of life.

As Powys grew older he simplified his thematic presentation, tending towards barer exposition, towards direct statement and argument. He abandoned, for the most part, detailed settings, involved plots, and complex characters in favour of dramatized debate (*The Inmates* is typical). While the drama is often lively, it lacks causal patterns; hence it is implausible on the level of realistic or naturalistic narrative. The people, regardless of their eccentricity, warmth, or intensity, are likewise unconvincing as whole human beings: they frequently remain static — however keenly personalized — representatives of various ideas. The achievement of the last four novels relies on imaginative authenticity. Fantasy is used as a means to approach the universal problems of the life-experience as they appear divorced from the normal contingencies of everyday living.

We certainly leave the ordinary world behind in *All or Nothing*. Faced with an assortment of monsters and giants, varieties of interstellar travel, numerous spokesmen from the inanimate, animal, and psychic levels of existence, we are required to exercise much more than a "willing suspension of disbelief"; we must be prepared to abandon all our preconceptions and to trust blindly to the whims of Powys's inventive genius. We are asked to accompany a group of teenagers — John o'Dreams, his twin sister Jilly Tewky and their friends Ring and Ting, children of the sadistic giant Urk — on their extraterrestrial voyages to the personified Heart of our sun, the planet Vindex in the Milky Way, and to a self-created orb in the outermost reaches of empty space. With them we meet twelve-year-old Lalanika the falling star, a delicate nymph-like creature who bursts into flame and vanishes soon after a short stay on earth; we meet the Horners, the original inhabitants of Vindex, some of whom speak fluent English and live a very British life in cosy cottages. We are introduced to Bog, King of the Milky Way — the end of his penis "decently slung over his left shoulder" — and to his servant the Cerne Giant — "his colossal sexual organ exposed to the sight of all". The latter kills his master to join the children on subsequent journeys. Other travelling companions include Wug and Zug, respectively a boy-worm and a girl-slug who stand over four feet tall and have human faces, legs and arms, "though with grotesquely clumsy hands and feet".

Bubble and Squeak are at the centre of all this activity. These two inanimate objects — the one a bursting bubble of water, the other a fossilized skull — are situated side by side at the Fountain near John o'Dreams' home. There they engage in endless debate about the relationship of being and nothingness: hence the book's title *All or Nothing* [10]

Squeak instigates the first venture into space. Although he explains that a person can go from place to place in an *aura* of personality, he decides that John o'Dreams must retain his bodily form as a more substantial shield against possible danger. From then onward, no attempt is made to continue the more ethereal method of transportation which seems to approximate astral-travel. Characters move independent of atmospheric barriers, untroubled by distance and speed.

Each episode of the book allows Powys to stage an impromptu symposium on some aspect of universal experience. Debate is sometimes violent: John kills Urk when the ogre tries, in a moment of sadistic nihilism, to devour the Heart of the sun; the Cerne Giant bludgeons Bog after he learns that Ballytogerattero, not Cerne, is his full name. (The act seems to climax a sort of identity crisis). More peaceful exchanges include discussions about God, consciousness, dreams, sex, and multi-dimensional realities. These conversations are never conclusive, nor are they especially penetrating. Our attention is caught by the novelty of their presentation rather than by the insights they provide.

Two arguments do stand out, however; these are, characteristically, about sex. The first is earth-bound and involves the question of virginity. A dialogue – faintly reminiscent of Ivy Compton-Burnett's – between the two servant-girls, Laura and Jessica, culminates in the following speech:

'I think when girls fall in love, something happens to them. It has nothing to do with the man or the youth or even the boy! He may . . . be in one sense completely discounted. I mean it's just a chance, an accident, *who he is* . . . It doesn't matter a drop in the bucket, my dear child, who he is, *as long as he's there*; as long, that is to say, as he carries on him, with him, about him, the thing that takes our virginity! He can be an absolute nondescript, with nothing about him to attract anybody's attention, but as long as he can pierce our maiden shield, it doesn't matter a bit what a fool he is! . . . But he must be there! What you *can* discount . . . *is your being in love with him*. Being given a baby by a male is the great thing'. (V36-7)

Since the marriages and offspring of John o'Dreams and

Ting, Ring and Jilly Tewky are described in an extremely telescoped manner during the last pages of *All or Nothing*, we can infer that a practical exercise of the generative principle is being advocated. This more natural development of sexual relations is counterbalanced, nonetheless, by a second attitude towards phallic power. This counter opinion is summarized by the Cerne Giant:

'In the matter of sex, Bog taught me that what in the English language is called masturbation — that is to say, the excited emission of semen by the use of our imagination — is a much more important and creative act than ordinary and natural fornication or the raping, if we are male, of our feminine opposite. Bog used to tell me that I always ought to be thinking sufficiently erotic thoughts to keep my penis in a state of erection.' (XXVII, 192)[11]

It is worth noting that copulation and reproduction are understood as completely physical acts, while masturbation is primarily an imaginative force. In the Powysian context, imagination can transform all activity, including the sexual urge, into unlimited, universal energy with creative or destructive powers (the lodestone and Brazen Head exemplified this). Seen thus, masturbation is "much more important and creative" than ordinary sex. Both means of fulfilment are available; they may, perhaps, be combined or practiced separately: the choice rests with the individual.

The novel's concluding paragraph — a fitting valediction — contains the seed of Powys's life-vision:

'But remember when you hear those two [Bubble and Squeak] disputing . . . that All is not Nothing, neither is Nothing All, but both of them have one home-star, where they can sink to eternal quiescence, or mount to everlasting activity, and that home-star, my children, is the heart in every one of us. So goodbye, my dears.' (XXXI, 219).

[1] J.C. Powys, *The Inmates*, London: Macdonald, 1952.

[2] Mao Tse-Tung, *Quotations from Chairman Mao Tse-Tung*, 2nd ed., Foreword by Lin Piao. Peking: Foreign Languages Press, 1967, pp.11-12.

[3] For references to psychic phenomena, see II, 26, 31, 39-40; IV, 84; VI, 97; VII, 135; VIII, 139, 142; IX, 157; XI, 180; XII, 204; XVI, 307. Students of Powys will find G. Wilson Knight's *Neglected Powers: Essays on Nineteenth and Twentieth Century Literature* (London: Routledge & Kegan Paul, 1971) indispensable in these matters. See especially Chapter I, "Poetry and Magic"; Chapters V and VI on Powys's lyrical poems.

[4] J.C. Powys, *Atlantis*, London: Macdonald, 1954. Throughout I retain Powys's spelling of Greek words.

[5] W.H. Auden, "Atlantis", *Selected Poems*, London: Faber & Faber, 1968, p. 47.

[6] J.C. Powys, *The Brazen Head*, London: Macdonald, 1956. My discussion of the Head, science, and the lodestone is partially based on notes I made in answer to a query from G. Wilson Knight. In a letter of 12th March 1969, Professor Knight asked me to check, among other things, a contrast he had made of the Head as science with the lodestone as sexual-energy. My reply argued that they were parallel rather than opposing forces; this interpretation forms the central idea in my present discussion. I am pleased to note that Professor Knight does not contradict the broad outlines of my interpretation in his comments on *The Brazen Head* in *Neglected Powers*, pp. 217-18. He acknowledges my assistance in the Preface (p. 11) to that book.

[7] For parthenogenesis, see VI, 81-3; XIV, 209-11; XIII, 207; XVIII, 271; XXII, 341. For *energeia-akinesis*, see XVII, 251-5; V, 76; XXII, 341. For apocalyptic humanism, see XIV, 209-10; XVIII, 270, XIV, 219; XX, 286; VI, 82.

[8] For the encounter between Head and lodestone, see XXII *passim* especially 347-8.

[9] For random examples, see: *Biblical* I, 10, 12-13, 24; II, 30; V, 75, 77; VII, 94, 95, 96; VIII, 102, 106, 107; IX, 130, 132; X, 136, 141, 146, 150-1, 152; XI, 158; XII, 177; XIII, 190, 195, 197, 206, 208; XIV, 213; XVI, 241, 244; XIX, 274, 275; XX, 287. *Celtic* I, 9-11, IV, 61; VIII, 106; X, 143, 144, 149; XVI, 236, 239; XVII, 245,

246-7, 248; XIX, 272; XX, 284, 290, 291, 294; XXI, 302; XXII, 325. *Psychic* I, 13; II, 31-3; III, 51; IV, 61; V, 71, 72; VI, 83; VII, 89, 95, 96; IX, 117, 118; X, 141, 152; XI, 153, 163, 166; XII, 185; XIII, 204; XVI, 235, 236, 239; XVII, 249, 256; XVIII, 259; XIX, 281-2; XX, 295, 296. *Magic* I, 18; IV, 61-2; V, 68, 69; VII, 89, 92; VIII, 106; IX, 122; XI, 157; XII, 177; XIII, 188, 203; XIV, 214; XIX, 276-7, 278; XX, 284, 293, 296; XXI, 300, 305. *Elements* IX, 131; XI, 160, 161, 166; XVI, 243; XVIII, 260. *Excrement* IV, 59; V, 64-5, 72, 73, 74, 77; VII, 89; VIII, 99, 107; XI, 157; XV, 227; XVII, 246; XIX, 277; XXI, 303, 304, 307, 316. *Sadism* I, 14-15, 22; III, 55; V, 73; VIII, 104, 113-14; IX, 116, 117; XII, 176, 183, 187; XIII, 191; XIX, 280-1; XX, 295, 296, 298; XXI, 305, 306; XXII, 323. *Sex* I, 11, 22; III, 51, 52-3; V, 77; X, 135, 136, 137; XII, 183; XV, 226; XVI, 235, 238, 240-1, 243; XX, 286, 288, 289; XXII, 336. *New Revelation* see note 7 above.

[10] J.C. Powys, *All or Nothing*, London: Macdonald, 1960. Bubble and Squeak is in fact a main dish — a fried mixture of potatoes and cabbage.

[11] For a lucid and convincing discussion of Powys's attitude to masturbation, see Wilson Knight's *Neglected Powers*; Ch. V, "Mysticism and Masturbation . . . ." pp. 156-96; the Cerne Giant's doctrine is discussed on pp. 164-5; see also Index B under "masturbation", p. 514.

VI

Powys's work as a novelist covers a span of forty-five years — from 1915 to 1960. During that period, momentous changes occurred in both literature and society. Two great wars, a number of minor ones, the Russian and Chinese revolutions, the discovery of atomic and nuclear power, major economic depression, the rise and establishment of socialism, dramatic urbanization, industrial and technological proliferation, unprecedented breakthroughs in medical science — these were but a few of the influences that shaped the century's mentality. The impact reverberated throughout English literature. The "War Poets", Wilfred Owen, Siegfried Sassoon, Charles Sorley, Rosenberg, and others, initiated us into the stark no-man's land of cataclysmic awareness; T.S. Eliot echoed the ideological aftermath of devastation in *The Waste Land*; the whole was transcribed by Ford Madox Ford in his Tietjens series. Thomas Hardy felt the subtle unrest of post-war life, while Auden and Spender recorded its more strident aspects. Society was placed under the microscope as Evelyn Waugh and Anthony Powell satirized the feeble frenzy between the wars; Virginia Woolf dissected the minutiae of human consciousness with Proustian thoroughness. Even more experimental James Joyce was structuring temporal, verbal patterns in a paradoxical quest: to transcend time and space by diffusing individual behaviour into an historical and cosmic perspective. The horrors of political and scientific technocracy were grimly forecast by Aldous Huxley in *Brave New World* and later by George Orwell in *Nineteen Eighty-Four*. William Golding's *Lord of the Flies* dashed Ballantyne's coral-coloured dream, while his *Inheritors* was a devastating riposte to H.G. Wells's *Outline of History*.

And where does Powys appear to be during all this furore? At first glance, the answer is almost embarrassing: he seems firmly ensconced in a deep armchair, busily compiling a Victorian three-decker. He is scarcely innovative in his literary technique. Characters are carefully worked through a series of episodes which subscribe to a regular chronological pattern. Psychological insight is delineated with the carefully self-conscious precision of George Eliot. Rural settings and descriptions of nature contribute universality to the whole by relating man to vast organic processes. Where forms of Dickensian vitality exert themselves – as they frequently do in peripheral, or flat, eccentric characterization – they do so within the conventions of nineteenth century economic morality. (Dolores's harassment by the ringmaster in *Wood and Stone* is a case in point.) All this detail requires expatiation; the combined rusticity, chronological expansiveness, external characterization, and moral preoccupation are decidedly in the Victorian tradition of the novel. Add to this, the stylistic deliberateness of periodic prose used in summary, digression, or explanation and the argument seems conclusive.

But there is another side to the Powys-novel – the thematic or, more aptly perhaps, the visionary quality of its intent. This vision, we discover, is urgently contemporary – prophetic at times; it transmutes those nineteenth century techniques into a powerful expression of "felt life", to use James's phrase. In novel after novel, Powys questions orthodoxy of various sorts – religious, philosophical, psychological, sociological – as it relates to man in the twentieth century. His grasp of modern consciousness is comprehensive. Expressed in dualistic terms, he parallels or contrasts the reality of a personal, inner world reflecting doubt and disorder with an outer, social world dependent on causal laws of necessity and chance.

His first two novels, *Wood and Stone* and *Rodmoor,* are an excellent introduction to his quest for meaning through fiction. The former depicts external reality in its arguments about the social placing of industry, religion, philosphy, and art; the latter exposes the psychological crisis of a person unable to compromise inner vision with outer necessity. Both books fail, however, because Powys himself was unwilling to accept the implications of his discoveries. The tensions, explored in the two early novels, crystalize in the personality of Rook Ashover of *Ducdame.* Here for the first time, we see the protagonist isolated from his fellows as a result of his break with tradition. Rook's decision to live according to a personal mandate deprives him of both past and future. His alienation epitomizes the modern condition of disrupted continuity. This state is described in moral as well as philosophical terms. Sexuality is seen as the central issue as it involves acceptance or rejection of life's basic premise — generative responsibility. *Ducdame* attempts, although unsuccessfully, to resolve the dichotomy through an imaginative solution which encompasses a multiplicity of human experiences. In doing so, it affirms the value of each man's struggle to go on living in the face of nearly overwhelming odds.

Technical mastery is lacking in *Wood and Stone, Rodmoor*, and *Ducdame:* Powys seems unable to fit his presentation to his ideas. There is, in other words, a discrepancy between the vehicle and the tenor of his thought. That difficulty is overcome in *Wolf Solent* where, with unprecedented exactness, he relates economic necessity, social hypocrisy, and sexual ethics to the incommunicable isolation of an individual. The novel, structured with an intricate blending of symbol, image, and thought, leads towards a definition of human values on the purely personal level. Wolf's achievement in uniting the unconnected strands of his personality into an expression of his integrity is an imaginative triumph. Powys manages to infuse purpose where none existed, and to communicate fully the complexity of living according to totally individual moral standards.

Having established the solitary consciousness of man at the centre of all life's meaning, Powys goes on to explore other facets of experience. *A Glastonbury Romance*, *Weymouth Sands* and *Maiden Castle* survey the twentieth century context emphasizing respectively the erosion of orthodox religion, the deterioration of human relationships, and the disappearance of traditional perspectives. Each of these novels advances a fresh approach to the problems of reconciling the inner and outer worlds. Sam Dekker and Johnny Geard develop an earth mysticism (the contradiction is inherent in the "flesh-spirit" nature of actual life) which coalesces in Sylvanus Cobbold's "cap-ut-anus" philosophy. Dud No-man's death quest is turned into a life-quest; his cerebral necrophilia is shown as inferior to generative sex. We recognize a developing pattern: sex and the imagination are key-factors in the process of self-revelation. Both are energizing forces, both relate to our human condition as expressions of our fundamental duality as physical and mental beings. Sex, imaginatively guided, becomes our best means of integrating ourselves with the external world.

Parthenogenesis — Powys's term for the sex-imagination relationship — operates on different levels. It can be cathartic and redemptive, as Sam Dekker discovered, when

used to transform base experience into mystical illumination; or it may occur as a subliminal activity
whereby maleficent urges are overcome and replaced by
beneficent ones. In either case, it generates a new
revelation. Perhaps Powys's novels were products of
parthenogenesis, for they are increasingly concerned with
visionary moments. As the vision strengthened, it broadened; in consequence Powys appears to have felt confinement to a relatively "realistic" world uncomfortable.
Morwyn breaks the limitations of orthodox fiction completely, but in so doing comes to even more immediate
grips with the modern world. Scientific and religious
dogmatism is attacked with unstinted ferocity. In its place,
qualities of humane sympathy and tolerance are advocated. These are seen as the ends of the imaginative
quest – their final expression being a return of the Age of
Gold. The more relaxed frame of reference allows Powys
to draw together the Celtic material scattered throughout
his earlier work. These myths and legends are given point
in *Owen Glendower* and *Porius*. Both novels are conceived
on a vast scale which sets individual men and women into a
cosmic as well as an historical perspective. Although
Powys's techniques are still in the nineteenth century
tradition, they carry a burden as ambitious as Joyce's.
Their concern with the fragmentation of society and its
ideologies is a precise *critique* of our present-day world;
while their emphasis on revolution and anarchy disturb-
ingly suggests the probable direction of events in the last
decades of this century.

Powys's prophetic vision grows even stronger in the
fantasy of his last four novels. Anarchy and mental illness
are seen as the counterparts to an apathetic, dehumanized
society; absolute individualism relying on a sustained
imaginative approach to life is the unique hope of human
salvation. *The Inmates* is an extreme book, but its

forebodings are echoed in *Atlantis* where revolt is again a basic rhythm. Powys refuses, however, to see man finally defeated; the phallic power of Odysseus wins over the scientific pronouncements of the Atlantean Ruler. Yet the possibilities of biogenetics are frighteningly real; so too are the computeristic and cybernetic techniques hinted at in *The Brazen Head.* The only relevant answer to these manifold perplexities is confirmed in *All or Nothing:* it is to be found in "the heart" of every human being.

The fourteen novels we have been examining seem to have developed along exceptionally logical lines. An early period of vacillation and experimentation, during which Powys tried to find his own fictional voice, was followed by a series of attempts to engage twentieth century experience directly; after these, the Welsh novels tried to place man in a great continuum where myth, legend, and history expanded his significance, and, through distancing, gave added sharpness to comments on the present world-order; the fantasy of the final novel dealt with the truly unimaginable prospects of our age in what is perhaps the most honest way — maybe the only way — they can be considered. Powys's conviction that our essentially human natures are being subverted and destroyed by technocracy is convincing; his belief in the cyclical phases of cultural evolution puts him in the company of Spengler, Sorokin, Yeats, and Joyce.

Powys's success in communicating his vision is his success as a novelist. Discussing particular novels, we noted the subtle architectonics of his best work: a technique of paralleling and balancing action and character; a use of symbol and image to give resonance to thought and feeling; an accumulation of detail to give incontrovertible reality to his fictional world. The failure of a certain novel often results from an excess of qualities rather than from a lack of any particular quality. Thus, an overabundance of detail may slow down the story; too many characters may be portrayed too deeply; an excessive stressing of parallels may impose a rigid pattern of "posed" contrasts which impedes the organic growth of the whole. While the structural achievement of many of Powys's novels is apparent, an even greater, more fundamental ability is his use of language. Powys shows extraordinary ability in his manipulation of words: vocabulary, diction, and syntax are harmonized with amazing power. Even more impressive is his sense of speech rhythms. The prose of these novels is extremely varied, ranging from West-country dialect to academic disquisition. Although cliched at times, over-decorative or awkward at others, the whole is infused with a delicate sensibility to the aural, visual, emotional, and intellectual potency of language. That this is a fact rather than a judgement is immediately obvious when an extended exerpt from a Powys-novel is contrasted with a similar exerpt from almost any other modern writer; for example, Ivy Compton-Burnett's desiccated prose — even allowing for differences of intention — seems so much straw set against the cadenced variety of Powys's writing.

The language-depth of these novels contributes much to their scope. The exploration of mythic overtones, psychic phenomena, open dimensionality, ideological theories, and sexual nuances requires imaginative versatility of expression. In the interrelation of levels of meaning, Powys has compressed and fused the actual, the symbolic, and the mythopoeic in clearly understandable language. Lying behind the novels' total organization is, of course, Powys's imagination. This power informs and unites the vision and the method.

When most successful — as in *Wolf Solent, A Glastonbury Romance, Maiden Castle, Owen Glendower,* and *Porius* — Powys's abilities as thinker and writer are one. Our general examination of his fiction brings numerous aspects to light: these deserve extended treatment else-where. His novels need to be placed in a literary perspective by assessing the influences on them (a formidable task), also by noting their influence on other writings; distinct elements in his novels merit close analysis — the Celtic references, the role of nature, the historical commentary, the philosophical argument, the stylistic form; subsequent investigations will undoubtedly reveal further areas — Powys's debt to oriental thought, for instance. My own purpose has been to establish a basis for future study by demonstrating the importance of these novels in terms of their literary achievement and their contemporary relevance.

Bibliography

Auden, W.H. *Selected Poems*. London: Faber & Faber, 1968.

Auerbach, Erich. *Mimesis: The Representation of Reality in Western Literature*. Translated by Willard R. Trask, Princeton, N.J.: Princeton University Press, 1953.

Bayley, John. *The Characters of Love: A Study in the Literature of Personality*. London: Constable, 1960.

Booth, Wayne C. *The Rhetoric of Fiction*. Chicago and London: University of Chicago Press, Phoenix ed., 1967. First published 1961.

Brebner, John A. "*Owen Glendower*: The Pursuit of the Fourth Dimension," *The Anglo-Welsh Review*, XVIII, 42 (February 1970), 207-16.

Brooke, Jocelyn. "On Re-reading A Glastonbury Romance," *London Magazine*, III, 4(1956), 44-51.

Byatt, A.S. *Degrees of Freedom: The Novels of Iris Murdoch*. London: Chatto & Windus, 1965.

Flaubert, Gustave. *November*. Translated by Frank Jellinek; introduction by J.C.Powys. Manufactured for John Lane The Bodley Head Ltd., in the U.S.A., first published in England, 1934. Limited ed.

Graves, Robert. *The White Goddess* (amended and enlarged ed.). New York: Vintage Books, 1948.

Gruffydd, W.J. *Math vab Mathonwy: An Inquiry into the origins and development of the Fourth Branch of the Mabinogi with the text and a translation*. Cardiff: The University of Wales Press Board, 1928.

Knight, G.Wilson. *Neglected Powers: Essays on Nineteenth and Twentieth Century Literature*. London: Routledge & Kegan Paul, 1971.

————. *The Saturnian Quest*. London: Methuen, 1964.

Langridge, Derek. *John Cowper Powys: A Record of
Achievement*. London: The Library Association, 1966.

Lovett, R.M. and H.S.Hughes. *The History of the Novel
in England*. London: Harrap, 1932.

The Mabinogion. Translated with Notes by Lady Charlotte Guest. London: Everyman's Library, 1906.

The Mabinogion. Translated and introduced by Gwyn
Jones and Thomas Jones. London: Everyman's Library,
1966. First published in Everyman's series, 1949.

Mao Tse-Tung. *Quotations From Chairman Mao Tse-
Tung*. Foreword by Lin Piao. Peking: Foreign Language
Press, 1967, 2nd ed.

Mathias, Roland. "Gwlad-yr-Haf," *Dock Leaves: A John
Cowper Powys Number*, VII, 19(Spring 1956), 20-9.

Mayoux, Jean-Jacques. "L'extase et la sensualité: John
Cowper Powys et Wolf Solent," *Critique* (Paris), XXIV,
252(Mai 1968), 462-74.

Murdoch, Iris. *The Flight From the Enchanter*. London:
Chatto & Windus, 1956.

Onions, Oliver. *Widdershins*. London: Chatto & Windus,
1968. First published 1911.

Pater, Walter. *Imaginary Portraits*. London: Macmillan,
1920.

————. *The Renaissance*. London: Macmillan, 1920.

Powys, J.C. *All or Nothing*. London: Macdonald 1960.

————. *Atlantis*. London: Macdonald, 1954.

————. *The Brazen Head*. London: Macdonald, 1956.

————. *Ducdame*. Garden City, N.Y.: Doubleday, Page
1925.

————. "England Revisited," *Scribner's Magazine,*

XCVIII, 3(September 1935), 141-6.

_____ . *A Glastonbury Romance*. New York: Simon & Schuster, 1932. New ed. London: Macdonald, 1955.

_____ . *The Inmates*. London: Macdonald, 1952.

_____ . *Maiden Castle*. New York: Simon & Schuster, 1936. New ed. London: Macdonald, 1966.

_____ . *Morwyn or the Vengeance of God*. London: Cassell, 1937.

_____ . *Owen Glendower*. New York: Simon & Schuster, 1940, 2 vols; reprinted London: John Lane The Bodley Head, 1941, identical pagination.

_____ . *Porius: a romance of the Dark Ages*. London: Macdonald, 1951.

_____ . *Rabelais*. London: The Bodley Head, 1948.

_____ . *Rodmoor*. New York: G.A.Shaw, 1916.

_____ . *Weymouth Sands*. New York: Simon & Schuster, 1934. Modified version as *Jobber Skald*. London: John Lane, 1935. New ed. Macdonald, 1963.

_____ . *Wolf Solent*. New York: Simon & Schuster, 1929, 2 vols. New ed. London: Macdonald, 1961.

_____ . *Wood and Stone*. New York: G.A.Shaw, 1915.

Rhys, Sir John. "Introduction" to Thomas Malory's *Le Morte d'Arthur*. London: Everyman's Library, 1963, I, v-xxiv. First published 1906.

Robillard, Douglas. "Landscape with Figures: The Early Fiction of John Cowper Powys," *Studies in the Literary Imagination*, I, 2(1968), 51-8.

Steiner, George. *Language and Silence: Essays 1958-1966*. London: Faber & Faber, 1967.

Stevenson, Lionel. *The English Novel: A Panorama*. Boston: Houghton Mifflin, 1960.

Sullivan, H.R. "The Elemental World of John Cowper Powys," Ph.D. dissertation, University of Georgia, 1960. Ann Arbor, Michigan: University Microfilms Inc., Mic 60-4656.

Wilson, Angus. " 'Mythology' in John Cowper Powys's Novels," *A Review of English Literature*, IV, 1(January 1963), 9-20.

Note: Mr. Derek Langridge's remarkably complete bibliography — *John Cowper Powys: A Record of Achievement*, lists works by and about Powys. Few significant items have appeared since then; I have mentioned these in my cited material.

Index

Adam, Villiers de l'Isle, 143

All or Nothing 220-23, 225, 231.

    characters: Bog, 221, 222, 223; Bubble, 221, 223; Cerne Giant, 221, 222, 223, 225; Horners, the, 221; Jessica, 222; Jilly Tewky, 221, 223; John o'Dreams, 221, 222; Lalanika, 221; Laura, 222; Ring, 221, 223; Squeak, 221, 223; Ting, 221, 223; Urk, 221, 222; Wug, 221; Zug, 221

    fantasy of, 220-21

    masturbation theme in, 223, 225

    places: Milky Way, 221; planet Vindex, 221

    sex in, 222-3

    space travel, 221, 222

Amis, Kingsley, 140

Anglo-Welsh Review, The, 192

Aristotle, 214

As You Like It, 88

Atlantis 190, 203-12, 214, 224, 231

    anarchy of the imagination, 212

    characters: Ajax, 206; Atropos, 204; Enorches, 203, 206, 208; Krateros Naubolides, 204; Nausicaa, Princess, 206, 210; Nisos Naubolides, 209, 210, 211; Odysseus, 203, 204, 205, 207-11 (every page), 231; Petraria, 210; Ruler of Atlantis, 209, 231; Telemachos, 203; Zeuks, 204-5, 212

    Club of Herakles, 203, 208, 209

    connections with *Iliad* and *Odyssey*, 203

    generative symbolism in, 208

    masculine-feminine duality, 210

    Odysseus' urge to voyage, 204

    philosophy of Zeuks, 205-6, 207

    places: Atlantis, continent of, 208; Ithaca, 203, 205, 210; Manhattan, 211; Temple of Athens, 203

    revolt of women, 210-11

    sex in, 208, 209, 210, 212

    sub-human creatures in, 203

Auden, W.H., 226

"Atlantis", 224

Auerbach, Erich, 86, 90

Austen, Jane, 66, 70

Beautiful Losers , L. Cohen's, 72

Black Mischief, Evelyn Waugh's, 76

Blake, William, 64, 189

Blick, Calvin, 85

Brave New World, Aldous Huxley's, 227

Brazen Head, The, 212-20, 224, 231

    activation of the Head, 213

    Brazen Head, the, 212-13, 214, 215, 216, 217, 223, 224

    characters: Albertus Magnus, 217; Bacon, Roger, 212-19

(every page); Bonaventura, 218; Boncor, 218; Ghosta, 213, 214; John, 218-19; Lilith, 217, 218; Lilt, Lady, 218; Lil-Umbra, 218; Maldung, Baron, 218; Mort, Lord of Roque, 216, 218, 219; Peregrinus, Peter, 215, 216, 217, 219, 220; Pole, Dod, 218;
characters as symbols, 218
doctrine of Peregrinus, 215-16
faults of, 219-20
lodestone of Peregrinus, 215, 216, 217, 219, 223, 224
magical setting of, 212
parthenogenesis, theme of, 213-14, 215
philosophy of, 217-18
places: Bumset Priory, 212; Cone Castle, 212, 218; Fortress of Roque, 212, 218, 219; Lost Towers, 212, 218
sex in, 217
Brebner, John A., "*Owen Glendower*: The Pursuit of the Fourth Dimension", 192
Brontë, Emily, 29
Brooke, Jocelyn, "On Re-reading A Glastonbury Romance", 88
Butor, Michel, 140

Characters of Love, The, John Bayley's, 89
Cohen, Leonard, 72, 89
Compton-Burnett, Ivy, 222, 232
Critique, 89
Dante, 155, 160
Decline and Fall, Evelyn

Waugh's, 76
Dee, River, 162
Defoe, Daniel, 73
Degrees of Freedom: The Novels of Iris Murdoch, A.S. Byatt's, 90
Descartes, René, 73
Dickens, Charles, 152, 161, 190, 192
Do It!, Jerry Rubin's 188
Dock Leaves: A John Cowper Powys Number, 138
Donne, John, 63, 73
Dorchester, 141, 148, 151, 152, 190
Ducdame, 38-57, 58, 88, 109, 134, 151, 194, 228
black magic in, 42, 56
characters: Ashover, Lexie, 38, 50-55 (every page), 58, ·59; Ashover, Rook, 39, 42, 45, 46, 48-53 (every page), 55-9 (every page), 88, 202, 228; Ashover, Sir Robert, 49; Ashover, Squire John, 38, 42; Cooper, Betsy, 42, 43, 44, 56; Cooper, Nancy, 42; Gore, Ann Wentworth, 39, 41, 42, 43, 46, 48, 55, 56; Hastings, Nell, 40, 46, 50, 51, 55; Hastings, William, 29-44 (every page), 48, 49, 50, 183, 194; Page, Netta, 43, 46, 48, 49, 50, 55; Poynings, Lord, 39; Roger, Lord of Ashover, 38
contact with the dead, theme of, 38, 48-9
continuing Ashover line, theme of, 38-9
death-urge exemplified by Hastings, 39, 40-41, 44, 56

Hastings' "Book of Annihilation", 39, 40-41, 42, 43
irony in, 50-51
merits of, 56-7
places: Ashover, 38; Ashover Church, 48; Ashover House, 43, 48, 49; Cimmery Land, 44
Rook's philosophy of life, 46-7
weaknesses of, 52-5, 228
white magic, 42-3, 44, 45, 46

Eliot, George, 227
Eliot, T.S., 138, 226
Elwin, Malcolm, 190
English Novel: A Panorama, The, Lionel Stevenson's, 90
Essays on John Cowper Powys, B. Humfrey's (ed.), 192

Finnegans Wake, James Joyce's, 176
Flaubert, Gustave, 86, 90
Flight from the Enchanter, The, Irish Murdoch's, 90
Ford, Ford Madox, 226

Gargantua and Pantagruel, Rabelais', 191
Glastonbury Romance, A, 91-124, 134, 138, 139, 153, 189, 202, 218, 229, 232
characters: Barter, Tom, 95, 96, 102, 139; Beere, Angela, 139; Crow, Canon, 92; Crow, John, 92-8 (every page), 101, 102, 103, 107, 108, 110, 111, 115, 116, 118, 120; Crow, Mary, 93, 94, 95, 96, 101;

Crow Philip, 92, 95, 110-12, 113, 114, 120, 121, 123, 139; Dekker, Rev. Mat, 103, 104, 105, 109-10, 116; Dekker, Sam, 103-10 (every page), 115, 118, 120, 122, 123, 125, 138, 159, 181, 229; Drew, Euphemia, 94; Evans, Cordelia, 102; Evans, Owen, 93, 94, 98-9, 100, 101, 102, 103, 107, 108, 109, 110, 115, 116, 120, 157, 175; Geard, John, 92, 93, 94, 99, 102, 111-24 (every page), 188, 198, 229; Legge, Mother, 110; Mad Bet, 101; Petherton, Tittie, 117; Robinson, Red, 113, 139, 162, 218; Spear, David, 112-13; Spear, Persephone, 112, 139; Trent, Paul, 113; Zoyland, Nell, 103, 104, 105, 109, 138; Zoyland, William, 103, 104, 112, 139
Commune, 111, 112, 113, 115, 123
Evans as Christ-figure, 100, 101
Evans' morbidness, 101-2
Evans' sadism, 98-9, 100, 102, 103, 138
flood, the, 110, 121, 122
Grail, the, 98, 102, 106-10 (every page), 120, 121, 124, 159
homosexual bond between John Crow and Barter, 95-6
King Arthur, romances of, 97
midsummer pageant, 94, 99,

116
money theme, 92
places: Abbey House, 94;
Brue, River, 97; Chalice
Well, 116, 117, 120; Dye-
Works, 111, 114; Glaston-
bury, 91, 93, 101, 114,
122; Mark's Court, 118;
Pomparles Bridge, 97;
Ruins, the, 93; Whitelake
Cottage, 104; Wookey
Hole caves, 112, 114
wide subject matter, 91
Golding, William, 140, 227
Gray, Dorian, 12
Graves, Robert, 88, 160, 191
Greening of America, The,
Charles A. Reich's, 188
Gruffydd, W.J., 167, 192
Gutenberg Galaxy, Marshall
McLuhan's, 192

Hard Times, Charles Dickens',
150, 151, 152
Hardy, Thomas, 29, 60, 64, 150,
151, 152, 161, 190, 202,
226
Harvey, E.R.H., 139
Hemingway, Ernest, 73
Henry IV (Bolingbroke), 161,
163, 171, 174
Henry IV, 192, 193
History of the Novel in England,
R.M. Lovett and H.S.
Hughes', 90
Homer, 155, 160, 190
Homer and the Aether, 190
Hopkins, Gerard Manley, 89,
192
Huxley, Aldous, 227
Huysmans, 143

Iliad, the, 203

Imaginary Portraits, Walter
Pater's, 37
Inheritors, William Golding's
227
Inmates, The, 194-202, 210, 218,
220, 224, 230-31
allegorical technique of,
195-6
characters: Cochineal, Colonel, 201; Commander, the,
196, 200; Cuddle, Cogent,
199; Echetus, Dr., 194,
199; Gewlie, 194, 199;
Hush, John, 195, 197,
200, 201, 208; Katch-as-
Kan, 197, 198; Mor-
simmon Esty, 199; Panta-
mount, Mr., 196; Sheer,
Tenna, 200, 201, 208;
Squeeze, Bill, 200; Toby,
Father, 201. Ursie Mum,
201; Yew, Nancy, 197,
199; Zeit-Geist (Marquis
of the Fourth Dimension or
Professor Zoom), 196, 200
magic in, 199-200
period and setting, 194
"Philosophy of the Demen-
ted", 195, 196, 201
places: Glint Hall, 194, 199
rationale of, 201-2
revolt, theme of, 202
sadism in, 194
sex in, 200-201
themes propounded in, 196-7
violence in, 199
vivisection as theme in, 194
wisdom of insanity, theme of,
197-8

James, William, 196, 227
Jellinek, Frank, 89
Joan of Arc, 193-4

Jobber Skald 139

Joyce, James, 124, 176, 190, 226, 230, 231

Keats, John,
"Ode to Autumn", 62

Kipling, Rudyard, 192

Knight, G. Wilson, 190, 224

Lady Chatterley's Lover, D.H. Lawrence's, 89

La Nausée, J.-P. Sartre's, 139

Language and Silence: Essays 1958-1966, George Steiner's, 192

Lawrence, D.H., 64, 87
"The Ship of Death", 190

Le Morte d'Arthur, Malory's, 191

Le Mur, J.-P. Sartre's, 139

Le Chemin de la Liberté, J.-P. Sartre's, 139

L'Etranger, Albert Camus', 139

London Magazine 88

Lord Jim, Joseph Conrad's, 81

Lord of the Flies, William Golding's, 227

Mabinogion, The, Gwyn Jones & Thomas Jones' translation, 191

McLuhan, Marshall, 76

Madame Bovary, Gustave Flaubert's, 86

Maiden Castle, 141-53, 161, 179, 190, 191, 207, 229, 232
  characters: Cask, Roger, 153; Cumber, George, 153; Dearth, Jenny, 153; Derfel, Saint, 149; No-man, Cornelia, 142; No-man, Dud, 141-53 (every page), 187, 190, 191, 207, 229; No-man, Mona, 142, 143; Popsy, 151, 152; Quirm, Enoch (Uryen), 146-7, 148, 149, 156, 157, 175, 198; Quirm, Nance, 149, 150; Ravelston, Lovie, 144, 145, 149; Ravelston, Wizzie, 143, 144-5, 148, 149, 150, 151; Urgan, Ben, 143, 145, 149, 151, 152; Urgan, Grummer, 151; Wye, Dunbar, 153, Wye, Teucer, 153; Wye, Thuella, 153
  Dud's death-quest, 143 145-6
  literary connections with Hardy and Dickens, 150-52, 161
  places: Amphitheatre, 150; Durnovaria, 144, 148; King's Arms, 150; Maiden Castle, 146, 148; Max Gate, 150; St. Peter's Church, 150
  symbolism, 142
  three principal characters symbolized, 148-9

Mao Tse-Tung, on revolution, 198-9

Marx, Karl, 73

Math vab Mathonwy, W.J. Gruffydd's, 167, 192

Mathias, Roland,
"Gwlad-yr-Haf", 138
"The Sacrificial Prince: A Study of *Owen Glendower*", 192

Mayor of Casterbridge, The, Thomas Hardy's, 150, 152, 190

Mayoux, Jean-Jacques,
"L'extase et la sensualité:

John Cowper Powys et
Wolf Solent", 89
Middlemarch , George Eliot's,
127
Mill on the Floss, The, George
Eliot's, 74
Milton, John, 160
*Morwyn or The Vengeance of
God,* 153-61, 179, 190,
191, 193, 202, 230
characters: Black Peter, 154,
158; Captain, the, 154,
155, 156, 157, 159, 160,
175; De Sade, Marquis,
154; 155, 156, 158, 160,
175, 191; Mr. ———.
154, 158, 159; Rabelais,
159; Rhadamanthus, 157,
158; Socrates, 157-8, 159;
Taliesin, 156, 158, 191;
Tityros, 158; Torquemada,
154
explorations of myth, 157
failure of, 160-61
letter form of, 153-4
sadists in, 154-5
set in a sadist's hell, 153, 154
vivisection, theme of, 154,
157, 158, 159, 161
Murdoch, Iris, 140

Neglected Powers, G. Wilson
Knight's, 224, 225
Nietzsche, 156
Nineteen Eighty-Four, George
Orwell's, 227
Novembre, Gustave Flaubert's,
89

Oberammergau, 94
*Odyssey, The,*155, 203
Old Wives' Tale, Arnold Ben-
nett's, 86

Onions, Oliver, 37, 77
"Benlian", 37
Orwell, George, 227
Outline of History, H.G. Wells',
227
Owen Glendower, 161-77 179,
191, 192, 193 , 202, 218,
230, 232
characters: Arglwyddes,
164, 165; Brith, 173;
Broch, 168, 169; Brut,
Walter, 162, 169; Catha-
rine, 164, 166, 169, 170,
174; Crach Ffinnant, 162,
173; Derfel, Saint, 162,
173, 174; Glendower,
Owen, 162-75 (every
page), 188, 198; Griffith
Llwyd, 164, 165; Hopkin
ap Thomas, 171, 174; Iolo
Goch, 164, 166, John ap
Hywel, 162; Mad Huw,
162, 163, 164; Mortimer
Sir Edmund, 170, 174;
Rhisiart ab Owen, 161-8
(every page), 170, 172;
Rhys the Black, 170; Sparrow, Philip, 162, 218;
Tegolin, 163, 164, 171,
172, 173
Owen's last appearance,
175-6
Owen's last campaign, 174
Owen's magic powers, 166-8
Owen's plans for Wales, 169
places: Bangor Cathedral,
175; Bryn Glas, battle of,
170; Dinas Bran castle,
161; Edeyrnion, 171, 175;
Glyndyfrdwy, court of,
162, 164, 167, 168, 169,
175; Harlech, 171, 173;
Mathrafal, 168, 175;

Meifod, 168; Milford Haven, 173. Mynydd-y-Gaer, 175; Snowdon, 169, 173; Tywyn, 170; Woodbury Hill, 174; Worcester, 174, 175

Powys's first historical novel, 161-2

prose style, 163-4

universality of, 176-7

Owen, Wilfred, 226

Parthenogenesis, 213-14, 215, 229-30

Pater, Walter, 12, 13, 37
"Leonardo da Vinci", 37
"Sebastian Van Storck", 37

Plato, 73, 200

Plutarch, 191

Porius: a romance of the Dark Ages, 177-89, 193, 202, 207, 218, 230, 232
argument of, 178-81, 187
characters: Arthur, King, 177, 183, 184, 188; Emperor, the, 177, 178, 183; Euronwy, 183; Galahaut, Prince, 177; Gogfran Derwydd, 179, 180; Lot-el-Azzis, 189; Medrawd, 177, 183, 193, 207; Myrddin Wyllt, 177, 179, 180, 182-6 (every page), 193, 198, 205; Neb ap Digon, 179; Nineue 177, 183, 184, 185; Pelagius, 178; Porius, 177-8, 181-7 (every page), 218; Rhun, 178; Taliessin, 177, 181, 182, 193, 198; Teleri, 183
code of behaviour, search for, 186-7
expression of Powys's life-vision, 189

places: Corwen, 177; Dee valley, 177; Edeyrnion, 177; Glyndyfrdwy, 177; Harlech, 186; Wyddfa, 184; Ynys Prydein, 186
power, problem of, 179
religious confrontation, 179-80
scepticism of Porius, 178
setting and period, 177
sorcery in, 179
style, 188

Powell, Anthony, 140, 226

Powys, John Cowper,
"England Revisited", 138

Powys's novels,
general analysis, 29-36, 57-8, 60-61, 85-7, 226-33
mental illness as subject, 194
minds as subject, 31-2
prose style, 191-2, 232
questioning of orthodoxy in, 227-8
span of, 226
truth of fantasy in, 202-3
Victorian image of writer, 227
visionary quality, 227

Quotations from Chairman Mao Tse-Tung, 224

Rabelais, 159, 160, 175, 208

Rabelais, John Cowper Powys's, 191

Renaissance, The, Walter Pater's, 37

Representation of Reality in Western Literature, The Erich Auerbach's, 90

Review of English Literature, A, 190

Rhys, Sir John, 146, 191

Richard II, 163, 164, 165

Robbe-Grillet, Alain, 140
Robillard, Douglas,
    "Landscape with Figures:
    The Early Fiction of John
    Cowper Powys", 88
Rodmoor 9-29, 30, 32, 37, 38,
    39, 50, 55, 56, 57, 125,
    194, 228
author's interpolations, 34
centred in Adrian's mind, 11,
    19, 29
characters: Doom, Rachel,
    10, 15, 20, 22; Herrick,
    Linda, 10, 12, 15, 16, 17,
    18, 20, 22, 28, 30; Her-
    rick, Nance, 10-16 (every
    page), 18, 19, 20, 22-8
    (every page), 59; Raughty,
    Fingal, 27; Renshaw,
    Brand, 15, 16, 17, 18, 20,
    22, 23, 27, 28; Renshaw,
    Philippa, 15, 16, 17, 18,
    20-25 (every page), 28, 58;
    Ricoletto, 23; Sorio,
    Adrian, 10, 11, 13, 14, 15,
    18-26 (every page), 28, 39,
    41, 47, 57, 58, 194; Sorio,
    Baptiste, 10, 13, 14, 15,
    20, 23, 24, 25; Stork,
    Baltazar, 10, 12, 13, 14,
    15, 16, 20, 22; Traherne,
    Hamish, 23, 27
depth of perspective, 32, 33
freedom of individual, 25-6,
    28-9, 31, 36
incest in, 16
lack of technical mastery,
    228
law of ebb and flow, 18
pairing of characters, 12,
    15-16
places: County Asylum, 19,
    20, 24; Dyke House, 16,

22; Mundham, 18, 19, 24;
    Oakguard House, 15, 23;
    Ravelston Grange, 18, 19;
    Rodmoor village, 10, 11,
    14, 25, 26-7, 28
sea, omnipresence of the, 26,
    27-8
seasonal pattern in, 30
verbal impasse, 31
view of life, 35-6
Rosenberg, Isaac, 226

Sarraute, Nathalie, 80, 140
Sartre, Jean-Paul, 73, 131
Sassoon, Siegfried, 226
Saturnian Quest, The, G. Wilson
    Knight's, 140
Scott, Sir Walter, 161
Scribner's Magazine 138
Sexus, The Rosy Crucifixion,
    Henry Miller's, 140
Shakespeare, William, 63, 192
Sorley, Charles, 226
Sorokin, 231
Spender, Stephen, 226
Spengler, 231
Steiner, George, 191, 192
*Studies in the Literary Imagina-
    tion*, 88
Sullivan, H.R.,
    "The Elemental World of
    John Cowper Powys", 193

Tennyson, Alfred, Lord,
    "Lady of Shalott", 139
Trask, Willard, R., 90
Trilling, Lionel, 91

Ulysses, James Joyce's, 176

Vile Bodies, Evelyn Waugh's, 76

Waste Land, The, T.S. Eliot's,

226

Waugh, Evelyn, 76, 140, 226

Weymouth Sands, 124-38, 139, 141, 153, 179, 193, 194, 229

"advantages of prostitution", 132-3

characters: Ballard, Sippy, 125, 127; Brush, Dr. Dan, 125, 133, 134, 135, 136, 140, 158, 194; Cattistock, Benny, 126; Cattistock Dogberry, 125, 127, 128, 136; Cobbold, Jerry, 131-2, 133; Cobbold, Mrs. Jerry (Lucinda), 126, 127; Cobbold, Sylvanus, 125, 126, 129-31, 133, 134, 181, 198, 229; Gipsy May, 125, 126, 130, 135; Girodel, Dr., 132, 133, 140; Lily, Hortensia, 127, 128; Muir, Magnus, 126, 127, 128, 129, 133, 136, 139; Skald, Adam (Jobber), 125, 127, 128, 129, 136; Tissty, 133; Tossty, 133; Wane, Perdita, 126, 127, 128, 129, 133; Wix, Curly, 126, 127, 132, 136; Zed, Larry, 125, 135

importance of, 137-8

occult, interest in, 126, 134-6

places: Brush Home (Hell's Museum), 130, 131, 158, 194; Sark House, 132, 140; Weymouth, 124

subject matter, 125

vivisection, attack on, 133-4, 153

weaknesses of, 136-7

White Goddess, The, Robert Graves', 88, 191

Widdershins, Oliver Onions', 37

Wilde, Oscar, 13, 76

Wilson, Angus, " 'Mythology' in John Cowper Powys's Novels", 190, 193

Wolf Solent, 58-87, 88, 89, 91, 153, 179, 194, 228-9, 232

arrangement, 60

characters: Beard, Josh, 75; Carfax, Lord, 59, 75-6, 77, 85; Gault, Selena, 75; Malakite, Christie, 59, 64, 66-72 (every page), 79, 80, 84, 90, 128; Manley, Mr., 74. 79, 82, 85; Martin, Mrs., 75; Olwen, 74; Otter, Darnley, 75; Otter, Jason, 74, 75, 76, 90; Round, Mr., 75, 194; Smith, Mattie, 74, 75; Solent, Mrs. (Wolf's mother), 74. 75, 79, 82, 85; Solent, William, 75; Solent, Wolf, 59-86 (every page), 90, 96, 103, 110, 124, 128, 159, 181, 187, 202, 207, 229; Stalbridge, Mr., 74, 76; Stone, Dimity, 75; Torp, Gerda, 59, 76, 77, 79, 82, 84, 85, 96; Torp, John, 75; Urquhart, Squire, 59. 74, 79, 80, 82, 85; Valley, Rev. T.E., 74-5, 85

contemporaneity of, 74

economics and sexuality, 75-6

imagery, 69-70

places: Blacksod, 59, 77, 85; Farmer's Rest, 75; King's Barton, 59, 74; Lenty Pond, 83; Nevilton, 75; Ramsgard, 59

portrayal of economic pres-

sures, 74
resumé, 59-60
symbolism in, 68-9, 71-2
technical mastery of, 228-9
use of physical setting, 61-6, 71, 72, 73
Wolf, an anti-hero, 59, 77-8
Wolf's crisis and resolution, 79-85
Wolf's "mythology", 78-9, 81, 84, 85
Wolfe, Tom, 76
Women's Liberation Front, 188, 210
Wood and Stone, 1-9, 10, 11, 30, 32, 37, 38, 50, 55, 57, 60, 151, 187, 194, 228
author's interpolations, 3-4, 34
character motivation, 3
characters: Andersen, James, 2, 3, 7, 51, 58, 194; Andersen, Luke, 2, 3, 4, 5, 6, 7, 50, 51, 58, 202; Clavering, Hugh, 2, 4; Dangelis, Ralph, 2, 7, 8; Dolores, 5, 37; Goring, John, 3, 4; Quincunx, Maurice, 2, 3, 5, 6, 9, 37; Romer, Gladys, 2, 4, 5, 6, 8, 30; Romer, Mortimer,
1-2, 4, 5, 111; Seldom, Mrs., 2; Seldom, Vennie, 2; Taxater, Francis, 2, 4, 5; Traffio, Lacrima, 2, 3, 5, 9, 37, 128; Witch-Bessie, 42; Wone, George, 14
earth-bound nature of, 29
emphasis on individuality, 31, 36
Holy Rood of Waltham, 1
lack of dogmatism, 5
lack of perspective, 32, 33
lack of technical mastery, 228
places: Leo's Hill, 1; Nevilton, 1, 8; Nevilton Churchyard, 4; Nevilton Manor, 7; Nevilton Mount, 1; Weymouth, 6, 8
sex in, 6
time and place in, 8-9, 30
verbal impasse, 31
view of life, 35-6
Woolf, Virginia, 66, 73, 226
Wordsworth, William, 87
"Intimations of Immortality...", 90

Yeats, W.B., 218, 231